PRAISE

R KATHRYN TROUTMAN'S PASSION FOR HELPING PEOPLE APPLY FOR FEDERAL JOBS:

Kathy Troutman genuinely looks out for the Federal worker. I know this first hand. Last year when our workers at the Marine base were notified that their jobs would be put on the bidding block in an A-76 study (commercial outsourcing where the lowest bidder wins), our workers were in a panic. Few of us knew how to properly write a winning resume in the Navy's new electronic resume system, Resumix. I asked Kathy if she were willing to come down to our base and provide training. Since we were unable to obtain funds to pay for her services, Kathy took it on her own, flew to Hawaii, and provided training to over 700 Navy, Marine, and Human Resource civilians at the Pearl Harbor Naval Shipyard. At no cost to the government. For many of our workers, one person made all the difference.
✪ Dennis Chiu - Honolulu, Hawaii

I met Kathy while trying to produce a training program on how to assist individuals with disabilities in getting a Federal job. Kathy quickly grasped the unique issues facing the disabled job seekers and put her incredible resources and energy into designing training tailor-made for vocational rehabilitation professionals. Since our training she has continued to pursue ways to assist my agency and others like it in making a Federal job search more workable.
✪ Lisa Marcucci - Springfield, VA

As a manager of a Federal Career Counseling Program, I have had Kathy teach Federal Resume Writing workshops to my customers on a monthly basis from 1995 to present. She consistently does outstanding presentations as evidenced by high numerical scores received on participants' evaluations, reinforced by glowing comments. Her workshops extend beyond resume writing—she is a dynamic motivational speaker, an excellent educator, very resourceful, and manages to engage the entire group in workshop activities. People depart from her workshops highly energized and enthusiastic. I recommend her without reservation!
✪ F. S. Williamson, Ed.D. - Baltimore, MD

I have been a Federal HR specialist for over 30 years and I share Kathy's frustrations with some of the antiquated approaches some Federal agencies continue to use in their recruitment efforts. I have also observed Kathy's efforts over the last several years to do something to remedy this situation. I am constantly impressed with the quality of Kathy's work, her persistence, and her commitment to the goal of helping the Federal government attract and select highly qualified employees. Kudos to Kathy!
✪ John Palguta - Vienna, VA

Ms. Troutman's new Federal Resume format helped me get a job in the Federal government by making me look like a young professional with potential, rather than a new grad. I don't think the 171 could highlight my expertise and skills as well as the new and improved format. I am grateful that I didn't have to fill out that terrible 171 form. I am proud of the way my new resume makes me look.
Thanks, Ms. Troutman—you're a genius!
✪ Scott Holland - Tulsa, OK

That Kathryn was able to slice through the Federal government's job hiring bureaucracy is nothing short of astonishing. Not only has she greatly simplified the process for prospective employees, she has improved the whole process for government agencies as well. Now that Americans want to serve their government more than ever before, Kathryn has greased the tracks for anyone trying to transition from the private sector into a rewarding and secure government job.
✪ Bill Cavdek - Campbell, CA

Kathy is a dynamic leader. She has a knack of communicating in a way that the general public can understand Federal requirements. She has been a great asset to the Office of Personnel Management in spreading the word about Federal employment, and providing a way for the public to apply for and get Federal jobs.
✪ Rosemary Downing - Arlington, VA

She (Kathryn) is a very determined lady and she makes things happen. As her story shows, she is persistent in getting things that matter happen. The Federal government needs more advocates like her.
✪ Ligaya Fernandez - Alexandria, VA

And they say the Government can't be changed. Obviously, they hadn't met Kathy before they said that. Her innovation has made a real difference.
✪ Margaret Dikel - Rockville, MD

When I was looking for a book to teach high school students how to write a resume, I stumbled over Kathryn's name and sent her an e-mail. She responded immediately and worked out a deal so that I could participate in a trial run of her new book and receive free resume books for my whole class. This is important in a school with one of the highest poverty rates and lowest achievement scores in the state. The school has benefited greatly from her kindness and attention.
✪ Joseph Meersman - Sunnyside, WA

These reviews were written for Kathryn Troutman, nominated for a Fast Change Agent competition sponsored by Fast Company, Fall 2001.

Ten Steps
to a Federal Job

Navigating the Federal Job System
Writing Federal Resumes, KSAs and
Cover Letters with a Mission

Kathryn Kraemer Troutman

With contributions by Laura Sachs, Mike Ottensmeyer,
Mark Reichenbacher, Jessica Coffey

The Resume Place
Professional Resume Writing for Federal Government

TEN STEPS TO A FEDERAL JOB

Copyright 2002 by Kathryn Kraemer Troutman
ISBN 0-9647025-3-3
Published by The Resume Place, Inc.
89 Mellor Avenue
Baltimore, MD 21228
Phone: (888) 480-8265
Fax: (410) 744-0112
Email: resume@resume-place.com
Website: www.resume-place.com

OTHER BOOKS BY KATHRYN KRAEMER TROUTMAN

Electronic Federal Resume Guidebook & CD-ROM
Federal Resume Guidebook & PC Disk, 1st & 2nd Editions
    (3rd edition coming in 2003)
Reinvention Federal Resumes (out of print)
The 171 Reference Book (out of print)
Creating Your High School Resume (2nd edition coming 2003)
Creating Your High School Resume, Teacher's Guide

See the back of this book for Resume Place titles and ordering
information. Quantity discounts are available.

We have been careful to provide accurate information throughout
this book, but it is possible that errors and omissions have been
introduced. Web site addresses and Federal job information may
be updated and revised at any time. The resume samples in the book
and on the CD-ROM are of real people who have given permission
to use their resumes in this book. Their names, social security
numbers, and other specific job information have been changed.

Trademarks: Resumix™ is the registered trademark of HotJobs.com.
Ltd. All brand names used in this book are registered trademarks
of their respective owners.

Printed in the United States of America by UtiliMedia –
www.utilimedia.com

Development Editor
Barbra Guerra

Interior Layout Designer
Paulina Chen
thedesignzoo@yahoo.com

Cover and CD-ROM Designer
Brian Moore
MJR Media
www.mjrmedia.com

Proofreader
Bonita Kraemer

Resume Designs/Appendix
Bonny Day
Laura Sachs
Jessica Coffey
Evelin Letarte
Jackie Allen
Carla Waskiewicz
Alan Cross
Mark Reichenbacher

Glossary
Ligaya Fernandez

Index
L. Pilar Wyman
Wyman Indexing
www.wymanindexing.com

Editorial Assistant
Sarah Blazucki

TABLE OF CONTENTS

PART VII APPENDIX 243

CD-ROM – TEMPLATES / SAMPLE FEDERAL RESUMES AND KSAs

IS THIS BOOK FOR YOU?

This book is written for several audiences, including:

- ✪ First-time Federal job seekers
- ✪ Returning Federal job seekers who are not familiar with the new Federal job application processes
- ✪ Career counselors who advise people in applying for Federal jobs
- ✪ College students who are considering professional positions, internships, and summer programs
- ✪ Federal employees who want to review the new ways of applying for Federal jobs
- ✪ Military personnel seeking Federal jobs

WHAT THIS BOOK COVERS

Each of the Ten Steps to Getting a Federal Job has its own chapter.

Introduction Have you made a decision to try to land a Federal job?

Step 1 Network – Who do you know that works for the government?

Step 2 Review the Federal Job Process – Learn the Federal job titles, grades, occupational series, salaries and other important Federal job search considerations.

Step 3 Research Vacancy Announcements – Start reading about the Federal jobs.

Step 4 Analyze Federal Core Competencies – Integrate your Core Competencies with your duties and accomplishments in order to stand out above the competition.

Step 5 Analyze Vacancy Announcements for Keywords – Match yourself to the announcement language for a more successful package.

Step 6 Write your Federal and Electronic Resume – Your critical package for a Federal job! Write two resume formats and you are 80% ready to apply for any Federal job.

Step 7 Write your KSAs and Cover Letter – Some announcements ask for Knowledge, Skills and Abilities. Learn how to write compelling essays of your skills and accomplishments.

Step 8 Apply for Jobs and Submit your Resume – No more thinking about it. Play the Federal Job Search Game. Start applying and see what happens.

Step 9 Track and Follow-up on Applications – Secrets to following-up with your packages. Ways to patiently communicate with Federal human resources offices.

Step 10 Interview for a Federal Job – Success! If you can get an interview, you are almost there! Tips for Federal job interviews – panels, one-on-one, telephone techniques.

Appendix Glossary of Federal terms, 8 outstanding Federal resumes and example of a KSA Statement, About the Author and Writers, Resume Place Books and Services, Index

CD-ROM Nine outstanding Federal resumes and KSA samples + Federal Resume, KSA and Cover Letter Builders – easy to use to build your Federal application content.

What work can be more important at this time of crisis and national need than a career in Federal service? And what aid can be more useful to you in this great endeavor than Kathy Troutman's masterful book on how to go about the daunting task of applying for a job with the Federal government?

The process of applying for a job in the Federal government these days is complex—more than it should be. To compete successfully, you need the time, energy, and know-how to write the correct resume and to apply in the right way for the right job for you.

After a career of 30 years in the Foreign Service and three tours as Ambassador, it is fair to say that I understand the importance and impact of working for the government that serves us all. I especially understand the importance of a government that is open to all persons with talent and dedication. We need good government and good people to make it so.

This is why I am so enthusiastic about Kathy Troutman's latest contribution to the world of Federal service. She demystifies the application process and makes it accessible to the kinds of people who need to be in Federal service.

In today's world of danger and opportunity, there is no higher calling than public service. No other job affords you the chance to impact people's lives for the better, promote their safety and health, and open access to public services. As a Federal worker, you administer the laws that our government adopts while contributing to the policy decisions that guide the implementation of these laws. In a myriad of ways, you are of assistance to the public...in such diverse agencies as the Social Security System, the Food and Drug Administration, the Department of Defense, and the National Park Service. Meaningful positions such as these are attainable by dedicated and talented individuals who rely on Kathy Troutman's book to guide them through the complicated business of applying for such positions.

From my own experience, I can attest to the satisfaction that Federal service can bring to employees who know they are making a difference for the good in the lives of others. Among these personal experiences, I count helping one country to hold the first democratic elections in its history and another to rid itself of murderous terrorists. Both contributed to the well-being of Americans, not only those who visited overseas, but those at home.

This book is intended for those thinking about Federal employment for the first time. I hope that it helps open the door to this world and sheds light on the paths to the kind of satisfaction I took from my own career in Federal service.

ALVIN ADAMS
United States Ambassador (retired)

PREFACE

DEAR FEDERAL JOB SEEKERS,

Every day I receive phone calls from people who say, "I'm considering Federal employment for the first time, but I don't know where to start." Since the private industry job market is at around 6 percent unemployment and the Federal government has about 50,000 jobs open, it's time for an easy step-by-step guidebook on how to apply and write a resume for Federal jobs!

With the terrorist acts of September 11, the role of government is more important than ever! The government needs all the help it can get to manage homeland security, public administration, defense, and services to the American public for our future.

I have attempted to make the Federal hiring process seem as simple as possible in this book, and it wasn't easy to do this. I created *Ten Steps to a Federal Job* for a workshop I was teaching for unemployment counselors for the Department of Labor. They needed a simple process to share with unemployed people who were anxious to apply for Federal jobs.

I truly believe that Federal jobs are good and are worth the effort to understand the whole process—the agency missions and the jobs, the vacancy announcements and core competencies, the "how to apply" instructions, and the interview process.

Whereas my other two publications on Federal resume writing focus on writing the application, this guidebook is an inclusive book taking you from the first decision to search for a Federal job through the final interview in a government agency.

When you finish this book and submit your first application, tear out the **Ten Steps to a Federal Job Certificate** on the last page of this book. Hang it proudly on your wall! Maybe you will land a promotion or new Federal job because of your time and energy in completing this difficult job application.

I hope this book inspires you and keeps you encouraged through your Federal job search. It's worth your patience, time, and effort. The government needs you.

Sincerely,

KATHRYN KRAEMER TROUTMAN

Author, Trainer, and President
The Resume Place, Inc. and www.resume-place.com

DEDICATION

This book is dedicated to the workers who lost their lives on
SEPTEMBER 11, 2001—Defense Department employees who lost
their lives while working to protect our nation at the Pentagon and
others who had just arrived at work on a busy Tuesday in the New
York financial district.

This book was written to help thousands of sincere, dedicated, hard-
working, and persevering new applicants apply successfully for jobs
that will protect our country, our families, and our homes, and support
our Defense department and military personnel worldwide.

And finally, remembering Ned Lynch, my senior writer, who was
a good friend and a great civil servant for more than 28 years
with the Immigration and Naturalization Service and U.S. Civil
Service Commission.

ACKNOWLEDGMENTS

My knowledge of the Federal hiring process and "how to apply" to Federal jobs has come from many sources. I want to thank the many people in the government for their insight and those who are trying to get in for the first time for their job search stories and strategies. The emails, resumes, and insight have made this book more than an instructional book, but an inspiring book that can help thousands of people apply more successfully for Federal jobs.

Federal Human Resources Policy-Makers and Senior Managers: John Palguta, Vice President of the Partnership for Public Service and previously Vice President of the Merit Systems Protection Board. Also Ligaya Fernandez and Paul VanRijn of the Merit Systems Protection Board, who wrote many emails about vacancy announcements, "how to apply" instructions, rating and ranking and the elimination of the SF-171. Richard W. Whitford, Acting Associate Director, Employment Information, Office of Personnel Management, who answered many questions regarding announcement instructions, agency requirements, and improving application processes.

Training Coordinators: My Federal Training Coordinators have introduced me to their Human Resources and Civilian Personnel Office Center Directors and staff who have explained the internal workings of Federal Resume and KSA Writing, Core Competency Development, Resumix, and Quickhire. As a trainer on these topics for Federal employees, I have learned "both sides of the desk" so that I can write insightful instructions for job applicants. I'd especially like to thank Faith Williamson, Training Coordinator, Health Care Financing Administration and now Food and Drug Administration for her support in my training career.

Federal websites and Federal HR Information: I'd like to thank Tom Shoop and Brian Friel at www.govexec.com for the great Federal job and HR information. Scott Thompson from www.fendonline and their newsletter have given me insight into the Federal HR decision-makers. Dennis Damp, publisher of www.federaljobs.com gives great Federal job information and has been supportive in my publishing career.

Clients: Many resume clients have volunteered their resumes to this publication in order to help other first-time or returning Federal employees understand the process better. All sample resumes are real and are volunteered for this book. Resume clients who graciously volunteered to provide their resumes as samples for others:
Bill Cavdek, Sheila Tavakolian, Erika L. Herold, Scott Lee Cromwell, Lauren Nopulos, Angela Moore, Michael Maloof, Jose Luis Bedoy, Carolyn J. Leep, R. Brian Richter, James P. Vares, William Seiler, Lora J. Bogda, Raja Nassar, Ken Hunter, Jr., Randolph D. Sanford, and Scott Holland.

Career Corner mailing list readers, especially those who helped me write Step 9 – "Tracking and Following Up with Your Application" with their stories and experiences with human resources and applications also offered help.

PLANNING YOUR FEDERAL JOB SEARCH PROJECT

Introduction: Make a decision

Step 1: Network

Step 2: Review the process

Step 3: Research vacancies

Step 4: Analyze core competencies for language

Step 5: Analyze vacancy listings for keywords

Step 6: Write your Federal and electronic resume

Step 7: Write your KSAs and cover letter

Step 8: Apply for jobs

Step 9: Track your applications

Step 10: Interview for a Federal job

PLANNING

"In this time of unparalleled national challenges, Americans are increasingly looking to their government for guidance. ...Therefore, focusing on how to get the right people in place to pull everything together and executive plans of action needs to be a top priority."

Kay Cole James,
Director Office of Personnel Management,
The HR Paradigm Shift and the Federal Human Capital Opportunity,
The Public Manager, p. 13

Is it worth your while to invest your time and effort in searching for and applying for a Federal job?

Deciding to pursue a Federal job is a commitment and a decision. What are your personal and professional reasons for seeking Federal employment? To find Federal job leads, you can't just look up the recruitment ads on www.monster.com under your job title and email your resume and letter, (although some Federal jobs are listed on commercial on-line databases now.) The process for finding and understanding the jobs, agencies, and application instructions requires a commitment and determination. The Federal job search process is also a "project," not just sending in a resume and cover letter to an ad. You will see with the Ten Steps in this book that you have to take each step seriously if you are going to be successful landing a Federal job.

Lots of people are deciding to pursue a Federal job these days. With the telecom, dotcom, aviation, manufacturing, retail, and other industries downsizing and laying off, displaced people need jobs. Jobseekers have to make a conscious, serious decision to pursue a Federal job. The government as an employer is so huge and intimidating that it's a challenge to understand how to "get in." Here are a few examples of real people who have decided to pursue Federal employment. As you'll see, their reasons for making the commitment to pursue Federal jobs are all different.

A Silicon Valley Information Technology professional writes: "Since this is the first time I have ever tried to obtain a government job, I have no clear idea of what to do, what to expect, when to expect it, or if I am even going about it in the best manner. I share the public's perception of government jobs that it takes an inordinate amount of red tape and months or years to get hired. Many others in my situation are really tired of the job hopping in Silicon Valley that has been going on for so many years (the greener pastures syndrome), to say nothing of the massive ranks of high-tech workers there who are now unemployed. It has become quite apparent in the last few years that the days of long-term employment with a particular company no longer exist."

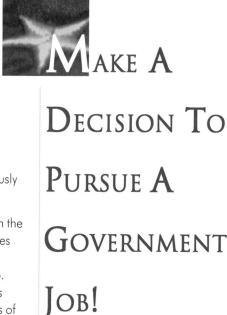

MAKE A DECISION TO PURSUE A GOVERNMENT JOB!

A graduate student who walks dogs to pay his way through college wrote: "I'd like to apply for positions with the CIA as an Analyst. My degree in political science, my analytical and writing skills, as well as my creativity in supporting myself throughout college might be of interest to the CIA."

A Las Vegas police officer wants a Federal job fighting terrorism: "I've always read and dreamed about a law enforcement job in government, but I didn't really know what the jobs were. I am hearing on the news about the FAA's recruitment of Federal Air Marshals and Trainers at the Tech Center in Atlantic City. This is the career for me!"

A general manager for a commercial meat manufacturer writes: "I have a great civilian job now with a great salary. But I have no 401(k), no retirement opportunity, only my Social Security to look forward to when I'm 65. I am 32 years old now and need something to support my family and me in the future."

A former Federal employee writes: "Applying for Federal employment is daunting and intimidating, to say the least. I go back to the days of the 171s."

A banking assistant/junior analyst with a bank asks: "I was wondering what are the best resources for obtaining a government job in the social services? I want to work in that area in a supervisory position."

A successful veterinarian who specializes in equine care writes: "I have a successful equine practice, but it's routine now. I'd like to work at NIH in a veterinary research institute where I can contribute my expertise and knowledge. I'm not concerned with salary. I'd like to contribute toward research and policy-making that will improve the quality of feed for horses."

A fish breeder writes: "I have been breeding fish and marketing and selling them to retail stores for the last 10 years. I know that NIH does fish research and I'd like to work in a breeding and research institute where I can contribute my expertise."

A social worker writes: "I went back to school a year ago to study bioterrorism and epidemiology. I'm not finished with the degree program yet, but I'd like to begin my search for a Federal job with the Centers for Disease Control, Environmental Protection Agency, or other Health and Human Services agency NOW. They need me now!"

A recent college graduate says: "I have a degree in psychology and political science. I speak three languages. Can I get a job in government?"

"Fortunately, government jobs are now perceived much differently, and favorably, by people than they were in the past. It now seems to be the ultimate answer to unstable and unpredictable employment, along with so many benefits that it provides, especially being able to move within agencies while still maintaining the same benefits."

- Bill Cavdek
Downsized IT Professional
Silicon Valley

A crisis management consultant writes: "I am interested in re-instatement in the Federal government (GS-14, Series 1035, Supervisory Public Affairs Specialist) to help with communications/crisis management programs related to Operation Enduring Freedom. Do you have any ideas about how I might proceed?"

A frustrated, laid-off IT worker writes: "I would really like to work for the Federal government. I am an IT professional currently, but believe myself to be underqualified for a lot of government IT jobs. I get disheartened when I see a four-year degree required, plus clearances, etc., but I am very capable and a quick learner, which can be proven by some excellent references. In other words, I am definitely open to another career field, particularly in the intelligence area with the CIA, for example."

WHAT ARE YOUR REASONS FOR SEARCHING FOR A FEDERAL JOB?

All of these Federal job seekers have decided to try to find a Federal position for different reasons. What are your reasons?

- Fighting terrorism
- Homeland Security
- Public service / Mission oriented
- Better retirement
- Better pay
- Career change
- Returning to government
- Steady employment
- Government is the best employer in town

Always keep your objective visible during your Federal job search. At times, you may become frustrated at the process. Keep your goal clear and persevere!

"Stability, purpose, and a bevy of openings make Uncle Sam an employer of choice for many. Amid rough economic seas, an uncertain world, and an unfamiliar job market, what do American workers now want most in a job? Security."

Career Guide 2002, p. 37, U.S. News & World Report, Feb. 19, 2002, Matthew Benjamin

Federal Job Statistics — What Are the Odds?

Since the Federal job search is so daunting, it's good to feel positive that the effort is worthwhile. This chapter includes employment statistics for Federal jobs and Federal employees so that you can feel that your time could pay off—if the stars are lined up for you. Ligaya Fernandez is the Project Manager for an important study by the Merit System Protection Board, a government agency that oversees the Office of Personnel Management. Ligaya Fernandez and team member Paul VanRijn have been analyzing Vacancy Announcements and Federal jobs because of the new popularity of Federal employment. Here are some of their interesting findings that are all in favor of investing the time necessary to find and land a Federal job.

Vacancy Announcement Study — Early Results

These results are based on an analysis of 10,000 vacancy announcements randomly sampled from a total of 188,000 vacancy announcements posted in USAJOBS during FY2001.

- Outside applicants can apply to about 60 percent of the announcements (including 20 percent open to both outside AND internal candidates). The other 40 percent are for internal candidates only.

- 85 percent of the announcements are for single vacancies.

- 50 percent of the jobs are professional or administrative in nature.

- 75 percent of the jobs were advertised from December through April and then very little until August and September—probably coinciding with appropriations and end-of-year budget considerations.

- Occupations with the most vacancy announcements are: clerk, secretary, general administration, computer specialist, and management/program analyst.

- About 50 percent of the announcements are open for application between two weeks and one month.

Ten departments account for 75% of the postings. In order from most postings to least, these are: Army, Interior, Agriculture, Air Force, Navy, HHS, State, Justice, Defense, Treasury, and Commerce.

"The federal government employs over 1.8 million civilian employees and this does not include military personnel or postal service employees. In FY 2001, the federal government hired just over 100,000 new, permanent employees. Most of those hires were to replace employees who retired or resigned from among the 1.8 million. Given that approximately 40 percent of the current federal workforce will be eligible to retire in the next five years, the number of new hires for replacement purposes is unlikely to decline anytime soon. In addition, the President's budget for FY 2002 and 2003 anticipates filling over 63,000 new positions to meet homeland security needs. Therefore, in the next two years alone, the federal government will need to hire over 250,000 new employees.

Further, there is a growing realization within the government that the concept of filling professional and administrative positions primarily at the entry level is outdated. Historically, federal agencies have only filled between 5 to 15 percent of their positions at the GS-12 to 15 grade level with individuals from outside government but this is likely to change. Following a period of almost 8 years of downsizing, the federal government now has a 'thin bench' at the mid-career level in a number of federal agencies. In addition, a growing percentage of individuals—particularly new college graduates—entering the workforce no longer anticipate spending their entire career with one employer and may well move among the private, public, and not-for-profit sectors throughout their career.

Most federal managers and HR staffs understand that they will need to cast a 'wide net' in their recruitment efforts in order to ensure that an adequate number of well-qualified and experienced candidates are available to fill their vacancies, including those above the entry level. This is likely to lead to a greater percentage of mid-career level positions in the federal government being filled with candidates from outside the government. In short, there will be some terrific opportunities within the federal government at all grade levels for well-qualified job applicants over the next several years."

John M. Palguta
Vice President, Policy and Research
Partnership for Public Service
Washington, DC
www.ourpublicservice.org

"In short, there will be some terrific opportunities within the federal government at all grade levels for well-qualified job applicants over the next several years."

How long does it take to get a federal job?

The real truth here is that it takes anywhere from two to six months. The Federal agencies are striving to cut down the time from the announcement to the interview. The time is decreasing every month because the need to hire employees is more and more critical. The electronic job application process is typically faster than the paper application process.

Steps 8 and 9 in this book will tell you how to manage and follow-up on your applications.

How many jobs are there?

The Federal government is the largest employer in the United States. According to the *Federal Civilian Workforce Statistics*, an Office of Personnel Management publication, there are 1.8 million full-time Federal civilian employees, excluding the U.S. Postal Service and foreign nationals employed overseas.

The Federal government is the largest employer in the U.S. with 1.8 million employees. Walmart employs 1.3 million.

How many jobs are open at any one time?

The typical average number of jobs open at any one time is approximately 20,000. But since September 11, the number of jobs has risen. Since that time, an average of 40,000 to 50,000 Federal jobs has been open at any time. The number of government contractor jobs is in the thousands as well.

Career Growth will be great in the next 10 years in government.

What's the career growth potential for government jobs for the future?

Great! With approximately 60 percent of the entire Federal government workforce retiring in the next 5 to 10 years, there will be tremendous growth opportunities for management professionals. The average age of the Federal worker is 49.5. Many will retire and leave outstanding jobs open for newly hired employees. Here are a few Federal agencies' strategies for workforce planning, retirement, and recruitment written by Brian Friel in *Government Executive* magazine:

"Typically, the Army hires 17,000 civilians a year. Because of a retirement bulge in coming years, the Army predicts that they will need to increase annual hiring by about 8,000 people—up to 25,000 new hires a year. The Army has filled many of its positions in recent years by hiring people already working in government. Now civilian officials are developing a marketing campaign aimed at potential civilian workers. 'We haven't had practice in building a recruiting and advertising program, but we'll be ready by 2003,' says Army Human Resources Chief Elizabeth Throckmorton.

"About 15 percent of the 56,000-person workforce will retire by 2006, according to the GAO estimate. Health and Human Services Human Resources Chief White says the agency will be looking for new employees with strong analytical skills currently lacking in the workforce. The department also wants to hire nurses, doctors, and other much-in-demand health professionals."

"The Army has filled many of its positions in recent years by hiring people already working in government.

Now civilian officials are developing a marketing campaign aimed at potential civilian workers."

CAN ONE PERSON REALLY MAKE A DIFFERENCE IN A GOVERNMENT JOB?

Here's a story about Nyetta Patton, an employee at the Center for Medicare and Medicaid. She made a difference to thousands of women who applied for bone density tests through Medicaid. Now these women can get the test without a problem because she resolved the bureaucracy involved in this test request and subsequent payment.

"I am the only clinical person in the Managed Care Branch in Seattle, WA. Most people do not know who I am or what I do here at the Centers for Medicare and Medicaid Services (CMS). Staff members who know me think that I am a nurse. Most of them do not know that I am a nurse practitioner. As a Clinical Specialist for managed care (CMS, Seattle), I am constantly faced with researching physician requests for medical tests that have been turned down by HMOs. The policies and procedures for requesting tests through HMOs are not clear. An irate and frustrated physician called requesting his patient receive coverage for a bone density test. The HMO was stating that the test was not covered. I reviewed the HMO's osteoporosis and practice standards. It was obvious that the Plan B Carrier, HMO, and HCFA policies for bone density coverage for this were not up-to-date."

RESULT: Because of Nyetta, Medicare patients can now receive bone density tests more easily through their HMOs.

"We're developing an Army civilian brand that says: Come to work with the Army. We have wonderful missions. People don't realize all that civilians do in the Army."

Elizabeth Throckmorton

If making a difference is one of your career goals for searching for a Federal job, this is real. Individual Federal employees can make a difference.

FEDERAL JOB SEARCH DECISION CHART

1. Do you need a good job with good pay, benefits, career growth opportunities, and stability?

   Yes or **no**

2. Can you handle a job search that might take two to six months?

   Yes or **no**

3. Can you spend one to three hours per day researching job announcements, mission statements, agency programs, preparing applications, and updating your application list?

   Yes or **no**

4. Are you organized and efficient in preparing and saving your applications and announcements?

   Yes or **no**

5. Are you determined to persevere at searching for a career-type position?

   Yes or **no**

6. Do you want a job where you can make a difference for many people?

   Yes or **no**

If you've answered **yes** to four out of six of the questions above, then you should begin your Federal job search right now.

"I left a good job for meaning. Some have responded to September 11 by trading stability for fulfilling careers."

Career Guide 2002,
U.S. News & World Report, p. 37,
Feb. 19, 2002, Angie Cannon

Creativity, nerve, resourcefulness, and a positive attitude can win!

Some people think that the only way you can apply for a Federal job is through a posted vacancy announcement at www.usajobs.opm.gov or other Federal job-posting sites. You need to know that it is possible to learn about upcoming jobs, changing and growing organizations, internship opportunities, and personnel changes through your network of contacts.

NETWORK— WHO DO YOU KNOW?

STRATEGIES FOR SAVVY, CREATIVE NETWORKERS

Here are two examples of clever people who are marketing themselves through their network of friends and well-connected business acquaintances.

One savvy networking woman in Washington, D.C., gave her resume to her realtor. The million-dollar realtor sold houses to many of the presidential appointees who buy houses about every four years in Washington. This friendly, informed, and knowledgeable realtor also acted as an informal public relations representative for friends and family.

Another person wrote her resume and made it look and sound great so she could hand it out at a holiday party. She wanted everyone to know her background and interests in finding a certain job in the Washington area. As a result of her resume distribution method, her friends became more aware of her skills and experience and she gained the opportunity to interview for a job in development with one of the Smithsonian Institutions. She was subsequently hired into a much-sought-after Smithsonian position.

Your network is important—even with an official Federal job search. Your contacts probably won't be able to GET you a Federal job, but they will give you the information you need to know what's going on in the agency and when they might be hiring.

"I called my neighbor, who is a GS-14 at SSA. She watched for vacancy announcements for me and kept me up-to-date. Finally a job was posted that fits my skills!"

INTERVIEWING YOUR NETWORK

How do you go about using your network once you've identified it? The following sections detail some of the specific ways you go about interviewing your network contacts—both formally and informally.

Federal Employees

If you have a friend, relative, or neighbor who is a Federal employee, you need to meet with or call that person. If he or she works in an agency that would be of interest to you, that's even better. You need to ask questions.

Here are a few questions you can ask at your first or second contact:

Is your department hiring?
What agency do you work for?
What office are you in?
Do you travel?
What do you like about your job?
What do you do?
Do you like the people you work with?
Who are your customers?
What are your programs or services that you provide?

Be prepared to give your contacts your resume. They will ask for it! Have lunch with your contact if possible. Go to the Federal building, get through security, walk down the halls, look at the offices, "feel" yourself there in the building. This immersion will help you write better Federal resumes for the jobs. It will help you understand the job descriptions better. The physical buildings will help you realize that a government job is not just a government job.

Who you know is important even when seeking a Federal job. Don't be bashful when you're looking for a job. This is the time to tell people what you're looking for.

Friends and Relatives of Federal Employees

If you don't know anyone who is a Federal employee, survey everyone you know locally and long-distance. It is quite likely you have a friend in this widening networking sphere who knows a Federal employee. Ask your friend to introduce you to the Federal employee. Explain that you are in a Federal job search and are making as many contacts and inquiries as possible. You might hear that you will have to apply for jobs through the Office of Personnel Management Web site. You can say that you know that, but you are trying to find any inside information about jobs, customer services, agencies, and hiring practices for particular agencies. Everything you learn will help you understand the Federal job search process.

Federal employees know that the government is anxious to hire quality people, so they should be helpful and informative about the job search process. They also know it is complex, difficult, and hard to understand, so they will help you interpret a vacancy announcement if they can. If you can befriend a Federal employee (or Federal manager), this will be a great benefit to you.

Almost Strangers

Don't forget neighbors and people you don't know very well who work for the government. Yes, these people are important too. If you have any outgoing spirit, you should introduce yourself. Simply tell them you are a neighbor and that you have decided to begin the Federal job search. You know that they work for the government and that you would appreciate ten minutes of their time to talk about their job and their agency. (Don't ask about jobs right away.) Get them to talk to you—at their convenience—about their jobs. Ask them how they make a difference in their work. After they have talked for 10 minutes, then you could begin to talk about yourself and what you are looking for in a government job. They will come up with ideas about how you could fit into their agency. It's very possible they will be hiring sometime in the near future. These contacts could be your eyes and ears for vacancy announcements that will be coming up.

Y ou have to be your own public relations agent when you're job-seeking. You have to know what you want, know what you have to offer and be able to speak it quickly.

Agencies are growing, changing and relocating. Ask questions about job opportunities with your friends and relatives who work for the government.

CORRESPONDENCE CAMPAIGN

Keep your friends and contacts in the loop on your job search. Tell them about the agencies and job titles that you have found. Always write—either by email or regular mail—when you receive a letter, telephone call, interview invitation, or job offer. Keep in touch with your friends and contacts so that they will remember your campaign—in case a job lead comes up. They will start to root for you and probably want to help you with your campaign. Sound excited, enthusiastic, and positive (even if you're not).

P.S. Even if you don't land a Federal job from one of these leads, one of your contacts will probably recommend you to A JOB because he or she is so impressed with your perseverance, attitude, and hard work!

PART I SUMMARY

Now that you've decided to pursue a Federal job and you've built your networking list, you're ready to begin the actual job search. Part II will lead you through the websites and information you need to make informed choices about job titles, grades, and agencies that best fit your qualifications and skills. The more you know about government jobs, the better you can match your resume to a Federal job and the more successful you will be with your Federal job campaign.

Even in the electronic resume writing application where you post your resume to a database, it helps to know people in the agency who know what jobs are coming up.

RESEARCH
THE FEDERAL
JOB INFO

"OPM Chief pledges to simplify federal hiring processes. It's not always easy to apply for a federal job."

Kay Cole James,
Director, Office of Personnel Management,
Brian Friel, www.govexec.com, April 22, 2002

The Office of Personnel Management has a fresh vision for the new millennium that will be implemented in 2002. According to Acting Associate Director for Employment Dick Whitford, the OPM plans to improve its overall image and recruitment procedures this next year with the intent of hiring thousands of Americans to fill critical open positions within the Federal government.

REVIEW THE FEDERAL JOB PROCESSES

Unraveling the Federal hiring process is not easy. To the external applicant, it is difficult to understand the hiring process. Yet, the Federal sector is a major employer in the United States, with talented people from all walks of life. How did these employees get their jobs in the first place? Let's take a look at some of the Federal personnel terminology and try to understand what happens in the Federal hiring process.

UNRAVELING THE TERMINOLOGY AND PROCESSES

The good news is that many Federal agencies are using new "e-Government" programs to improve the hiring time, efficiency, and responsiveness to customers/applicants. Most Federal agencies are in a hiring mode all the time. Given all of the opportunities that exist for employment in the Federal sector, the Federal Government is working hard to catch up with the private sector in automated hiring procedures. Consequently there is a lot of great information for outside job applicants on the Office of Personnel Management's website (www.opm.gov).

Here is the Three-Step Process promoted by the Office of Personnel Management. This book examines and explains ten steps to a Federal job. You can decide which is more accurate when you finish this book.

STEP 1

Use any of the Automated Components of the Federal Employment Information System.

The Federal government's employment information system provides worldwide job vacancy information, employment information fact sheets, job applications and forms, and has online resume development and electronic transmission capabilities. In some cases, people who seek Federal employment can apply for positions online, but you will notice that most Federal jobs open to outsiders still require a written resume. USAJOBS is updated every business day from a database of more than 12,000 worldwide job opportunities. USAJOBS is available to job seekers in a variety of formats. This ensures access for customers with differing physical and technological capabilities. It is relatively convenient, accessible through the computer (www.usajobs.opm.com) or telephone (478-757-3000 or TDD 478-744-2299), and available 24 hours a day, seven days a week.

This 3-step process is correct, but you will have to follow the announcement's directions on "how to apply" instructions. Each agency is unique.

STEP 2

Obtain the Vacancy Announcement.

Once you have identified a job announcement that interests you, you will need more information on the specific job as well as the appropriate application forms. Many of your questions will be answered as you read through the announcement. For example, announcements provide closing/deadline dates for applications, a brief synopsis of the duties of the position, whether or not a written test is required, educational requirements, duty location, salary, and other such information.

STEP 3

Follow the Application Instructions.

You may apply for most jobs with a resume. For jobs that are filled through automated procedures, Federal agencies may require you to submit an electronic resume and/or other specialized forms. Jobs with unique requirements may occasionally require special forms, and frequently require you to write out detailed statements outlining your knowledge, skills, and abilities related to the specific job announcement.

HOW FEDERAL JOBS ARE FILLED

Most Federal agencies fill their jobs basically the same way as private industry by writing a vacancy announcement, describing the job, and requesting applications sent directly to the agency. Previously, the Office of Personnel Management (OPM) maintained a list of applicants and required standardized written tests. You no longer need to complete the SF-171 or the OF-612. You can submit a resume that looks like a traditional chronological resume you would submit in the private sector, as long as you include the "compliance" information mentioned in the side box, and any other specific information that is requested in the job announcement.

All jobs are required to be posted on www.usajobs.opm.gov.

Agencies in the competitive service are required by law and OPM regulation to post vacancies with OPM (for positions lasting more than 120 days) whenever they are seeking candidates from outside their own workforce. (*Agency,* in this context, means the parent agency—such as Agriculture, Department of Defense, and so forth.) These vacancies are posted on OPM's USAJOBS and are also posted with state employment service offices.

Classes of Federal Employees

The two classes of jobs in the Federal government are *competitive* and *excepted service*. To be eligible you must be a citizen of the United States. There is no maximum age limit for appointment to most positions in the competitive service, but some jobs, such as law enforcement officers and firefighters, do have limits.

Competitive service jobs are more typical. These are the jobs that are announced on www.usajobs.opm.gov. They are subject to the civil service laws passed by Congress to ensure that applicants and employees receive fair and equal treatment in the hiring process.

Excepted service jobs are the jobs with agencies that set their own qualification requirements and are not subject to the appointment, pay, and classification rules in Title 5, United States Code. However, they are subject to veterans' preference. Some Federal agencies, such as the Federal Bureau of Investigations (FBI) and the Central Intelligence Agency (CIA), have *only* excepted service positions. In other cases, certain organizations within an agency or even specific jobs may be excepted from civil service procedures. Positions may be in the excepted service by law, by executive order, or by action of OPM. These excepted agencies are able to be more flexible with recruitment incentives, salaries, promotions and other personnel matters.

Your Federal resume must contain the following information:

Job Information
Announcement number, title, and grade.

Personal Information
Full name, mailing address (with ZIP code), day and evening phone numbers (with area code), social security number, country of citizenship, veterans' preference, reinstatement eligibility, highest Federal civilian grade held.

Education
High school name, city and state; colleges or universities, name, city and state; majors and type and year of any degrees received (if no degree, show total credits earned and indicate whether semester or quarter hours).

Work Experience
Job title, duties and accomplishments, employer's name and address, supervisor's name and phone number, starting and ending dates (month and year), hours per week, salary and indicate whether or not your current supervisor may be contacted. Prepare a separate entry for each job.

Other Qualifications
Job-related training courses (title and year), job-related skills, job-related certificates and licenses, job-related honors, awards, and special accomplishments.

Sources of "Eligibles"

Eligibles is the Federal term for job candidates who meet the Federal requirements for hiring eligibility. In filling competitive service jobs, agencies generally choose from among three groups of candidates:

✪ A competitive list of eligibles administered by OPM or by an agency under OPM's direction. This is the method that centers around USAJOBS announcements online and is the most common method of entry for new employees.

✪ A list of eligibles who have civil service status and are currently working in government.

✪ Non-competitive eligibles: Special non-competitive appointing authority established by law or executive order. People with special status include: Veterans' Readjustment Appointment (VRA), people with disabilities, the special authority for 30 percent or more disabled veterans, and the Peace Corps.

FREEDOM TO MANAGE FOR FEDERAL RECRUITERS

As you can tell by reading through this chapter, the Federal hiring process is complex. Although put on the back burner by the September 11 terrorist attacks, plans are afoot in both the White House and Congress for civil service reforms. Changes may be formally unveiled to bring about the Bush administration's idea of a *freedom to manage* proposal, backed by much-needed legislation. Both Democrats and Republicans are interested in simplifying and speeding up the Federal hiring process, expanding the concept of pay for performance, and implementing hiring incentives. Freedom to manage also focuses on training and other career development issues to enhance the benefits of Federal employment.

The Federal Human Capital Act of 2001 (S1603), introduced by Senator George Voinovich (R-OH) and unveiled at an October 2001 event hosted by the newly-formed Partnership for Public Service, is designed to empower Federal agencies to recruit and retain skilled workers and better manage the workers they have now. The proposed legislation calls for reforms in Human Capital Management and the inclusion of Human Capital Strategic Planning in agency program performance reports to Congress and the Office of Personnel Management (OPM). ("Human Capital Management" means human resources management and

"One of the most difficult problems facing federal managers will be what to do about the thousands of experienced homeland security professionals who are expected to retire soon. A third of employees at the Coast Guard, the Federal Emergency Management Agency, the Animal and Plant Health Inspection Service, the Customs Service and the INS will be eligible to retire in the next five years. About 12.5 percent of federal law enforcement professionals are expected to retire from 2001 to 2005, up by nearly 40 percent over the previous four years."
Katherine McIntire Peters, "The Challenge," www.govexec.com, July 15, 2002

strategic planning for better HR management in government wording.) Among the highlights of the bill is the creation of a "Chief Human Resources Capital Officer" in major agencies to oversee management reforms and to plan for future needs. According to Senator Voinovich, one of the chief reasons he has pushed for reform legislation is that, in his words, "we're not using common sense and modern techniques in recruiting people."

See http://thomas.loc.gov for information of current legislation.

DECIDE ON AGENCIES

To make a decision about which areas and functions of the Federal government interest you, you need to learn more about the workings of Federal agencies. You can find a discussion to help you gain this knowledge of the missions of the various government agencies at http://www.firstgov.gov/featured/usgresponse2.html#agencies.

What Agency Is Right for You?

You will need to make several decisions regarding your Federal agencies. First will be a **geographic** one. Do you want to stay in your current city or would you consider relocating? The second is the **industry or services** of the agency. Do you have a preference for the mission of the agency? Or will you accept a good job in any agency with any mission that you can support?

Geographic Decision

Do you want to relocate? Can you relocate? Are you staying right where you are?

The best way to decide on an agency is to know what Federal agencies are in your local geographic area. You can look up Federal agencies in your government section of your phone book. Or you might know about agencies in your area. For instance, here in Baltimore, we have Social Security Administration (headquarters center for all of SSA); Centers for Medicare and Medicaid (handles all of the Medicare and Medicaid for the entire U.S.); a District Internal Revenue Services office; the U.S. Coast Guard (at the Baltimore Harbor); Ft. Meade Army Base; National Security Agency (NSA); U.S. Army Corps of Engineers; Defense Investigative Services Agency; and a few others. That's quite a few government agencies in the local Baltimore area.

"I have to stay local because of my husband's position and children in school. We can't move. I'll have to target Bureau of Land Management, Dept. of the Interior, Forest Service and the Corps of Engineers because they are the major federal employers in Salem, Oregon."

Deciding on your agency is like deciding on an industry in private industry. You might have been in the financial services field before, now you'd like to stay in finances and accounting, but you should focus on an agency. Defense Finance Accounting Services, General Services Administration, U.S. Treasury, Internal Revenue Service and other agencies are principally financial and accounting in services. It's great to look for jobs by going to the agency website directly. Read the mission, the recruitment ads and the services. Get to know your prospective agency.

You can search for agencies by state and town very easily at the www.Federaljobsearch.com Web site. You can see how many jobs are open in a specific town any day of the week. For instance, in Portland, Oregon, today there are 90 jobs; in Roseberg, Oregon, there are 5 jobs. In Alaska there are 128 Federal jobs open right now.

Mission Decision

Another way to make an agency decision is by the mission and purpose of the agency. You know what your special interests are. You know what education and training you have. You should try to match your interests to the mission of the agency, unless you are technical and administrative. If you are a generalist with skills needed by any agency, such as computer, contracts, administrative, or administrative support, then any Federal agency can use your skills. If you have a passion for a particular service or program, then pick your agency by its mission.

If you are a scientific researcher and interested in health, animals, wellness, and medicine, the **National Institutes of Health** would be a great place to work. Check them out at http://www.nih.gov/icd/.

> **NIH Mission:** Founded in 1887, the National Institutes of Health today is one of the world's foremost medical research centers, and the Federal focal point for medical research in the U.S. The NIH, comprised of 27 separate Institutes and Centers, is one of eight health agencies of the Public Health Service, which, in turn, is part of the U.S. Department of Health and Human Services.

If you like the outdoors, streams, trees, land-use, and communities, then you could consider the Department of Interior agencies.

> **Bureau of Land Management Mission:** To protect the country's land, trees, streams, wildlife, and community resources.

If you are interested in healthcare policies and issues, the Department of Health and Human Services agencies would be of interest to you.

> **Department of Health and Human Services Mission:** The Department of Health and Human Services is the United States government's principal agency for protecting the health of all Americans and providing essential human services, especially for those who are least able to help themselves.

If you like housing, real estate, contracts, and property management, the General Services Administration would be a great agency for you because they own and manage so much real property.

GSA National Account Program Mission: We have designated National Account Executives and Regional Account Managers to work with our clients to understand their changing organizations and workspace requirements, make it easier for them to do business with us, and provide smart advice about their real estate portfolios.

If you are a medical professional, the Veteran's Administration is serving thousands of veterans with medical, housing, education, and financial services.

Veteran's Administration Mission: To serve America's veterans and their families with dignity and compassion and be their principal advocate in ensuring that they receive medical care, benefits, social support, and lasting memorials promoting the health, welfare, and dignity of all veterans in recognition of their service to this Nation.

If you are an engineer, scientist, or administrative, technical, logistics, or transportation person and would enjoy the Defense world, then you might like to submit your resume for civilian jobs with Navy, Army (including U.S. Army Corps of Engineers), Marines, or Air Force where you can support the warfighters on ships and overseas. It is exciting and meaningful work.

Navy Mission: We ensure that the right people are in the right place at the right time to support the mission of the Department of the Navy.

U.S. Army Corps of Engineers Mission: The United States Army Corps of Engineers (USACE) is made up of approximately 34,600 civilian and 650 military men and women. Our military and civilian engineers, scientists, and other specialists work hand in hand as leaders in engineering and environmental matters. Our diverse workforce of biologists, engineers, geologists, hydrologists, natural resource managers, and other professionals meets the demands of changing times and requirements as a vital part of America's Army.

If you like finance and accounting, you would like working for Defense Financing and Accounting Services, any agency of the Department of Treasury, and any other government agency. (Extensive accounting, finance, budget, and contracting jobs can be found in all areas of government.)

DFAS Mission: To provide responsive professional finance and accounting services to the people who defend America.

" I have been employed by the Federal government for over 18 years, and I thoroughly enjoy the challenges as well as flexibility of my job. Not only do I work on projects that are important, but I am able to telecommute two days each week from my home. I also earn an average of 45 days each year for holidays, vacations, sick leave and family leave days. I can donate my vacation days to colleagues if they need them for extended medical emergencies. Over the years, I have found the Federal government to be very flexible in terms of time-off to care for my family. You can't beat government benefits. "

Contract Specialist,
Wright-Patterson AFB, Ohio

Treasury Mission: Promote prosperous and stable American and world economies; manage the government's finances; safeguard our financial systems; protect our nation's leaders; secure a safe and drug-free America; and continue to build a strong institution.

Federal agencies are diverse and provide various services and missions for the American public. Reading the agency's mission statements is an important part of your Federal job search. If you don't understand or know the agency's mission, you might not be successful with your application. You need to understand and integrate your interests and skills into meeting the needs of the agency's mission.

REVIEW JOB TITLES, OCCUPATIONAL SERIES, AND MATCHING QUALIFICATIONS

You can find the "Handbook of Occupational Groups and Families" at http://www.opm.gov/fedclass/text/HdBkToC.htm to learn more about how the Federal government organizes job categories.

Before you can find vacancy announcements that are appropriate for your experience, education, and skills, you will need to know what job title is correct. Some Federal job titles are not the same as private industry. For instance, here's a good example. If you are a university researcher and writer, you could be very well qualified for a Management or Program Analyst position in government. How would you know this if you didn't study the Federal government's job title scheme? The Civil Service System and job titles were created in 1949. The job titles need to be updated, and as of the publishing date of this book, the job titles are not state-of-the-art for 2002.

Below is a list of Occupational Groups and Series and Families that could give you some clues as to your job title and series number for your job search. Two of the occupational groups are difficult to understand but are important for private industry applicants. The **300 General Administrative** and the **1100 Business and Industry Group series** have a lot of positions that equate well to private industry jobs. The job titles are not the same in government as in private industry.

"I know I can do a job in government, but I can't find anything that matches my skills on www.usajobs.opm.gov. I guess I just don't know the job titles that would be equal to my job. I work as a Catering Manager for an Event company. I have administrative skills and good people skills. What job titles would work for me?"

ANSWER:
Administrative Assistant,
Administrative Officer,
Program Assistant,
Security Screener,
Border Patrol Agent,
Management Assistant.

STEP TWO   FEDERAL JOB PROCESSES

Definitions of General Schedule Occupational Groups and Series

GS-0000 - Miscellaneous Occupations Group

GS-0100 - Social Science, Psychology, and Welfare Group

GS-0200 - Human Resources Management Group

GS-0300 - General Administrative, Clerical, and Office Services Group

> This series includes Program Analyst, Management Analyst, Administrative Officer, Secretary (Office Automation), Executive Secretary, Clerical positions.

GS-0400 - Biological Sciences Group

GS-0500 - Accounting and Budget Group

GS-0600 - Medical, Hospital, Dental, and Public Health Group

GS-0700 - Veterinary Medical Science Group

GS-0800 - Engineering and Architecture Group

GS-0900 - Legal and Kindred Group

GS-1000 - Information and Arts Group

GS-1100 - Business and Industry Group

> This series includes contracts, business analysts, marketing, business-related positions.

GS-1200 - Copyright, Patent, and Trademark Group

GS-1300 - Physical Sciences Group

GS-1400 - Library and Archives Group

GS-1500 - Mathematics and Statistics Group

GS-1600 - Equipment, Facilities, and Services Group

GS-1700 - Education Group

GS-1800 - Investigation Group

GS-1900 - Quality Assurance, Inspection, and Grading Group

GS-2000 - Supply Group

GS-2100 - Transportation Group

GS-2200 - Information Technology Group *NEW SERIES* for computer professionals

Gs-2200 Information Technology Group includes: Network Managers, Webmasters, Database Managers, Programmers, Administrative Support in IT, User Support, Trainers

Definitions of Federal Wage System Job Families and Occupations

WG-2500-Wire Communications Equipment Installation and Maintenance Family

WG-2600-Electronic Equipment Installation and Maintenance Family

WG-2800-Electrical Installation and Maintenance Family

WG-3100-Fabric and Leather Work Family

WG-3300-Instrument Work Family

WG-3400-Machine Tool Work Family

WG-3500-General Services and Support Work Family

WG-3600-Structural and Finishing Work Family

WG-3700-Metal Processing Family

WG-3800-Metal Work Family

Teachers can find positions in the 1700 series, Education Group.

WG-3900-Motion Picture, Radio, Television, and Sound Equipment Operation Family

WG-4000-Lens and Crystal Work Family

WG-4100-Painting and Paperhanging Family

WG-4200-Plumbing and Pipefitting Family

WG-4300-Pliable Materials Work Family

WG-4400-Printing Family

WG-4600-Wood Work Family

WG-4700-General Maintenance and Operations Work Family

WG-4800-General Equipment Maintenance Family

WG-5000-Plant and Animal Work Family

WG-5200-Miscellaneous Occupations Family

WG-5300-Industrial Equipment Maintenance Family

WG-5400-Industrial Equipment Operation Family

WG-5700-Transportation/Mobile Equipment Operation Family

WG-5800-Transportation/Mobile Equipment Maintenance Family

WG-6500-Ammunition, Explosives, and Toxic Materials Work Family

WG-6600-Armament Work Family

WG-6900-Warehousing and Stock Handling Family

WG-7000-Packing and Processing Family

WG-7300-Laundry, Dry Cleaning, and Pressing Family

WG-7400-Food Preparation and Serving Family

WG-7600-Personal Services Family

WG-8200-Fluid Systems Maintenance Family

WG-8600-Engine Overhaul Family

WG-8800-Aircraft Overhaul Family

WG-9000-Film Processing Family

A Sales Director can become a Business Analyst, Marketing Analyst or Contract Specialist in the GS 1100 series.

A K-Mart Cashier can become an Administrative Assistant, Clerk-Typist, or Receptionist in the GS-0300 series.

Two Important Job Series that Relate to Private Industry Job Skills and Titles

The 300 Series is the most difficult to understand for private industry people interpreting their job titles and skills into Federal job titles. Here are a few of the significant titles and expanded descriptions in the 300 series that could help you in your Federal job search.

GS-0300 - General Administrative, Clerical, and Offices Group

This group includes all classes of positions the duties of which are to administer, supervise, or perform work involved in office management and administration; management analysis and research; administrative assistant; word processing, correspondence, and secretarial work; mail and file work; office equipment operations; mail processing equipment; copier/duplicating equipment; and other work of a general clerical and administrative nature.

GS-0301 - Miscellaneous Administration and Program Series**

This series includes positions the duties of which are to perform, supervise, or manage two-grade interval administrative or program work for which no other series is appropriate. The work requires analytical ability, judgment, discretion, and knowledge of a substantial body of administrative or program principles, concepts, policies, and objectives.

GS-0302 - Messenger Series*
GS-0304 - Information Receptionist Series*
GS-0305 - Mail and File Series*
GS-0309 - Correspondence Clerk Series*
GS-0312 - Clerk-Stenographer and Reporter Series**
GS-0313 - Work Unit Supervising Series**
GS-0318 - Secretary Series*
GS-0322 - Clerk-Typist Series**
GS-0326 - Office Automation Clerical and Assistance Series**
GS-0340 - Program Management Series *(In private industry this job could be called: researcher, analyst, team leader, project manager, manager, operations manager, service manager, assistant manager, operations manager, administrative manager. Under this series there is no subject-matter expertise required. There are many jobs with this title in government.)*

Line manager or director of one or more programs, including appropriate supporting service organizations. The primary qualification requirement is management.

GS-0341 - Administrative Officer Series** *(In private industry this job could be called: office manager, operations manager, administrative manager, assistant manager, supervisor, team leader, general manager.)*

Provide a variety of management services essential to the direction and operation of an organization. Extensive knowledge and understanding of management principles, practices, methods and techniques, and skill in integrating management services with the general management of an organization.

GS-0342 - Support Services Administration Series*

Supervising, directing, or planning and coordinating a variety of service functions that are principally work-supporting; i.e., those functions without which the operations of an organization or services to the public would be impaired, curtailed, or stopped. Such service functions include (but are not limited to) communications, procurement of administrative supplies and equipment, printing, reproduction, property management, space management, records management, mail service, facilities and equipment maintenance, and transportation.

GS-0343 - Management and Program Analysis Series** *(In private industry this job could be called: researcher, analyst, statistician, project manager, team leader, coordinator, liaison, representative, change agent, policy analyst, writer-editor, financial analyst, budget analyst, statistical analyst, program planner, efficiency expert, spokesperson, negotiator, briefer, problem-solver.)*

Analysts and advisors who manage the evaluation of the effectiveness of government programs and operations or the productivity and efficiency of the management of Federal agencies or both. Positions in this series require knowledge of: the substantive nature of agency programs and activities; agency missions, policies, and objectives; management principles and processes; and the analytical and evaluative methods and techniques for assessing program development or execution and improving organizational effectiveness and efficiency. Some positions also require an understanding of basic budgetary and financial management principles and techniques as they relate to long-range planning of programs and objectives. The work requires skill in: application of fact finding and investigative techniques; oral and written communications; and development of presentations and reports.

GS-0346 - Logistics Management Series**

This series covers positions concerned with directing, developing, or performing logistics management operations that involve planning, coordinating, or evaluating the logistical actions required to support a specified mission, weapons system, or other designated program. The work involves: (1) identifying the specific requirements for money, manpower, materiel, facilities, and services needed to support the program; and (2) correlating those requirements with program plans to assure that the needed support is provided at the right time and place. Logistics work requires: (1) knowledge of agency program planning, funding, and management information systems; (2) broad knowledge of the organization and functions of activities involved in providing logistical support; and (3) ability to coordinate and evaluate the efforts of functional specialists to identify specific requirements and to develop and adjust plans and schedules for the actions needed to meet each requirement on time.

GS-0350 - Equipment Operator Series*
GS-0360 - Equal Opportunity Compliance Series*

This series includes positions performing, supervising, or managing analytical, evaluative, and interpretive equal opportunity and civil rights compliance work. Positions in this series are concerned with the application of civil rights and equal opportunity laws, regulations, and precedent decisions to eliminate illegal discrimination and to remove barriers to equal opportunity. This work involves analyzing and solving equal opportunity and civil rights problems through factfinding, problem analysis, negotiation, and voluntary compliance programs. The work requires judgment in applying equal opportunity principles to solve problems or recommend action. Many positions in this series require specialized knowledge and skill in investigating and resolving allegations of discrimination. This series also includes equal opportunity or civil rights positions of an analytical, evaluative, and interpretive nature that are not properly classified to another series.

GS-0361 - Equal Opportunity Assistance Series*
GS-0391 - Telecommunications Series*

This occupation includes positions that involve: (1) technical and analytical work pertaining to the planning, development, acquisition, testing, integration, installation, utilization, or modification of telecommunications systems, facilities, services, and procedures; (2) managerial and staff work in the planning, implementation, or program management of telecommunications programs, systems, and services; or (3) line supervision over communications operations, when such work includes responsibility for management functions such as planning, recommending changes, determining organizational structure, staffing, training, and budgetary requirements.

GS-0399 - Administration and Office Support Student Trainee Series

GS-1100 - Business and Industry Group

This group includes all classes of positions having to do with business and trade practices, characteristics and use of equipment, products, or property, or industrial production methods and processes, including the conduct of investigations and studies; the collection, analysis, and dissemination of information; the establishment and maintenance of contacts with industry and commerce; advisory services; the property management; and administration of regulatory provisions and controls.

GS-1102 - Contracting Series*

> This series includes positions that manage, supervise, perform, or develop policies and procedures for professional work involving the procurement of supplies, services, construction, or research and development using formal advertising or negotiation procedures; the evaluation of contract price proposals; and the administration or termination and close-out of contracts. The work requires knowledge of the legislation, regulations, and methods used in contracting; and knowledge of business and industry practices, sources of supply, cost factor, and requirements characteristics.

GS-1103 - Industrial Property Management Series*

> This occupation includes positions that primarily require a knowledge of business and industrial practices, procedures, and systems for the management and control of Government-owned property. These positions involve technical work in the administration of contract provisions relating to control of Government property in the possession of contractors, from acquisition through disposition. Also included are positions that involve providing staff leadership and technical guidance over property administration matters.

GS-1104 - Property Disposal Series*

> This series includes administrative, managerial, and technical work required to redistribute, donate, sell, abandon, destroy, and promote the use of excess and surplus personal property. Employees must know: (1) characteristics, proper identities, and uses of property items; (2) merchandising and marketing methods and techniques; and/or (3) property disposal policies, programs, regulations, and procedures.

GS-1105 - Purchasing Series*

> This series includes positions that involve supervising or performing work to acquire supplies, services, and construction by purchase, rental, or lease through (1) delivery orders and/or (2) small purchase procedures. The work requires knowledge of policies and procedures for delivery orders and small purchases. This series also requires knowledge of commercial supply sources and common business practices related to sales, prices, discounts, units of measurement, deliveries, stocks, and shipments.

GS-1106 - Procurement Clerical and Technician Series*

GS-1107 - Property Disposal Clerical and Technician Series*

GS-1130 - Public Utilities Specialist Series

GS-1140 - Trade Specialist Series**

> This series includes positions where the duties are to administer, supervise, or perform promotional, advisory, or analytical functions pertaining to the commercial distribution of goods and services. The work performed concerns and requires a practical knowledge of market structures and trends, competitive relationships, retail and wholesale trade practices, distribution channels and costs, business financing and credit practices, trade restrictions and controls, and principles of advertising and consumer motivation.

GS-1145 - Agricultural Program Specialist Series*

GS-1146 - Agricultural Marketing Series*

GS-1147 - Agricultural Market Reporting Series*

Knowing your Occupational Series can help you LAND A FEDERAL JOB!

GS-1150 - Industrial Specialist Series*

This series includes positions that require primarily a practical knowledge of the nature and operations of an industry or industries, and the materials, facilities and methods employed by the industry or industries in producing commodities. These positions involve the administration, supervision, or performance of one or more of the following functions: (1) developing and carrying out plans for the expansion, conversion, integration or utilization of industrial production facilities, either to meet mobilization or strategic requirements or to strengthen the industrial economy; (2) furnishing technical information, assistance, and advice concerning facilities, machinery, methods, materials and standards for industrial production (that may include exploration, extraction, refining, manufacturing and processing operations); (3) developing and/or administering provisions or regulations covering such matters as materials allocation, tariffs, export-import control, etc.; (4) conducting surveys of industrial plants to evaluate capacity and potential for production of specific commodities; (5) planning, evaluating, and maintaining technical surveillance over Government production operations, either in contractor plants or in Government-operated plants; or (6) performing related functions that require essentially similar knowledge as the functions listed above.

GS-1152 - Production Control Series*

This series includes positions involved in the supervision or performance of planning, estimating, scheduling, and expediting the use of labor, machines, and materials in specific manufacturing or remanufacturing operations that employ mechanical or automated production systems and methods in the fabrication, rebuilding, overhaul, refurbishing, or repair of any type of Government-owned, controlled, or operated equipment, systems, facilities, and supplies.

GS-1160 - Financial Analysis Series*

This series includes all positions the duties of which are to direct or perform analytical and evaluative work requiring a comprehensive knowledge of: (1) the theory and principles of finance applicable to the full range of financial operations and transactions involved in the general activities of the various types of business corporate organizations; (2) the financial and management organization, operations, and practices of such corporate organizations; (3) pertinent statutory or regulatory provisions; and (4) related basic economic, accounting, and legal principles.

GS-1161 - Crop Insurance Administration Series*

GS-1162 - Crop Insurance Underwriting Series*

GS-1163 - Insurance Examining Series**

This series includes positions with the duties to direct, supervise, or perform work involved in insuring persons or property, determining that adequate insurance to protect Government or private interests has been provided, settling claims arising under insurance contracts, or performing other similar insurance examining work when the duties performed are of a technical, nonclerical nature requiring: (1) knowledge of insurance principles, procedures, and/or practices; the commercial insurance market; commercial insurance operations; or similar specialized insurance knowledge; (2) knowledge of pertinent statutory or regulatory provisions; related administrative regulations; and (3) some knowledge of contract law and of other laws related to the particular kind of insurance involved but not legal training equivalent to that represented by graduation from a recognized law school.

GS-1165 - Loan Specialist Series*

GS-1169 - Internal Revenue Officer Series*

This series includes positions involved in administering, supervising, or performing work related to collecting delinquent taxes, surveying for unreported taxes, and securing delinquent returns. The work requires application of a knowledge of: (1) general or specialized business practices; (2) pertinent tax laws, regulations, procedures, and precedents; (3) judicial processes, laws of evidence, and the interrelationship between Federal and State laws with respect to collection and assessment processes; and (4) investigative techniques and methods.

GS-1170 - Realty Series*

This series includes positions with the primary duties to perform, advise on, plan, or direct one or more of the following functions: (1) acquisition of real property; (2) management of real property in the administration of Federally owned, Indian-owned, leased, or consigned space or property; or (3) preparation for disposal; or (4) disposal of real property. The work requires a knowledge of real estate laws, principles, practices, and markets.

GS-1171 - Appraising Series*

This series covers positions that involve supervising or performing work in appraising and reviewing the appraisals of real or personal property or property interests. These positions require technical knowledge and skill in the application of the principles, practices, and techniques of appraisal.

GS-1173 - Housing Management Series*

This series covers positions that involve the following duties: (1) to manage or assist in managing one or more family housing projects, billeting facilities, or other accommodations such as transient or permanent individual and family living quarters, dormitory facilities and restricted occupancy buildings including adjacent service facilities and surrounding grounds; and/or (2) to administer, supervise, or perform work involved in the evaluation of housing management programs, the development of administrative procedures, and the provision of technical assistance to on-site housing management. Positions in this occupation require a variety of housing management and administrative knowledge and related practical skills in: operations and maintenance, procurement of services, cost management and financial planning, assignments and utilization, occupancy changes and periodic inspections, scheduled and special requirement surveys, new construction and improvements, control of furnishings and equipment, master planning, and management-tenant relations. While some positions may involve administrative or indirect supervision of trade or craft work, an intensive practical knowledge of skilled trade and craft work techniques and processes is not required.

GS-1176 - Building Management Series*

This series covers positions that involve management of buildings and other facilities to provide organizations with appropriate office space and essential building services. Employees in this series typically perform one or more of the following functions: (1) applying business knowledge to directly manage, or assist in managing, the operation of one or more buildings and the surrounding property; (2) directing comprehensive building management programs; or (3) performing staff level work in the study of building management methods and the development of standard building management practices.

GS-1199 - Business and Industry Student Trainee Series

You can go to http://www.opm.gov/fedclass/text/HdBkToC.htm at the Office of Personnel Management Web site and study more details of these positions so that when you write your resume, you can incorporate some of the keywords and descriptions in your job description write-ups.

REVIEW GOVERNMENT SALARIES TO DETERMINE YOUR GRADE LEVEL FOR YOUR GOVERNMENT JOB

"I currently make $75,000 in my current job, but I'd be willing to accept a GS 9 position, Step 10, in order to change my career. That would be $44,783. I know that the benefits are great in government and security is better than my current job."

Don't be deceived by the salaries on these schedules if they seem low. Remember that the government has reasonable salaries plus generous benefits, including holidays, vacation, family leave, health benefits, and retirement. Remember also that some government agencies will pay for recruitment bonuses if you have specialized skills that are needed by the agency.

Check the OPM Web site at http://www.opm.gov/oca/01tables/GSannual/html/2001gs.htm for current information about salaries.

The 2002 General Schedule Salary Table

The following table incorporates a 3.60% general increase, effective January 2002, and shows annual rates by grade and step.

Step \ Grade GS	1	2	3	4	5	6	7	8	9	10
1	14757	15249	15740	16228	16720	17009	17492	17981	18001	18456
2	16592	16985	17535	18001	18201	18736	19271	19806	20341	20876
3	18103	18706	19309	19912	20515	21118	21721	22324	22927	23530
4	20322	20999	21676	22353	23030	23707	24384	25061	25738	26415
5	22737	23495	24253	25011	25769	26527	27285	28043	28801	29559
6	25344	26189	27034	27879	28724	29569	30414	31259	32104	32949
7	28164	29103	30042	30981	31920	32859	33798	34737	35676	36615
8	31191	32231	33271	34311	35351	36391	37431	38471	39511	40551
9	34451	35599	36747	37895	39043	40191	41339	42487	43635	44783
10	37939	39204	40469	41734	42999	44264	45529	46794	48059	49324
11	41684	43073	44462	45851	47240	48629	50018	51407	52796	54185
12	49959	51624	53289	54954	56619	58284	59949	61614	63279	64944
13	59409	61389	63369	65349	67329	69309	71289	73269	75249	77229
14	70205	72545	74885	77225	79565	81905	84245	86585	88925	91265
15	82580	85333	88086	90839	93592	96345	99098	101851	104604	107357

If you are qualified for a certain grade, you can negotiate your step.

What the Salary Ranges Mean

The actual salary that the agency offers will be dependent on your qualifications. The general qualifications needed to receive that pay (and equivalent GS grade) are shown by the salary. Please see the announcement for specific education and experience requirements for the position.

$22,000–$39,000	Three years of general experience or at least one year of professional experience or a bachelor's degree (GS-5 and GS-8).
$33,000–$62,000	One or more years responsible and independent experience related to the job or a Masters or higher degree (GS-9 through 12).
$57,000–$88,000	One or more years highly responsible and independent experience directly related to the job to be filled (GS-13 to GS-14).
$79,000 and above	More than one year of highly responsible and independent experience directly related to the job to be filled, frequently requires supervisory or managerial skills.

The Senior Executive Service (SES)

The SES is a corps of men and women who administer public programs at the top levels of Federal Government. Positions are primarily managerial and supervisory. The SES is a gradeless system in which salary is linked to individual performance, not position. Basic annual salaries range from $109,100 to $125,700. Employees in most geographic locations also receive locality pay, with total pay ranging from $127,625 to $133,700. Some positions include additional recruitment incentives that are described next.

ES-1 must equal at least 120% of GS-15/1; however, basic pay may not exceed Executive Level IV. President adjusts rates annually; CY 2001 basic rates (excluding geographic locality pay):

ES-1 = $109,100	ES-3 = $119,400	ES-5 = $125,700
ES-2 = $114,200	ES-4 = $125,500	ES-6 = $125,700

The agency head sets basic pay at one of the six rates. Pay can be adjusted upward any number of rates once a year, but downward only one rate per year. In setting pay rates, agencies consider such factors as qualifications, performance, duties, and responsibilities of the position, and private sector pay.

Total compensation (including salary, cash awards for top performance, relocation, recruitment or retention allowances) may not exceed the pay for Executive Level I ($161,200 in CY 2001).

More information about SES can be found at http://www.opm.gov/ses/agencywebsites.html. How SES jobs are filled is detailed at http://www.usajobs.opm.gov/ei30.htm.

If you can accept one lower grade, you might get the job faster.

Then you can move up after you learn the government systems.

"I currently make $58,000. How does that translate into the government GS program?"

ANSWER: That would put you in the GS 9-12 range and depends on your specific experience and education and the job you are seeking.

Help wanted

"The role the vacancy announcement plays in government is perhaps the least appreciated of all. On the surface, a vacancy announcement merely lists roles, responsibilities and rewards and the criteria necessary to get them. The announcement does just what the name says: It announces a position that someone will eventually fill. Announcement written, position filled, case closed. Yet, in reality, the vacancy announcement is of irreplaceable, and unexpected, value. After all, employees are the lifeblood of the government; they're the ones who do the work and carry out the plans."

Susan Benjamin, Help Wanted, www.govexec.com, Feb. 4, 2002

RESEARCH VACANCY ANNOUNCEMENTS FOR JOBS

Once you have researched your appropriate Federal Job title and grade, you can look for job announcements that are of interest to you.

This chapter provides an analysis of a Federal vacancy announcement. The real announcement from www.usajobs.opm.gov had slightly more content. We deleted some of the repetitive information so that we could analyze the truly relevant content. Special comments are in blue print. Every announcement will be different. But certain features of the announcements are more important than others. You will have to analyze announcements carefully for the information important to you and the job. Generally Federal vacancy announcements are too long and are repetitive. You will have to be the selective editor to find the relevant information. This exercise will help you to analyze announcements for the pertinent information.

The announcement that we selected for this analysis is a real vacancy that was posted by the Immigration and Naturalization Service (Winter 2002).

You really cannot start your Federal job search until you study vacancy announcements.

Sample vacancy announcement

DEPARTMENT OF JUSTICE, IMMIGRATION & NATURALIZATION SERVICE (INS)
Vacancy Announcement Number: 01-49-DE002

> This announcement has a "DE" in the number. This means Delegated Examining Unit (DEU). This is the name for the personnel unit that reviews applications from non-Federal applicants. If you see other announcements that have DEU in the number, that means people outside of government can apply for this job.

Opening Date: 12/07/2001
Closing Date: 01/06/2002

> Closing date is very important. Later in this announcement the instructions tell you that the package has to be received in their office by CLOSE OF BUSINESS on January 6. Sometimes announcements will say that the package must be "postmarked" by a certain date.

> You should email or call the contact person at the end of the announcement to make sure the closing date hasn't changed. Many times the dates move up because of the lack of applications or a change in the announcement.

Position: COMPUTER ANALYST (SYSTEMS ANALYST)   GS-0334-13

> Sometimes you will see computer positions listed under the 2210 series number. This is the new classification number for computer and information technology professionals.

Salary: $63,211 - $82,180 per year

> You can negotiate your salary here. If you've been earning $82,000+ in your past jobs, you will probably be offered that salary in the government.

Duty Location: 1 vacancy at WASHINGTON, DC

> Later in this announcement under Special Notes, No. 5. it says that they will not be accepting applications from people who do not live in the Washington, DC metropolitan area and they won't pay for relocation.

SPECIAL NOTE TO APPLICANTS:

Due to current situations affecting the receipt of mail in the Washington, D.C. metropolitan area, the Immigration and Naturalization Service is unable to accept mail through the normal postal service. Therefore, we are continuing our policy that all applications must be postmarked by the closing date and received in the Human Resources Office within 5 calendar days of the closing date. We have established a special fax number dedicated to electronically receiving applications for our positions.
FAX: Headquarters Human Resource Office telephone: (815) 328-2872.

Electronic files cannot be accepted. Additionally, the application may be hand carried to a drop box on the Main Retail Level of the TechWorld Building at 800 K Street NW, in Washington, D.C., for during- and after-hours collection.

> Because of the problems with mail in DC, you should fax or hand carry the package to the dropbox.

TITLE, SERIES, GRADE: Computer Specialist, (Systems Analyst) GS-334-13
> Look for other Computer Specialist jobs under the 2210 series as well.

SALARY RANGE: GS-13: $63,211 - $82,180 (includes locality pay adjustment)

Note: Locality rates will increase once the new locality projections are final.

PROMOTION POTENTIAL (IF ANY): NONE
> This isn't very encouraging, but even if this position may not have promotion potential,
> you can find another job in the government that is a promotion.

VACANCY ANNOUNCEMENT NUMBER: 01-49-DE002

AREA OF CONSIDERATONS: All sources (all qualified candidates may apply for this position)
> Anyone can apply for this position. Inside or outside of government.

DUTY LOCATION: Immigration and Naturalization Service, Office of Executive Associate Commissioner,
Management, Office of Assistant Commissioner, Administration, Washington, DC.
> This would be an interesting place to work—Office of the Assistant Commissioner.

NUMBER OF VACANCIES: 1* Position (number of positions subject to change)
> Maybe they will hire more than one person if really good candidates apply.

DUTIES: The incumbent's primary responsibility is **oversight** of the **automation analysis** work necessary for
planning, defining requirements, and coordinating the design, integration, and/or modification of automated systems
for accomplishing **administrative management activities** by using computers. The incumbent is the Office of
Administration **point of contact for automation** with other organizations and participates in **developing business cases**
for enterprise resource planning, enterprise architecture, enterprise application **planning**, and the like. Plans and
coordinates the design of **sophisticated systems/subject-matter applications** in direct support of the Office of
Administration. Coordinates and interacts with the **Office of Strategic Information Technology Development (OSITD)
on IT investment issues.** Plans and participates in the **introduction of new and modified INS and Office of Administration
automated systems/subject-matter applications.** Provides **authoritative automation guidance** and assistance to Office of
Administration officials and personnel on INS and Office of Administration automated systems/subject-matter
applications and services. Provides, coordinates, and **conducts ADP/office automation training** for Office of
Administration personnel on Office of Administration specific systems. Serves as the **Office of Administration
Computer Systems Security Officer (CSSO).** This includes **communicating security standards** and requirements to the Office
of Administration staff, **assessing security practices**, and **correcting identified security deficiencies.** Coordinates Office of
Administration computer security activities with the **IRM Computer and Telecommunications Security Program Office.**
Ensures that Office of Administration staff attend and/or receive initial and required annual **computer security
awareness training** and education. Maintains and reviews **Certification and Accreditation documents.**

Performs other duties as assigned.
> This looks like a very challenging IT job with the responsibility for researching and
> implementing many changes and improvements that will affect all of INS. In order to match
> your resume to the duties in this position, you should analyze the keywords in this section and
> try to integrate them into your resume. The keywords are in bold. Use them in your resume
> if they are truthful.

QUALIFICATION REQUIREMENTS: To qualify for the GS-13 grade level, one (1) year of specialized experience equivalent to the next grade level (GS-12) is required.

> All you need to qualify for this position is one year at the salary and experience level in the duties. This looks like a responsible, challenging position, so you will have to demonstrate similar experience from your previous positions in your resume in order to qualify.

SPECIALIZED EXPERIENCE: Experience that demonstrated accomplishment of computer project assignments that required a wide range of knowledge of computer requirements and techniques pertinent to the position to be filled. This experience is generally demonstrated by assignments where the applicant analyzed a number of alternative approaches in the process of advising management concerning major aspects of ADP system design, such as what system interrelationships must be considered, or what operating mode, system software, and/or equipment configuration is most appropriate for a given project.

Alternative approaches in the process of advising management on ADP system designs. Also inter-relationships, configuration … computer consulting to senior management.

> There are some important keywords and skills in this paragraph.

EVALUATION METHOD: Applicants who meet the basic qualification requirements will be rated on their total background as it relates to the evaluation criteria. Applicants are encouraged to submit a separate Supplemental Qualifications Statement that addresses each Knowledge, Skill and/or Ability (KSA) listed in this announcement under EVALUATION CRITERIA and should provide detailed evidence of the KSAs in the form of clear, concise examples showing level of accomplishment and degree of responsibility.

> "Applicants are encouraged." This means that you should write the evaluation criteria or Knowledge, Skills, and Abilities statements with concise examples that show the level of accomplishment and degree of responsibility—hopefully at the level of the "duties" paragraph above.

EVALUATION CRITERIA:

1) Ability to communicate in writing regarding ADP matters.
2) Ability to function in a technical capacity or as a team member on ADP projects.
3) Ability to establish and maintain relationships and contacts inside or outside a particular environment in order to achieve coordination of a project, activity, or assignment.
4) Demonstrated knowledge of computer languages, utilities, machines, and access methods.
5) Demonstrated knowledge of database administration.
   > There are five KSAs with this application. If you study the KSA chapter in this book, you will be able to write these KSAs. Give examples of computer consulting, problem-solving, new systems integration, analysis, and training development that you have performed in past positions. The duties make it very clear what they are looking for in a top candidate.

HOW TO APPLY:

You may submit (1) a resume, the Optional Application for Employment (OF-612), the SF-171, or any other form of application. Whatever format you choose to describe your job-related qualifications must follow the guidelines outlined in the Office of Personnel Management pamphlet "Applying for a Federal Job" (OF-510). You may obtain the OF-510 from a Web site at www.opm.gov (click on Forms), from the INS office listed below, or by calling (202) 514-2530.

You can use a Federal-style resume as described in this book and samples in the index. You do not need to prepare an OF-612 or SF-171 in addition to the resume. You won't need the OF-510 pamphlet because the information on "what to include" in your Federal resume is in this book.

(2) In addition, applicants are encouraged to submit a supplemental statement addressing the KSAs listed above.

"Encouraged" means that you should write the KSAs or you won't be competitive.

(3) Applicants claiming veteran's preference must submit a copy of the DD 214. Veterans claiming 10-point preference must submit a copy of the SF-15 and required documentation.

Important for Veterans. The points are in your favor.

VETERAN'S PREFERENCE:

You must clearly identify your claim for veteran's preference on your application. If you are claiming a 5-point veteran preference, you must provide a DD-214, Certificate of Release or Discharge from Active Duty, or other proof of entitlement. If you are claiming 10-point preference, you will need to submit an SF-15, and the required proof (i.e., Veterans Administration letter dated within the last year, and the latest copy of report of separation from active duty (DD-214) to establish proof of honorable discharge). The Defense Authorization Act of November 18, 1997, extended veteran's preference to persons who served on active duty during the Gulf War from August 2, 1990, through January 2, 1992. The law grants preference to persons otherwise eligible and who served on active duty during this period, regardless of where the person served or for how long. The law also authorizes the Secretary of each military department to award the Armed Forces Expeditionary Medal for service in Bosnia during the period November 20, 1995, to a date to be determined. The award of the Medal qualifies for veterans' preference. More information on veterans' preference is available in the VetGuide that may be found at the U.S. Office of Personnel Management Web site at www.opm.gov.

Read these notes.

SPECIAL NOTES:

1)   All non-INS selectees are required to submit to a urinalysis test to screen for illegal drug use prior to appointment. This position may be subject to random drug testing.
2)   All applicants must meet all eligibility requirements as of the closing date of the vacancy announcement in order to be considered.
3)   This is a bargaining unit position.
4)   Relocation expenses are not authorized.
5)   Applications submitted from outside the area of consideration will not be considered.
6)   Appointment is contingent upon a favorable background security investigation.
7)   Applications must contain all required information in accordance with the instructions contained in this announcement (i.e., social security number and citizenship); incomplete applications will not be considered.

There is a security investigation for this position. Make sure you are able to make it through a favorable background security investigation. Don't apply for this position if you live in California or anywhere outside of the Washington, DC metropolitan area.

POINT OF CONTACT: Access Internet http:/www.usdoj.gov or {contact person}
CONTACT PHONE: (202) 514-2530
TDD: (202) 514-8988

You can call the contact person if you have questions. You might have to leave a voicemail message. Be informative when you leave a message. Tell him or her the announcement number of the position, ask what information you need, and allow enough time to call back. He or she might leave a response on your voicemail also, but you will be contacted.

CRITICAL ANNOUNCEMENT FEATURES:
Job Title, Series No., Grade
Agency, Location
Closing Date
Duties
Qualifications
How to apply

Summary of Important Vacancy Announcement Items

When analyzing vacancy announcements there are always major items that you search for quickly in order to determine if the announcement is still open and possible for you to apply. Here are the major items you should check quickly.

Title of Job and Grade and Geographic Location: Make sure it's correct for you.

Closing Date: If the date is too soon, it could be difficult for you to apply for the position. It will depend on whether you have your resume drafted and are ready to start applying for jobs now.

Do the instructions say that you have to have the package in the office by the end of the business day or can you have the package postmarked by that date? Should it be faxed? Can it be emailed? Should it be in the textbox or as an attachment? These days, the best way to submit is by fax if it is a "paper" application. If the package is automated, you should send by email or through the Resume Builder.

If the closing date says "Open Continuously," "Inventory Building," or has a date that is two years away, then this announcement is a database building announcement. This announcement represents

"If applicants don't have a clear picture of a job's requirements, they may understate their qualifications or place emphasis on the wrong factors."

many jobs that may open up at any time. The HR recruiters will search in this database for applicants who are qualified and have their resume in the database. These are good announcements and worth submitting your resume for. People are hired from the open continuously announcements everyday.

Who Can Apply: Open to Anyone With or Without Status. If the announcement says "Open to anyone," then you can apply. Status means that the person has worked for the government before or has a special status because of military or other special situation (more on this in the Index).

Location/Duty Station: Make sure you are willing to work in this geographic location. Check the announcement to see if people can apply who live outside the geographic region of the position.

Knowledge, Skills, and Abilities: Read the announcement to see if KSAs will be required to be written on separate sheets of paper, or if the KSAs can be included in the text of the resume.

If one of the KSAs seems to be IMPOSSIBLE to write because you have never worked in the agency and really do not know the agency's policies, procedures, regulations, or legislation, never fear. Read Chapter 7 on KSA writing. Read the "Writing the Unwritable KSA" segment. *You can write this KSA with honesty.*

Duties: Read the duties carefully because the title of the position may not reflect the duties of the job at all. The duties could represent a completely different job than the one you thought would be described. Sometimes the government job titles do not match the duties you would expect.

Qualifications: Read the qualifications to determine if you have the Generalized and Specialized Qualifications. If the announcement states one year, that means 52 weeks, 40 hours per week. This is the reason they ask for the number of hours you worked in your jobs for the last 10 years. They want to make sure you have the specialized experience they need to determine if you are qualified for the job.

How to Apply: Read the instructions on what to send with the application. Sometimes this is not very clear. You can contact the person on the announcement to make sure you have the right application format. The usual application includes a resume, KSAs (maybe), last evaluation (if possible), DD-214 (if you were in the military), transcripts (sometimes, not often).

"I was delighted to see you recommend www.federaljobsearch.com in your *Electronic Federal Resume Guidebook*. I found that site while researching Federal job search Web sites about 15 months ago, and thought its sorting feature by state/city/town was the greatest thing since sliced bread. We have been recommending it to anyone looking for a Federal job since."

- Air Force Family Support Center Counselor

Federal Job Web Sites with Vacancy Announcements

Searching for good vacancy announcements is hard work. If you can, sign up for automatic emails that could save you time. Both the OPM and the other website mentioned in this chapter can send emails if you sign up and create a profile of your interests. If you find good announcements, be sure to save or print them so that you can keep track of your applications. Here are the two Federal job websites that we recommend:

The official **Office of Personnel Management** website www.usajobs.opm.gov

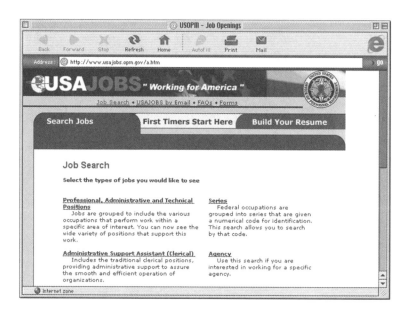

Federal Job Search.com
www.Federaljobsearch.com
Commercial site with better looking vacancy announcements by geographic region

Agency Website Employment and Career Pages

Check the specific agency website for their employment pages in case they have their own job listings. Many agencies have their jobs on www.usajobs.opm.gov and not on their own website.

Other websites: www.washingtonpost.com and www.monster.com sometimes will list Federal jobs. If you do find a Federal announcement on these two sites, the announcement will be short and sweet. It might not contain all of the needed information for you to be competitive against those who have read the announcement on the www.usajobs.opm.gov website.

Here are a few tips on making your search more fruitful:

✪ Bookmark these sites and check them every week or more frequently.

✪ Sign up for automatic emails with job listings.

✪ Study "how to apply" instructions on announcements.

Vacancy announcements aren't pretty, but they are very useful. Find the information you need and disregard the rest.

OPM pledges to change vacancy announcements to include:

A. A user-friendly application process that is not unduly burdensome nor time-consuming.

B. Clear, understandable job announcements and instructions for applying.

C. Timely and informed responses to questions about the requirements and the process.

D. Prompt acknowledgement that applications have been received.

E. Regular updates on the status of applications as significant decisions are reached.

F. A timely decision-making process.

"Successful professionals know that important projects need strategies and plans to be successful. Your long-term career strategy in the Federal workforce (or the private sector, for that matter) is one of the most important projects you'll ever tackle. Yet for most people personal career management is something we fit into the cracks while we're doing our work. Your career deserves your own best efforts. Organize, plan, and do the work—and do your homework by consulting the experts in the field, in person or in their writing."

- Michael Dobson, author of PRACTICAL PROJECT MANAGEMENT, MANAGING UP!, ENLIGHTENED OFFICE POLITICS, and others.

PART THREE

FIND YOUR
KEYWORDS
AND CORE
COMPETENCIES

ANALYZE

What are your best competencies for a Federal job? Are you flexible, hard-working, creative, resourceful, a good team member, customer-focused, a proven leader, a good listener, organized, able to handle change and pressure in the workplace?

What skills are government agencies looking for?

Federal agencies are looking for more than just the basic qualifications to do the job. For instance, for an Accountant, GS-7, you have to have one year specialized experience and 25 credit hours in accounting. How many hundreds of people have these qualifications? Lots. But do you also have the following traits?

- ✪ Proven experience working as a valuable member of a team
- ✪ Demonstrated your attention to customers
- ✪ Established your ability to meet strict deadlines
- ✪ Shown skill in discovering errors and saved customers thousands of dollars

If so, your resume will STAND OUT. These are your core competencies.

Supervisors are looking for the core competencies that will make you a high performer. Many human resource offices at Federal agencies are developing lists of "core competencies" that they would like to see in their employees—in addition to the generalized and specialized experience and education.

This step features the Veteran's Administration set of Core Competencies developed by a group of human resource and organizational development specialists in upstate New York. Their initial drive to create this set of eight core competencies was to improve the flexibility, interpersonal skills, and customer services skills of all employees in VA hospitals. They recognized that the employees were doing their jobs taking care of patients, but they weren't as customer-focused or flexible as they could be. Henceforth, the VA is hiring RNs, LPNs, and other health specialists who have the basic certifications and years of experience, as well as the ability to change and adapt as needed, manage multiple tasks, interact with patients and co-workers cohesively, and work effectively under pressure.

ANALYZE FEDERAL CORE COMPETENCIES FOR LANGUAGE

OPM defines competency as an "observable, measurable pattern of skills, knowledge, abilities, behaviors, and other characteristics that an individual needs to perform work roles or occupational functions successfully."

(U.S. Office of Personnel Management. Op. Cir., Glossary)

It is a recognized fact that these same competencies are needed in all agencies. An employee in a Defense agency has to change in a day's time when Congress asks for a new report on finances or other matters. An employee at the Center for Medicare and Medicaid has to change daily work efforts because of legislation sought by the President for improved services to Medicare customers. A fisheries biologist with the Bureau of Land Management has to change his focus because of an environmental committee or actions required by neighbors, industry, and Congress. All employees at the Department of Health and Human Services had to change their daily job routines following September 11. Now the focus is on healthcare, epidemiologic studies, environmental management, and security—not the former routine policies, procedures, and programs.

Core competencies should be considered and integrated into your resume along with your education and technical expertise. If you would like to learn more about core competencies, look for material on the topic of "emotional intelligence." Daniel Goleman is an expert in the field of emotional intelligence, which equates with core competencies. These are the valued skills in government and industry. The better you know and recognize your competencies and emotional intelligence, the better you will be able to market yourself and get ahead in the workplace.

HOW TO USE THESE SKILLS IN YOUR RESUME

While you are reading this chapter, use a pen to check off or underline language, skills, and information that you can use in your resume. You will, of course, have to be qualified with the right education and generalized or specialized experience, but to stand out among your competition, these core competencies can make the difference in your application.

Veteran's administration example

Core Competencies address the skills and attitudes most needed for today's work force challenges. These eight competencies form a natural progression toward interpersonal and organizational excellence. These core competencies should be demonstrated in most Federal applications—no matter what position you are seeking. This competency language can help you write a better Federal resume.

- ✪ Personal Mastery
- ✪ Interpersonal Effectiveness
- ✪ Customer Service
- ✪ Flexibility/Adaptability
- ✪ Creative Thinking
- ✪ Systems Thinking
- ✪ Technical Competency
- ✪ Organizational Stewardship

Include these skills and core competencies in your Federal resume. You will have the competencies to perform a Federal job. Are you creative? Do you have outstanding customer services skills? Do you continually strive to learn more? Are you flexible and adaptable? Say so in your resume. The government needs creative, flexible and customer-focused workers.

"Since the beginning of the 1990's, increasing attention has been focused on measuring competencies. One source defines competency as 'an underlying characteristic of a person which results in effective and/or superior performance in a job.'"

--Robert Wood and Tim Payne, *Competency-Based Recruitment and Selection: A Practical Guide*, John Wiley and Sons, New York, 1998, p. 24 (quoting in turn from G.O. Klemp, Jr.'s 1980 report to the National Institute of Education, titled "The Assessment of Occupational Competency.")

EXAMPLES FOR "OTHER INFORMATION":

Coach and Mentor, Big Brothers of America;
Member, Board of Directors, Homeowner's Association;
Amateur tournament golfer and enjoy family camping.

This resume information demonstrates:

interpersonal effectiveness,
organizational stewardship,
flexibility/adaptability,
and personal mastery.

Core Competency Descriptions for the High Performance Development Model

Personal Mastery

General Description:

- ✪ Assumes responsibility for personal development and career goals
- ✪ Takes time to reflect on personal satisfaction and balance between work and personal life
- ✪ Manages self effectively, including time and physical/ emotional health
- ✪ Takes initiative for continuous learning
- ✪ Actively seeks information on how one is perceived by others
- ✪ Improves behavior, skills, and knowledge as a result of evaluation and feedback
- ✪ Learns from setbacks or failures as well as from successful efforts

Resume Sample

PERSONAL:

Active leader in the community and school organizations. Continually strive for self-study in the most recent computer software. Attend professional conferences and read list-servers in my field of website development.

Resume and KSA Writing Tip

Personal mastery demonstrates your drive to improve your professional level. These skills are demonstrated by your professional memberships, conferences attended, professional training (college courses and developmental training), skills training, personal interests, non-profit activities, and volunteer participation. If you are a committee leader in your volunteer association, you will be demonstrating personal mastery. You can also demonstrate personal mastery by showing your career progression, accomplishments, committees, and tasks. Resumes that include only duties are not demonstrating personal mastery. You must write about accomplishments and other life components to show a well-developed person who is seeking improvement and personal mastery of skills.

Interpersonal Effectiveness

General Description:

- ✪ Builds and sustains positive relationships
- ✪ Handles conflicts and negotiations effectively
- ✪ Earns trust and holds respect
- ✪ Collaborates and works well with others
- ✪ Shows sensitivity and compassion for others
- ✪ Encourages shared decision-making
- ✪ Recognizes and uses ideas of others
- ✪ Communicates clearly, both orally and in writing
- ✪ Listens actively to others
- ✪ Honors commitments and promises

Resume and KSA Writing Tip

Interpersonal skills are a must in today's government and industry jobs. If you can't get along with others, your career will not progress. These skills and language can be used in a cover letter, KSA statements, or in the descriptions of your work experience. Being able to get along with co-workers, customers, contractors, and vendors can mean you are a valuable employee. This knowledge, skill, and ability is one of the most important in government. You can include this statement in your Profile Statement (as shown in the examples in the appendix)— for example, "Recognized for interpersonal skills with customers and co-workers."

"Team Capabilities

Creating Group Synergy in Pursuing Collective Goals

People with this competence:

Model team qualities like respect, helpfulness, and cooperation

Draw all members into active and enthusiastic participation

Build team identity, esprit de corps, and commitment

Protect the group and its reputation; share credit"

--Daniel Goleman, *Working with Emotional Intelligence*, 1998, Bantam Books, p.216

Defense Contract Management Agency

The "Goals"

Deliver great customer service.

Lead the way to efficient and effective business processes.

Enable DCMA people to excel.

Resume Sample

Experienced in customer services providing follow-up, research, and attention to detail to resolve problems.

Customer Service

General Description:

- ✪ Understands that customer service is essential to achieving the VA mission
- ✪ Models commitment to customer service
- ✪ Understands and meets the needs of internal customers
- ✪ Manages customer complaints and concerns effectively and promptly
- ✪ Designs work processes and systems that are responsive to customers
- ✪ Ensures that daily work and the VA's strategic direction are customer-centered
- ✪ Uses customer feedback data in planning and providing products and services
- ✪ Encourages and empowers subordinates to meet or exceed customer needs and expectations
- ✪ Identifies and rewards behaviors that enhance customer satisfaction

Resume and KSA Writing Tip

Most Federal agency mission statements include a comment about improving customer service. This is a critical skill in government because of the important focus on services to the American public and the Defense agencies. Always include your customer services experiences, knowledge, and focus in your Federal resume. You can include a customer services statement in your Profile Summary at the top of your resume—for example, "Recognize the importance of customer service. Received more than 25 letters from customers for outstanding service and efficient handling of priority situations."

Flexibility/Adaptability

General Description:

- ✪ Responds appropriately to new or changing situations
- ✪ Handles multiple inputs and tasks simultaneously
- ✪ Seeks and welcomes others' ideas
- ✪ Works well with all levels and types of people
- ✪ Accommodates new situations and realities
- ✪ Remains calm in high-pressure situations
- ✪ Makes the most of limited resources
- ✪ Demonstrates resilience in the face of setbacks
- ✪ Understands change management

"Change Catalyst

Initiating or Managing Change

People with this competence:

Recognize the need for change and remove barriers

Challenge the status quo to acknowledge the need for change

Champion the change and enlist others in its pursuit

Model the change expected of others"

--Daniel Goleman, *Working with Emotional Intelligence*, 1998, Bantam Books, p.193

Resume and KSA Writing Tip

Flexibility is almost mandatory in government. Each agency changes its mission, services, customers, and procedures regularly. The government is striving to recruit people who are flexible, willing to change, and demonstrate the ability to manage multiple projects and priorities. You can write a "flexibility" statement in your work experience summary or your Profile statement—for example, "Demonstrated flexibility in handling multiple projects across agencies. Worked successfully under deadlines to achieve program objectives. Willing and able to work extra hours and take over additional tasks to complete project."

Creative Thinking

General Description:

- ✪ Appreciates new ideas and approaches
- ✪ Thinks and acts innovatively
- ✪ Looks beyond current reality and the "status quo"
- ✪ Demonstrates willingness to take risks
- ✪ Challenges assumptions
- ✪ Solves problems creatively
- ✪ Demonstrates resourcefulness
- ✪ Fosters creative thinking in others
- ✪ Allows and encourages employees to take risks
- ✪ Identifies opportunities for new projects and acts on them
- ✪ Rewards risk-taking and non-successes and values what was learned

Resume Sample

Created a new on-line database to improve the management of client information for 12 professionals. Designed the data input forms and report formats.

Resume and KSA Writing Tip

Creative thinking is becoming more popular in government. We all know that the government is bureaucratic and it is challenging to change processes—even for the better. But the government is recognizing that change is important and inevitable. The government is recruiting creative people who are willing to try new processes, take calculated risks, and even demonstrate entrepreneurial behavior. You can write a "creativity" statement like this: "Created a new process to receive information for website content. Recognized the need for consistent formatting and receiving of information to more efficiently update the intranet site. Designed an online form to assist content editors with organization of thought and information. Resulted in saving 50% of my time."

Systems Thinking

General Description:

- ✪ Understands the complexities of VA healthcare and how it is delivered
- ✪ Appreciates the consequences of specific actions on other parts of the system
- ✪ Thinks in context
- ✪ Knows how one's role relates to others in the organization
- ✪ Demonstrates awareness of the purpose, process, procedures, and outcomes of one's work
- ✪ Consistently focuses on the core business of the organization
- ✪ Asks questions that help others to think in a broader context
- ✪ Encourages and rewards collaboration

Resume and KSA Writing Tip

Systems thinking means that you have to be able to work through a complicated system and process. The government is huge and achieving success means that you have to work through a system. You have to be able to push your idea, process, or customer service through barriers and steps to achieve success. You have to be patient in such a large organization as the government. A resume or Profile statement could be the following: "Improved the system of receiving and managing emails from more than 500 customers per week. Categorized the requests, organized the information, and wrote ready responses to consistent inquiries. Streamlined the response time from one day to one hour. "

Resume Sample

As a team member worked effectively toward the completion of the project on-time and within the budget. Developed a strategy to cooperate with other departments to utilize their resources in addition to ours in order to meet an almost impossible deadline.

Technical Skills

General Description:

- ✪ Displays knowledge and skills necessary to perform assigned duties
- ✪ Understands processes, procedures, standards, methods, and technologies related to assignment
- ✪ Demonstrates functional and technical literacy
- ✪ Participates in measuring outcomes of work
- ✪ Keeps current on new developments in field of expertise
- ✪ Effectively uses available technology (voice mail, automation, software, etc.)

Resume Sample

Experienced Systems and Network Administrator. Eight and nine years experience, respectively, performing Windows NT and UNIX systems and network administration. Extensive experience administering NT4.0/3.51, WIN98, WIN95, WFW, WIN3.1, and DOS. Substantial expertise supporting Silicon Graphics IRIX, including operating system upgrades and security patch installations.

Resume and KSA Writing Tip

You need technical skills for certain jobs. What technical skills you have, how you use them, and how you present them are the important elements. If you are a subject-matter expert, train co-workers, or serve as a user support professional, you continually upgrade technical skills. These are the important elements, as well as the technical skills themselves. Many government employees are involved in technology—secretary, contact representative, engineer, healthcare specialist, or disaster preparedness professional, to name a few. Improving the use of technology to improve job performance is one of the challenging jobs of government workers. There is so much to do and so much information to manage and disseminate, improving the use and facility of technology will provide better service to the American public. This is an important core competency.

Organizational Stewardship

General Description:

- ✪ Demonstrates commitment to people
- ✪ Empowers and trusts others
- ✪ Develops leadership skills and opportunities throughout organization
- ✪ Develops team-based improvement processes
- ✪ Promotes future-oriented system change
- ✪ Supports and encourages lifelong learning throughout the organization
- ✪ Manages physical, fiscal, and human resources to increase the value of products and services
- ✪ Builds links between individuals and groups in the organization
- ✪ Integrates organization into the community
- ✪ Provides developmental opportunities for employees
- ✪ Participates in and fully supports 360 degree assessment
- ✪ Accepts accountability for self, others, and the organization's development
- ✪ Works to accomplish the organizational business plan

"Collaboration and Cooperation

Working with Others Toward Shared Goals

People with this competence:

Balance a focus on tasks with attention to relationships

Collaborate, share plans, information, and resources

Promote a friendly, cooperative climate

Spot and nurture opportunities for collaboration"

--Daniel Goleman, *Working with Emotional Intelligence*, 1998, Bantam Books, p.211

Resume and KSA Writing Tip

Organizational stewardship is a core competency for managers, supervisors, and team leaders. It entails knowing, following, and introducing the agency's mission and strategic plan, as well as communicating these goals to all employees. Managers and executives should integrate this element into their application. Here's a good way of saying you have "organizational stewardship": "Dedicated, determined, and driven to achieve agency mission objectives." These skills and language can be used in a cover letter, KSA statements, or in the descriptions of your work experience.

Summary of Veteran's Administration Core Competencies

The VA has developed an excellent set of core competency skills and language that can be used in anyone's Federal resume, KSA, and cover letter. Using these skills and terminology will fit your experience toward the needs of Federal agencies successfully. The agencies are looking for flexibility, customer services, interpersonal skills, team membership, technical credibility, and continual learning skills in all Federal employees.

More Core Competencies

Center for Medicare and Medicaid (www.hcfa.gov) uses these Core Competencies to recruit the best managers and supervisors at the GS 13 and above levels. Five competencies are listed here; there are 27 competencies that can be useful for managers at CMS.

Leading People: Skills and Behaviors

1. **Managing Conflict**
   a.   Uses conflicts as occasions for mutual problem solving.
   b.   Focuses on issues and outcomes rather than personalities.
   c.   Helps parties with differing interests and viewpoints to maintain constructive work relationships.

2. **Managing Differences**
   a.   Recognizes the value of cultural diversity and other individual differences in the workforce.
   b.   Uses differences in combination to achieve a broader, more diverse perspective.
   c.   Ensures that the organization respects differences and that all employees are treated in a fair and equitable manner.

3. **Interpersonal Skills**
   a.   Maintains constructive relationships with staff, peers and managers.
   b.   Demonstrates ability to listen attentively to others.
   c.   Encourages the self-confidence and self-esteem of others.
   d.   Uses tact, patience and sensitivity when dealing with anger and other emotional behavior.

4. **Managing Performance**
   a.   Establishes clear performance expectations, provides regular performance feedback to staff.
   b.   Takes corrective action and provides coaching to help staff improve their performance.
   c.   Rewards and encourages positive results.
   d.   Ensures that staff receives necessary orientation, mentoring and training.

5. **Team Building**
   a.   Understands the stages of team development and helps teams progress to higher levels of performance.
   b.   Develops leadership abilities in others by providing coaching, mentoring and developmental assignments.

ANALYZE VACANCY

ANNOUNCEMENTS FOR

KEYWORDS AND

GOVERNMENT-TYPE

LANGUAGE

"The two biggest problems I see from applicants are:

1. Not reading and following the directions on the announcements exactly. We have a complicated system (blame Congress, not us) with many different appointing authorities.

2. Not reading, understanding and determining if they meet minimum eligibility requirements."

—Personnel Specialist, Army CPAC

It's important to understand how a government agency receives and reviews your resume. When you send your Federal resume, electronic resume, and/or KSAs to an agency, the ensuing review is a two-step process. Human resources receives your resume first. The personnel person is not the actual supervisor or hiring person. The human resources staff member screens the resumes to determine if you are qualified for the job. This same personnel person is probably the one who put the vacancy announcement together. He or she is familiar with the duties in the vacancy announcement and will be looking for "keywords and skills" from the announcement in your resume. This person probably will not have time to read your entire application in depth, but will simply look for words, skills, and experience that match the announcement. Therefore, it is very important to include language from the "duties" section in your resume.

We will analyze two vacancy announcement DUTIES sections and discuss how you can use the keywords and skills in your resume as long as it is truthful.

Federal personnelists are looking for the keywords from the announcement when they review your package.

CASE STUDY NO. 1: MECHANICAL ENGINEERING STUDENT – JUNIOR – SUMMER INTERN

Sample Announcement Abstract

MECHANICAL ENGINEER INTERNSHIP, Navy

Duties

Provides input on the design, construction, and modification of Military Sealift Command (MSC) ships to ensure that MSC requirements and standards are being adhered to, particularly in areas of operability, reliability, habitability, maintainability, life-cycle cost effectiveness, safety, and compliance with regulatory bodies.

Important Courses

Include differential and integral calculus and courses (more advanced than first-year physics and chemistry) in five of the following seven areas of engineering science or physics; (a) statics, dynamics; (b) strength of materials (stress-strain relationships); (c) fluid mechanics, hydraulics; (d) thermodynamics; (e) electrical fields and circuits; (f) nature and properties of materials (relating particle and aggregate structure of properties); and (g) any other comparable area of fundamental engineering science or physics, such as optics, heat transfer, soil mechanics, or electronics.

A successful Mechanical Engineering applicant for a summer internship will include this language in his or her resume in the following sections: Education, Coursework, and Projects.

Sample Resume Wording for a Mechanical Engineering Student Applicant

Education

University of Maryland, College Park, MD 1999–present

Major: Mechanical Engineering

Currently enrolled in University of Maryland Honors Program

Maryland Distinguished Scholar

86 Credits earned   1999–present

Overall GPA: 3.6/4.0   1999–present

Engineering GPA: 3.8/4.0   1999–present

Deans List (Semester Academic Honors) Spring '00–Fall '01

Significant Courses

Differential and Integral Calculus

Statics, Dynamics

Strength of Materials (stress-strain relationships)

Fluid Mechanics, Hydraulics

Thermodynamics

Electrical Fields and Circuits

Nature and Properties of Materials - particle and
     aggregate structure of properties

Fiber Optics

Group Semester Projects

Portable water pump design project
     (Introduction to Engineering Design)

On-campus traffic flow statistical analysis project
     (Statistical Methods for Product and Process Development)

Scale wind tunnel testing of a high-rise building
     (Fluid Mechanics)

Team design problem in materials selection
     (Engineering Materials and Manufacturing Process)

Analysis of stress, bending and failure in a lug wrench
     (Mechanics of Materials)

Be sure to use the same course titles as the announcement. If they ask for
22 credits in Math, include Math in your list of mathematics courses.

CASE STUDY NO. 2: ADMINISTRATIVE ASSOCIATE, GS-9

Sample Announcement (keywords in bold)

Administrative Officer
National Institute of Allergy & Infectious Diseases NIAID-01-179

GS - 341 - 9/11/12 ($53,156 - $69,099)
Montgomery County, MD
Closing Date: 3/8/02

The incumbent of this position serves as an Administrative Officer in one of three areas: Office of the Director (OD), Intramural Administrative Management Branch (IAMB), or the Extramural Administrative Management Branch (EAMB). The incumbent will provide **administrative support services** to OD, IAMB, or EAMB. The incumbent's specific responsibilities include: providing assistance in **developing budget requests,** developing options for allocation of assigned budget, **monitoring expenditures** throughout the fiscal year, and identifying current or **potential allocation problems** and recommending solutions; reviewing requests for **personnel actions** for adherence to policies and regulations, relevance and appropriateness to Program needs, providing advice on personnel options to **facilitate staffing needs** and human resource management priorities, and developing methods for monitoring and **controlling personnel ceilings**
for assigned areas; monitoring the status of **past, current, and future budgets**, reviewing and analyzing contract financial reports, and maintaining an accounting of the overall status of active and pending **contract actions and plans** for future activities.

This Administrative Officer applicant matched her resume to the duties in this announcement. The focus of the job is on budget management. There is some work in contracts and personnel actions, but the emphasis will be budget costs, expenses and meeting organizational objectives within the budget.

Sample Resume Wording with Keywords and Skills

Objective

Administrative Officer (GS-0301-09), Health and Human Services Administration, National Institutes of Health.

Skills and Qualifications

Articulate and energetic professional who holds a master's degree and additional graduate-level training in Public Health Administration. Strong desire to return to a career in public health administration and to make a difference in the world. Mature values coupled with creativity, patience, and enthusiasm.

Experienced Public Health Program Director. Have served for more than eight years as the director and chief administrator of a 90-bed in-patient drug rehabilitation program.

Budget management. Experienced in managing, controlling and monitoring operations budget. Effective at interpreting budget requirements and communicating budget availability to managers.

Human resources. Able to recruit and train new personnel, facilitate staffing needs and analyze workload.

Contract management. Managed staff, services, and facilities contracts. Negotiated terms and ensured quality services.

Effective administrative manager. Particularly enthusiastic to know more about management and program analysis, public health analysis, and financial administration, budget, or procurement. Masters new skills and material accurately and in short time.

Strong work ethic. Sees projects through to completion, overcoming resistance and obstacles. Will put in 100% effort. Takes work seriously.

Seasoned professional. Outstanding oral and written communication skills. Polished professional image. Self-starter with a can-do attitude. Skilled at identifying and solving problems. Proven track record for establishing and reaching goals.

Technically proficient. Adept at using Microsoft Windows 2000. Experienced and capable with all types of Internet navigation.

Employment History

MEDICAL BILLING ASSOCIATE   October 2000 – Present

Cardiac Consultants Chartered, 6410 Rockledge Drive, Bethesda, MD 20817   40 hours/week

Supervisor: Ms. Mary Jane Woodward, you may contact at (301) 888-8888 Salary: $32,000/year

Administer step-by-step collections program for a busy cardiology practice. Track, handle, and follow up with late payments from insurers and patients. Bill secondary insurers. Identify and correct errors in billing and coding.

DIRECTOR   October 1996 to October 2000

Drug Rehabilitation Center, Brownsville, TN 20901   40 hours/week

Supervisor: John Smith, M.D., (909) 777-7777   Salary: $37,000/year

Started and developed new drug rehabilitation program and a 90-bed in-patient unit for low-income males. Prepared monthly reports for the Ministry of Health on workload and patient status. Coordinated patient management health care team comprised of physicians and social workers. Developed policies and procedures.

Budget and Financial Manager. Managed and monitored operating budgets. Analyzed budget availability throughout the year. Monitored expenses and allocated funding based on year-end projections. Monitored status of past and future budgets.

Provided outreach and community drug education. Offered numerous educational programs to community members. Targeted extensive educational efforts to prostitutes.

Organized staff training. Scheduled training programs for center staff including lectures and seminars from national and international experts on substance abuse.

Directed job placements. Scheduled patients to appropriate occupational training programs. Worked extensively within the community to develop relationships with potential employers. Made job placements and followed up to provide ongoing support.

PRIVATE INDUSTRY TO FEDERAL TERMINOLOGY

The way you would write certain skills in your private industry resume is different from in your Federal resume. Here are just a few examples from the second case study above:

Government Verbiage	Private Industry Language
Administrative support services	Office management
Develop budget requests	Manage budget
Develop options for allocation of assigned budget	Allocate funds
Monitor expenses	Monitor expenses
Identify potential allocation problems	Identify budget and expense problems
Review requests for personnel actions	Advise managers in recruitment matters
Facilitate staffing needs	Recruit needed personnel
Control personnel ceilings	Monitor staffing requirements
Maintaining and account of contract action and plans	Manage contracts

Study the vacancy announcement terminology. Using common sense, use the terminology in your resume.

"I am writing to thank you for your book about Resumix. I am a previous civil service employee who has had great difficulty returning to Federal service. My husband is Army so it would be beneficial for me to return since he has 12 more years left.

I thought I understood Resumix since I used it to get my first civil service job. Thank you for your insight into how the system works and especially the project lists and buzzwords. I felt guilty using previous position descriptions to write my resume but now I see that these buzzwords really help to bring out my skills in terminology that the computer will pick up on.

After using your book I feel confident that this is a more accurate reflection of the work I did and am capable of. I had been hesitant to purchase it because there are so many useless guides that do not give specific advice concerning Resumix. I will let you know the outcome but I feel better already and think I've definitely improved my chances."

STEP-BY-STEP GUIDE FOR ANALYZING KEYWORDS IN VACANCY ANNOUNCEMENTS

I wrote a column for two years for the government website www.govexec.com. You should consider signing up for their daily email concerning government jobs, legislation, recruitment practices, and other interesting government initiatives that can relate to you if you want a job in government. My column was called *Career Corner* and covered many topics having to do with Federal resume writing, KSAs, electronic resumes, human resources automation, getting promoted, and other topics relating to government employment. One of my favorite subjects in workshops and in my columns was understanding, interpreting, and using the language from vacancy announcements. What follows is one of my favorite columns from *Career Corner*. The 12 tips here are used by thousands of Federal employees who are trying to move up and over, as well as private industry job applicants trying to use the right words in their resumes.

Deciphering Vacancy Announcements

Do you find that vacancy announcements are difficult to read in 9-point type? I do. Do you have a hard time reading 50 to 100 lines of text in one paragraph? I do.

My attention span has gotten much shorter since the dawn of the Internet. I can't focus on small type or big paragraphs anymore. The human resources recruiters who design vacancy announcements need to know that one of the reasons their carefully worded announcements aren't being followed by applicants is because of the document's lack of "readability."

When was the last time you really *read* a vacancy announcement? I know you "read" them because that's how you know when to apply for the position. But "reading" isn't the same as analyzing, interpreting, understanding, and even empathizing with the hiring manager who has struggled to get the position description, crediting plan, and KSAs written.

Follow the 12 tips for analyzing vacancy announcements. Enlarge the type of the Duties section so that you can read the words and description.

I have a special technique for analyzing vacancy announcements that I always follow when I am writing for a particular announcement. Here's my easy 12-step system for interpreting an announcement:

Read the agency's website, mission statement and press releases. Learn about the services the agency provides and how you can help.

Interpreting an Announcement

1. Save the vacancy announcement as an html file.
2. Copy and paste the duties and responsibilities and the KSAs out of the announcement into a Word or WordPerfect file.
3. Enlarge the type to 14 to 16 points so it is more readable.
4. Separate each sentence so that it is more clear.
5. Delete useless words such as "the incumbent will" or "duties will encompass a variety of tasks including."
6. Find keywords and skills that are significant to the position, such as "identifying deficiencies in human performance" and "recommending changes for correction."
7. Read the new document out loud slowly.
8. Try to understand the duties and responsibilities of the job.
9. Think about what the hiring manager really wants and needs.
10. Try to interpret the job situation and decide if you really want the job.
11. If you don't understand the job, go to their website and read more.
12. Now you can start considering this job as your next step in your career.

Here's an interesting announcement written by a U.S. Navy HR office for a Supply System Analyst position. After the announcement was enlarged, expanded, and read carefully, I found some wonderful plain language that explains how this Supply Analyst will be setting up new systems and resolving "human" problems. Here's an excerpt:

Interpreting an Announcement

Duties: Establish and implement long-range, intermediate and short-term supply and logistics plans and programs for the command's support of stocks in-transit including current Navy-owned material and newly-procured material;

Adapt and implement technically complex government-wide supply and logistics management policies, goals and objectives. Identify deficiencies in human performance and recommend changes for correction.

Adjudicate and write Requirements Statements for complex systems with many interfaces and in a wide range of media and forums, to include: conferences, print medium, presentations, active Ad Hoc participation in DOD-level task groups, and briefings.

The complex In-Transit accountability system design requires all of the skills listed plus the ability to effectively design and explain the system to GAO, Congress, SECNAV and OPNAV, in addition to other Flag and general Officers in the Navy and other DOD components.

The government speaks a different language than private industry companies. You won't be able to write in a complete bureaucratic style, but you can use a few words that could help your campaign: set policies, developed programs, implemented systems, wrote and edited manuals. If you look like a Federal employee on paper (even slightly), you can become one.

The second paragraph identifies obvious human problems in this job that need correction. The last two paragraphs contain the clues "ability to write and communicate," and the last paragraph also has a list of customers.

I actually enjoy reading and interpreting vacancy announcements. They are such a challenge. Sometimes I find good sentences like the one above, and others are amazingly boring and difficult to understand.

PART III SUMMARY

If you take the time to look for core competencies, skills, and keywords from government agencies and include these in your resume, your resume will look like a Federal Resume. The private industry resumes are not written the same. You have to add the bureaucratic skills, verbs, and nouns to your resume. The business of government is not the same as private industry. If you want to be successful with your Federal job search, your resume has to sound as Federal as possible.

WRITE YOUR APPLICATION PACKAGE

WRITING

"Can I submit one resume for all government positions and departments?"

"I am having a very hard time understanding just what the different government departments want and how to go about getting this done."

WRITE YOUR FEDERAL AND ELECTRONIC RESUME

GETTING STARTED

Writing your first Federal resume is challenging. You might have a one-page private industry resume that will need to be expanded. You might have a creative functional resume that will have to be converted to a chronological resume. You might not have any resume right now and will have to begin to build a Federal resume. You might have military evaluations and training forms that need to be organized and constructed into a Federal resume. You could have an old SF-171 that needs to be converted into a Federal-style resume. Or you could have a curriculum vitae that is long and skeletal without real specific descriptions of work and few references to accomplishments. Whatever resume format you have, you will need to study the Federal resume formats and lessons in this chapter to build a Federal resume that will get you qualified, impress the human resources staff and the hiring official, and get you HIRED. You will have to learn how to write a new resume format for your Federal job search.

Before you start writing your Federal resume, let's review the typical instructions that will be included in many Federal vacancy announcements. The instructions are slightly confusing and I'd like to make it clear right now that the agencies will accept a Federal resume (or electronic resume) for most every job in government.

Once you have your Federal (paper format) and electronic resume written, you are 70 to 80% ready to apply for any job in government.

Here's an example of the typical instructions that are not clear:

> Please submit the following documents to the address provided in this announcement:
>
> A written application for employment. You may use OF-612 (Optional Application for Federal Employment) a resume, or submit an alternative format. You must include all of the information specified in this announcement and all information listed in the Office of Personnel Management's brochure "Applying for a Federal Job" (OF-510). Applications must be typed or printed clearly in dark ink.

This paragraph could be translated into a more commonsense, direct phrase, such as:

> Please submit a Federal-style resume, including the specific information listed at the end of this vacancy announcement.

You will not need to use the OF-612, which is a short, unflattering employment form. You do not need a copy of the OF-510 because the instructions are simple and are usually included in every announcement. They are also in this chapter.

"I know that the attached resume is far too long for a standard resume, but am not sure how to make significant reductions in length while also making sure (as required by the position description) that the resume meets all the requirements of the OPM OF-510 which, I believe, seems to ask that one provides all of the information which was previously provided in the old SF-171, although not necessarily in the same format."

Federal Resume, OF-612, SF-171, and Private Industry Resume Facts

In order to understand that the new Federal resume is acceptable for a Federal application, rather than the forms, there are a few important things you have to know before you learn about writing a Federal resume.

✪ The Federal resume has replaced the SF-171 that was mandatory for nearly 40 years in government. The SF-171 was eliminated in 1995 with former Vice President Gore's National Performance Review.

✪ A Federal resume is not the same as a private industry resume because it includes certain information that typically is not included in a private industry resume. You can see the list of "compliance details" required in a Federal resume in the next section.

✪ The Federal resume is not the same as the OF-612 that is listed in most vacancy announcements. The Federal resume is better because it is more flexible.

✪ The Federal resume replaces both the OF-612 and the SF-171.

✪ Do not submit both OF-612 and Federal resume. The Federal resume will be a good application if it is done correctly.

✪ If the announcement states that you can submit "resume, OF-612, SF-171 or any format you choose," then you can submit a Federal-style resume as described in this chapter and this book.

✪ The Federal resume is typically three or four pages. There is no length requirement.

✪ Some Federal agencies are accepting resumes by email and online. However, you cannot include any formatting with an electronic Federal resume. Step 7 will review the formatting required for an electronic Federal resume.

What makes a resume "Federal" are the following "compliance details" that must be included in your Federal Resume. Here is the information from the OPM Web site (http://www.usajobs.opm.gov/EI25.htm) regarding what to include in your resume:

PLEASE INCLUDE THE FOLLOWING INFORMATION IN YOUR FEDERAL RESUME:

Job Information
Announcement number, title, and grade.

Personal Information
Full name, mailing address (with ZIP code), day and evening phone numbers (with area code), social security number, country of citizenship, veterans' preference, reinstatement eligibility, and highest Federal civilian grade held.

Education
Colleges or universities, name, city and state, majors and type and year of any degrees received (if no degree, show total credits earned and indicate whether semester or quarter hours). High school name, city, and state. (Some announcements do not ask for high school.)

Work Experience
Job title, duties and accomplishments, employer's name and address, supervisor's name and phone number, starting and ending dates (month and year), hours per week, salary, and indicate whether or not your current supervisor may be contacted. Prepare a separate entry for each job.

Other Qualifications
Job-related training courses (title and year), job-related skills, job-related certificates and licenses, job-related honors, awards, and special accomplishments.

"I have a current resume; may need help modifying for a Federal application. I am interested in a government position that would utilize skills learned in business continuity/disaster recovery department for the past seven years."

"I am a Registered Nurse, hold a BSN degree and an MS degree in business. I have been working for a Managed Care Organization for the past 6 years as a Regional Quality Management coordinator and now I am very much interested in finding a position at HCFA. However, I was told that in order to apply for a position with the Federal government, I have to write my resume in a specific format. I was also told that you could help me write my resume to fit the position I am applying for."

F ederal Resume Builders can help you "build" your resume content – see the CD-ROM.

Every Agency Has Different Application Requirements

Since every agency has its own way of recruiting and its own favorite application format, you will have to be prepared to apply for Federal jobs with two types of resumes—Federal-style "paper" and an electronic resume. Step 8 covers the various application requirements for government. Once you have a good Federal electronic resume, you will be ready to apply for any Federal job.

In Step 6 you will learn how to write the all-important Knowledge, Skills, and Ability (KSA) statements. And lastly, in Step 7, you will see how to use a cover letter to make your Federal application package stand out from your competition and present your interest in supporting the agency's mission.

This chapter takes you through the step-by-step process of writing your Federal and electronic resume. The appendix of the book has samples of private industry, military, and returning Federal job applicants' resumes, KSAs, and cover letters.

Introducing the Federal Resume Builders

This chapter refers to the Resume Builder, the online resume writing templates that can help you address all of the resume sections that need to be represented on your Federal resume. The Builder forms are printed in this chapter and the actual online builders are on the CD-ROM. The Federal resume templates are usable with PCs and Macs with Internet, a browser, and email. Simply fill in the fields and receive your content by email within minutes.

http://www.resume-place.com/fedres_builder/federal_a

FEDERAL VS. PRIVATE INDUSTRY RESUME

Federal resumes are different from private industry resumes for a number of reasons. Here is a quick list of differences to keep in mind when you are converting your private industry resume into a Federal resume.

Private Industry	Federal Resume
Focused on the mission of the business	Focused on the mission of the agency, programs, and services
Profit motivated	Grant and budget motivated
Customer service for customers who buy products	Customer service for millions of people as well as internal customers
Provides a product or service	Provides a program or service. Implements Congressional legislation and laws
Markets business to select customer base	Markets, introduces, and informs the American public (similar to private industry)
One or two pages	Three to five pages is acceptable
No social security number, supervisors, or salaries	Include SSN, supervisors' names, salaries
Fewer details in work descriptions	More details for work descriptions so that keywords demonstrate your qualifications for a job
Creative, graphic, functional formats are okay	Chronological, traditional format
Accomplishments are great	Accomplishments are great
Keywords are desirable	Keywords are needed
Emphasis on 10 years experience	Emphasis on 10 years experience
More succinct writing style	Concise, yet informative content
Honors, awards, and recognitions are important	Honors, awards, and recognitions are more important

CREATING THE FEDERAL RESUME

Writing your Federal and electronic resume is usually an exercise of expanding your private industry resume, de-militarizing your military resume, converting your old SF-171 into the Federal resume format, or focusing your current resume toward a particular Federal job.

The samples in this book, on the CD-ROM, and in this chapter will help you see what a Federal-style resume looks like. When you see the samples and read the 10 Lessons on writing a Federal resume, you will be less intimidated. To write a Federal resume that is focused and complete is a project that will take between three and ten hours. But if this effort gets you a good Federal position with career potential, good benefits, and a good paycheck, it will be worth your effort.

The sample shown here is for Barbara Wagner. She is trying to return to government. She was a Federal/Defense civilian employee for six years while she traveled with her husband who was in the military. He retired and they started a small business in Baltimore. Now, with the economy so uncertain, she wants to return to a government position. We have flipped her experience in her Federal resume so that the government position is first. Then her business experience is listed second. We wanted her Federal position and skills to be near the top of the resume. We listed her earlier positions in a short, succinct listing and put the emphasis on her last three positions. We also included her education, training, awards, and other information. Barbara is seeking a GS-7 position in the Administrative job series somewhere in the Baltimore-Washington area. She is flexible about working for either a Defense or non-Defense agency.

"**Y**our *Federal Resume Guidebook* was terrific in helping me revamp my application from 'SF-171-esque' to the more formal resume format."

— William Winsom, Senior Forecaster, National Weather Service

"I do a lot in my job. I'm not sure how to word it properly for the position."

Sample Federal Resume — Paper (pages 89-92)

The Federal resume sample that follows is an example of a "paper" resume—that is, one that includes the type of formatting typically found in a printed resume.

Sample Electronic Resume (pages 93-94)

This electronic resume could be copied and pasted into a resume builder or the textbox of an email to an HR office.

Barbara Wagner

2276 Community Dr.
Baltimore, MD 21228
Home: (301) 888-8888
Fax: (301) 888-8888
Email: BWagner@msn.com

Social Security Number:	222-22-2222
Citizenship:	United States
Federal Civilian Status:	Office Automation Assistant (GS-0326-07)
Veteran's Preference:	N/A
Highest Civilian Grade Held:	GS-0326-05, 10/1992 to 01/1994

OBJECTIVE:

Administrative Assistant, NIH, Announcement: NCI 02 1302, GS 0341-7

SUMMARY OF QUALIFICATIONS:

Experienced Office Assistant with 12 years diverse administrative experience including:
- Budget, payroll and financial management
- Personnel coordination, travel, and schedule management
- Personnel action reviews
- Property and space management
- Travel order production, voucher review, funds checking
- Administrative office flow
- Type correspondence, reports, financial tables, and personnel reports
- Database updating and management
- Forms design with Harvard Graphics and other software programs
- Keyboard 40 wpm

COMPUTER SKILLS:

Operating Systems:	Windows '98, ME
Word Processing:	Microsoft Word, Word Perfect
Internet:	Microsoft Explorer, Netscape, Outlook Express, email management
Other Business:	Form Tool, Quickbooks, Harvard Graphics, Enable, Excel

FEDERAL GOVERNMENT ADMINISTRATIVE EXPERIENCE:

DEFENSE LOGISTICS AGENCY   08/1991 to 01/1994
Defense Contract Management Office   40 hours/week
RAF Croughton, United Kingdom   Salary: $18,951.00/year
Supervisor: Colonel Mike Smith (703) 444-4444
Supervisor may be contacted

Office Automation Assistant (GS-0326-05/2)   12/1992 to 01/1994

Managed administrative operations for 35-person contracting office.

Maintained and coordinated contracting support for professional staff.

Received, reviewed, and typed correspondence, emails, and outgoing mail.

Prepared rough drafts for management signature. Utilized existing formats, referred
to style manuals and used independent judgment to ensure accuracy of document.

Researched information, records, and data to support office and program operations.

Received calls, visitors and responded to inquiries and made referrals.

Managed administrative appointment and meeting schedule.

Maintained computer-based records in databases and file system management.

Ordered and maintained agency publications, regulations, manuals, and pamphlets.

Researched and compiled contract administration data.

Office Automation Clerk (GS-0326-04)   03/1992 to 12/1992

Clerk-Typist (GS-0322-03)   08/1991 - 03/1992

Managed records and publications distributed to universities and centers internationally.

Devised spreadsheets to manage equipment and ADP inventories

Skilled in Harvard Graphics to develop slides, charts and organizational charts

Created forms, inventory sheets, and office informational charts.

Researched and compiled contract administration data concerning contracts, unliquidated
obligations, completed contracts, and delinquencies. Input contractor information into
software for Commander's monthly report.

DEPARTMENT OF THE AIR FORCE   10/1990 TO 08/1991
PACAF, 5AF, 475 Air Base Wing   40 hours/week
Fuels Management Branch
Accounting and Administrative Section

Clerk-Typist (GS-0322-03)

Word processing, accounting support, and administrative services to the
Fuels Management Branch.

BUSINESS EXPERIENCE:

WAGNER PLUS SURPLUS   06/1997 to Present
　1400 West Melvin Ave., Baltimore, MD 21228   40 hours/week
　Supervisor: Self   Salary: $27,254.00/year

Store Owner/Operator/Bookkeeper

Manage and run all aspects of a successful military clothing and surplus store, including sales; inventory management and ordering; credit card acceptance and management; sales tax collection and payment, business tax management and payment; annual inventory counts and analysis; rent payment; payroll; and bank deposits and bank account management.

Utilized Quickbooks to manage inventory, accounts payable, sales information, new client information, product returns, payroll, and credit card sales. Set up the Quickbooks system in addition to bank reconciliation and cash management.

Accomplishments

Built this business from "the ground up" to gross over $71,000.00 last fiscal year.

Increased net profit year to year by 25% with increase in sales of 14%

Managed $17,000.00 in inventory

OTHER WORK EXPERIENCE:

ARMY AND AIR FORCE EXCHANGE   1990 to 1990
　Pacific Field Office, Yokota Air Base, Japan
　Inventory Management Technician

DEPARTMENT OF THE AIR FORCE   1988 to 1989
　475 Comptroller Squadron, Yokota Air Base, Japan
　Teller/Accountability Clerk (GS-0530-05)

EDUCATION:

University of Maryland, Yokota Air Base, Japan and RAF Uxbridge, UK   1988, 1991
　Completed 11 Semester Hours - English and Microsoft Business Software

Defense Language Institute, Monterey, CA   1987 to 1988
　Completed 30 Semester Hours - Intensive Japanese Language Course

SAMPLE PAPER FEDERAL RESUME

AWARDS:

USAF Outstanding Performance Award, 1985, 1991, 1992

Defense Logistics Agency Performance Award, 1991, 1992, 1993

USAF Special Act or Service Award, 1991, 1992

AAFES Courtesy Award, 1984, AAFES Proficiency Award, 1983

FOREIGN LANGUAGES:

Thai, Japanese, in addition to fluent written and oral English

INTERNATIONAL TRAVEL:

Extensive foreign travel as military spouse. Born and raised in Thailand. Lived in Japan from 1977 to 1983 and 1988 to 1991. Lived in the United Kingdom from 1991 to 1994.

SPECIAL INTERESTS:

Thai cooking, dancing, vegetable carving, and flower arranging.

PROFESSIONAL TRAINING:

Customer Account Representative Course, RAF Uxbridge, UK	1991
Maintenance of Air Force Documentation Training, Yokota Air Base, Japan	1991
Freedom of Information and Privacy Act Course, Yokota Air Base, Japan	1991

Barbara Wagner, SSN: 222-22-2222
2276 Community Dr.
Baltimore, MD 21228
Home: 301 888-8888
Fax: 301 888-8888
Email: BWagner@msn.com

WORK EXPERIENCE

12/1992 to 01/1994. 40 hrs. per wk. OFFICE AUTOMATION ASSISTANT, GS-0326-5/2. Defense Logistics Agency, Defense Contract Management Office, RAF Croughton, United Kingdom. Supervisor, Colonel John Smith, 703 444-4444.

STAFF SUPPORT: Managed administrative operations for 35-person contracting office. Maintained and coordinated contracting support for professional staff. Received, reviewed, and typed correspondence, emails, and outgoing mail. Researched information, records, and data to support office and program operations. Researched and compiled contract administration data. Maintained computer-based records in databases and file system management.

OFFICE MANAGEMENT: Prepared rough drafts for management signature. Utilized existing formats, referred to style manuals, and used independent judgment to ensure accuracy of document. Received calls, visitors and responded to inquiries and made referrals. Managed management appointment and meeting schedule. Ordered and maintained agency publications, regulations, manuals, and pamphlets.

COMPUTER PROFICIENCIES: Windows 98/ME Operating Systems; Internet, Microsoft Explorer, Netscape, Outlook Express, email management; Microsoft Word, WordPerfect, Form Tool, Quickbooks, Harvard Graphics, Enable, Excel.

ACCOMPLISHMENTS: Logistics Agency Performance Awards for outstanding service and performance in contracting division, 1993, 1992, 1991.

06/1997 to present. 40 hrs. per wk. RETAIL STORE OWNER-OPERATOR-BOOKKEEPER. Military Plus Surplus, 1400 West Melvin Ave., Baltimore, MD 21228. Salary: $27,254.00/year. Supervisor: Self, 301 888-8888. May we contact your current Supervisor? Yes.

RETAIL MANAGEMENT: Manage and run all aspects of a successful military clothing and surplus store, including sales, inventory management, product ordering, credit card acceptance and management, sales tax collection and payment, business tax management and payment, annual inventory counts and analysis, rent payment, payroll, bank deposits, and bank account management.

FINANCIAL MANAGEMENT: Utilize Quickbooks to manage inventory, accounts payable, sales information, new client information, product returns, payroll, and credit card sales. Set up the Quickbooks system in addition to bank reconciliation and cash management.

ACCOMPLISHMENTS: Built this business from its inception to gross over $71,000.00 last fiscal year. Increased net profit year to year by 25 percent with increase in sales of 14 percent. Manage $17,000.00 in inventory.

SAMPLE ELECTRONIC FEDERAL RESUME

OTHER EXPERIENCE:

03/1992 to 12/1992. 40 hrs. per wk. OFFICE AUTOMATION CLERK, GS-0326-4.

08/1991 to 03/1992. 40 hrs. per wk. CLERK-TYPIST, GS-0322-3.

DATA MANAGEMENT: Managed records and publications distributed to universities and centers internationally. Devised spreadsheets to manage equipment and ADP inventories. Utilized Harvard Graphics to develop slides and charts, including organizational charts. Created forms, inventory sheets and office informational charts. Researched and compiled contract administration data concerning contracts, unliquidated obligations, completed contracts, and delinquencies. Input contractor information into software for Commander's monthly report.

1990. INVENTORY MANAGEMENT TECHNICIAN. Army and Air Force Exchange, Pacific Field Office, Yokota Air Base, Japan.

1988 to 1989. TELLER/ACCOUNTABILITY CLERK, GS-0530-5. Department of the Air Force, 475 Comptroller Squadron, Yokota Air Base, Japan

EDUCATION

University of Maryland, Yokota Air Base, Japan and RAF Uxbridge, UK. 11 Semester Hours, 1988, 1991.

Defense Language Institute, Monterey, CA. Major, Japanese language. 30 Semester Hours. 1987 to 1988.

TRAINING

Customer Account Representative Course, RAF Uxbridge, UK, 40 hrs, 1991.

Maintenance of Air Force Documentation Training, Yokota Air Base, Japan, 32 hrs, 1991.

Freedom of Information and Privacy Act Course, Yokota Air Base, Japan, 24 hrs, 1991

AWARDS

USAF Outstanding Performance Award, 1992, 1991, 1985.
Defense Logistics Agency Performance Award, 1993, 1992, 1991.
USAF Special Act or Service Award, 1992, 1991.
AAFES Courtesy Award, 1984.
AAFES Proficiency Award, 1983.
OTHER INFORMATION

PROFESSIONAL PROFILE: Experienced Office Assistant offering 12 years diverse administrative experience including: budget, payroll and financial management; personnel coordination, travel, and schedule management; personnel action reviews; property and space management; travel order production; voucher review; funds checking; administrative office flow; typing correspondence, reports, financial tables, and personnel reports; database updating and management; forms design with Harvard Graphics and other software programs;keyboard 40 wpm.

FOREIGN LANGUAGES: Thai, Japanese, in addition to fluent written and oral English

SPECIAL INTERESTS: Thai cooking, dancing, vegetable carving, and flower arranging.

If you compare the paper Federal resume to the electronic resume, you will see that the content is similar, but the format is different. The electronic resume must be more succinct and ready to copy and paste into an email textbox or resume builder. In today's job market you can't begin a job search—Federal or private industry—without both resume formats. These are your basic job search tools.

The next 10 Federal resume-writing lessons will help you build the content in your resumes—both the paper version and electronic resume. If you are writing an electronic resume with a three-page limit, then you should try to fill the three pages. The Federal paper resume does not have a page limit, but three to four pages is better than two pages. So, you need to have ideas of what to write in your Federal resume. The Federal personnelists and supervisors are depending on your words to get you qualified and to stand out so that you will go as far as an interview—and maybe get hired.

TEN FEDERAL RESUME-WRITING LESSONS

The following Federal resume-writing lessons are designed to help you write a Federal resume that gets you qualified for a Federal job. Read the lessons and then refer to the Resume Builder at the end of this chapter to begin building your Federal and electronic resume.

Read, think about, research, and write information for each of the resume-writing exercises. Take your time and you will be successful at being rated "Best Qualified" by Federal human resources staff. Be determined to make your resume outstanding.

The lessons correspond chronologically to each section of the Federal resume and the order in which you complete the tasks, as follows:

1. Format your name and address
2. Education and training
3. Other qualifications and skills
4. Work experience
5. Duties and responsibilities
6. Create your project list
7. Highlight skills that support the announcement
8. Include recognitions in job descriptions
9. Skills and talents in the future workforce
10. Write a profile statement

> " I suspect that my resume is too long at 8 pages. But I'm always concerned that the receiving personnel office will claim that I didn't give them the information they needed."

Lesson 1. Formatting Your Name and Address

Job Information and Personal Data

Your first impression is your name and contact information.

Your contact information should be organized so that it is accessible and easy to read for future contact by the selecting official who might want to call you for an interview.

Federal Job "Compliance" Information

Most Federal, state, county, and city applications require certain compliance information for civil service jobs. Check the application for the particular agency and add the information that is on the application. Some agencies may require that you fill out the application in addition to the resume. It would be preferable if you can provide the information they need in your resume. Here are the typical compliance details that civil service human resources offices require:

Federal Resume Builder - Template 1

Federal Resume and Resumix Resume Builder Part 1
Personal Information - Education - Training
Help | Sample

Personal Information
_____

KATHRYN KRAEMER TROUTMAN
2 Holmehurst Avenue
Baltimore, MD 21228
Home Telephone: (410) 777-7777
Office Telephone: (410) 744-4324
email: resume@resume-place.com

Social Security No: 000-00-0000
Federal Employment Status: Writer-Editor, GS-301-13,
November 1995 to present
Veteran's Status: Honorably Discharged, U.S. Army, 1970-1975
Citizenship: United States

Please type the above information in this field.

Objective
If you have a current announcement, insert the title of the

- Full name, mailing address (with ZIP Code) and day and evening phone numbers (with area code)

- Social Security Number

- Country of citizenship

- Veterans' preference

- Reinstatement eligibility (If you have been laid off, there could be special rules for reinstatement; you will need proof of your status.)

- Highest civilian grade held, job series, and dates

- Announcement number, title, and grade(s) of the job for which you are applying

Examples of Job Information and Personal Data

The following two examples include the personal information, job information, and compliance details required by the personnel offices. This information makes the resume recognized as a "Federal style." This is one of the big differences between a Federal resume and private industry resume. The personnel staff will depend on this information for contact, citizenship, veteran's information, and Federal civilian status. Many resumes written by unknowing private industry job applicants do not include this information in their resume. These applicants will be eliminated from consideration very quickly for not including these details in their resume!

ROBERTA A. SPENCER

ADDRESS:	124 3RD STREET, NE
	WASHINGTON, DC 20002
TELEPHONES:	HOME: (202) 566-8910
	WORK: (202) 267-9976
E-MAIL:	SPENCER@ARI.NET
SOCIAL SECURITY NUMBER:	345-57-6540
CITIZENSHIP:	UNITED STATES
FEDERAL CIVILIAN STATUS:	PUBLIC AFFAIRS SPECIALIST, GS-12
VETERANS' PREFERENCE:	10 POINTS, 1971-1975, U.S. ARMY
OBJECTIVE:	INTERNATIONAL AVIATION OFFICER, GS-0301-13/14
	ANNOUNCEMENT NO. AWA-AIA-96-1379-10590

SCOTT LEE CRIMSON

4225 HARNEY ROAD
HAGERSTOWN, MD 21787
HOME: (410) 777-7777
CELL: (410) 777-7777
SLCRIMSON@HOME.COM

CITIZENSHIP:	UNITED STATES OF AMERICA
SOCIAL SECURITY NO.:	222-22-2222
VETERAN'S STATUS:	NOT APPLICABLE
HIGHEST FEDERAL GRADE:	LOGISTICS SPECIALIST, DEFENSE LOGISTICS AGENCY, 1989-1992, GS-13

OBJECTIVE:

LOGISTICS PROGRAM SPECIALIST, DEPARTMENT OF HEALTH AND HUMAN SERVICES (HHS), OFC SEC HEALTH AND HUMAN SERVICES, VACANCY ANNOUNCEMENT #OS-01-123

Lesson 2. Education and Training

Your education and training can show that you are qualified for a certain Federal position. The Federal personnelist will consider your education when determining whether you qualify for a certain grade level. Review Step 2 "Salary Decisions" to determine what grade level is appropriate and reasonable for your job announcement selection and objective.

What goes first—education or experience? You can list your education before Work Experience or after Work Experience, depending on the importance and dates of your degrees. Many professional and technical applicants list the education before work experience so that it is easy to find—since this will be a qualifying factor.

There is a difference between education and training in a Federal resume. Education is college coursework and training is professional development courses to improve your skills and knowledge on the job.

Regardless of the format of the resume, the information should always be sufficient for the reviewer to determine whether the individual is basically qualified for the job being sought.

Federal Education and Training Requirements

Here is a list of the typical education information that must be included in your Federal resume.

- Names of colleges, including city, state, and ZIP code
- Degree, including major and date graduated
- If you have not graduated, provide the credit hours and courses that are important for your objective
- Number of credit hours completed
- Some announcements ask for name of high school, city, state, and year graduated

Other Academic Information

If you are a new graduate or a recently returning college student, you can include the following sections in your Education section that can help you pick up keywords, courses, skills, and papers or projects. You will be using your education to help you qualify for the position, so this information could be critical to your application.

Include important training from the last 10 years.

- Academic honors and awards
- Internships and residencies
- Major papers and projects (described)
- Lists of courses or course concentration
- Activities
- Scholarships
- Awards

Training Course Lists

You could name this section any of the following titles: TRAINING, PROFESSIONAL DEVELOPMENT, CAREER DEVELOPMENT, SELF-STUDY, or CONTINUING EDUCATION. Many people learn through self-study now because there are so many new computer programs. This is legitimate training that can help you qualify and also demonstrates "continual learning" as we described on the Core Competency section of this book (Step 4). For the last five to ten years, list the titles of the relevant courses and year. Include recent computer and technical courses.

Formatting Your Education and Training Section

Here are four examples that show you how to format this section of your Federal resume.

Continual learning must be part of your career in today's changing technology and job market. To stay marketable, always take courses!

Example # 1 EDUCATION

Pepperdine University, Los Angeles, CA 97801
    Completed 32 hours in post-graduate studies
    Major: Education, 1998 – present

San Francisco State University, San Francisco, CA 96810
    Master of Arts, Political Science, 1997

University of California, Los Angeles, CA 95701
    Bachelor of Arts, Speech and Communications, June 1995

Robert Fulton High School, Queens, NY 10065 - *Diploma,* 1989

Example # 2 TRAINING

PROFESSIONAL DEVELOPMENT:

Aviation Technical Courses:

    Air Traffic Control History (1999), 16 hours
    Managing Public Communication, 16 hours
    Management Development Courses: (All 1998)
    Discovering Diversity and Valuing the Diverse Workforce, 3 hours
    Management Skills for Non-Supervisors, 8 hours

Communications Training:

    Public Involvement Training (1998), 16 hours
    Constructive Communications (1996), 8 hours

EXAMPLES

Example # 3 TRAINING

Education:

Diploma. Francis Scott Key High School, Unionbridge, MD 21791, 1999.
Vocational Diploma, Machine Shop. Carroll County Vo-Tech, Westminster, MD 21158, 1996.

Example # 4 TRAINING

Training & Development:

Emergency Program Manager, National Fire Academy, 2001

Incident Command System, National Fire Academy, 2000

Terrorism, National Fire Academy, 2000

FIT Test for Self-Contained Breathing Apparatus, State of Maryland, 2000

Emergency Preparedness-USA, National Fire Academy, 2000

Radiological Emergency Management, National Fire Academy, 2000

The Professional in Emergency Management, National Fire Academy, 2000

Basic Farm Equipment Rescue, University of Maryland, 1992

Basic Rough Water Rescue, NASAR, 1992

Firefighter 1, University of Maryland, 1991

Lesson 3. Other Qualifications and Skills

The "Other Qualifications and Skills" sections can be very important toward your qualifications for the job and your "likeability factor." The likeability factor for your resume can help the human resources staff and supervisor remember you by your other qualifications and experiences you can offer. These sections can help you stand out from your direct competition.

Resume Headings

Examples of headings you can use on your Federal resume to identify other qualifications follow:

Associations	Honors & Awards	Presentations
Community Service	International Travel	Publications
Computer Skills	Languages	Special Interests
Conferences Attended	Memberships/Offices	Activities
Consultancies Part-time	Teaching Positions	Volunteer Services

Formatting Tips

These resume sections are usually placed after Work Experience unless they are so impressive that they should be included earlier.

Qualification Requirements for Outside Activities

There usually isn't any requirement for this resume information. However, it is to your benefit to present as much diverse information about your qualifications, experience, and contacts as possible. Human resources professionals want to know about your experiences outside of work. These outside activities demonstrate many core competencies, which can help them determine if you have the "value added" qualifications needed to perform a certain job. (Read more about core competencies in Step 4.)

Outside Activities

These are the types of activities that Federal HR professionals and supervisors like to see on resumes. These are unpaid, volunteer activities that show knowledge, skills, and abilities that can be used in a Federal position. These activities will show your core competencies as discussed in Step 4 that the government personnelists are looking for in certain positions.

✪ Girl Scout Leader – Provide leadership, counseling, mentoring, planning, scheduling, problem-solving, and supervising for a troop of 25 girls, ages 10 to 12.

✪ Soccer or Basketball Umpire – Use skills in coaching, counseling, leading, communication, scheduling, flexibility, problem-solving, and time-management. Supervise teams of 15 boys, ages 8 to 12.

✪ Home Owner's Association – Leadership responsibilities involve public speaking, teamwork, negotiations, presentations, meeting planning, and budget management. Direct a budget of $150,000 with a membership of 150 families.

✪ Choir Member – Active member and soloist in performance group. Additionally plan rehearsals, help manage music inventory, and coordinate events and programs.

Federal Resume Builder

Federal Resume Template Part III
Federal Resume Help | Draft Sample | Final Sample

Other Qualifications

Name:
email:

Licenses and Certifications

Honors and Recognitions

Professional Memberships

Conferences Attended

Presentations

Other Information will also demonstrate special *core competencies* (reviewed in Step 4). You can show that you are flexible, creative, have initiative, a valuable member of a team, can mentor others and communicate, and resolve problems.

Example of Other Qualifications Section

OTHER QUALIFICATIONS AND SKILLS

PROFESSIONAL PUBLICATIONS
> Co-author, Women & Minorities in Aviation in Hawaii, Hawaii Office of Education, 1998
> Aviation Progress in the Pacific, FAA World, October, 1999

PROFESSIONAL PRESENTATIONS
> Hawaii Conference on Women and Minorities
> National Congress on Aviation & Space Education

PROFESSIONAL MEMBERSHIPS & AFFILIATIONS
> Air Traffic Advisory Committee (Chair, two years)
> Air Force Association
> Hawaii Aerospace Development Corporation
> Federal Women's Program

HONORS & AWARDS
> Outstanding Performance Ratings seven consecutive years
> Award for Excellence in Aerospace Education from Civil Air Patrol

LANGUAGES
> Fluent Spanish, Moderate German and French

PART-TIME TEACHING
> Adjunct Instructor, Aviation Management, Montgomery Community College, Montgomery, MD, Fall 2002 to present

VOLUNTEER ACTIVITIES
> Girl Scout Troop Leader since 2001. Mentor, counselor and activities leader for 14 girls, ages 8 through 14.
> Finance Manager, Maryland Public School, Montgomery County, MD. Manage a $25K annual budget,
> including fundraising management and event planning.
> Monopoly World Champion, 1999, Monte Carlo, Monaco.

Lesson 4. Work Experience

Prepare an Outline of Positions

Creating an outline of your work history can be a great help in determining which jobs you are going to list in your Federal resume and which jobs you can eliminate or combine. The Federal announcements state that work history should include recent and relevant positions. So if you held a job for three months, you might decide to eliminate this position. Or if you held three or four positions that were short-term, you might want to combine these. (See Barbara Wagner's sample on page 89). You can also decide, when you see the chronology if the Straight Reverse Chronology is going to work for you. If the second job is more significant than the first job, you might want to change the Work experience from the Straight Reverse Chronology to a Work Experience Subject Category format. Barbara Wagner's resume listed her second position first in the chronology, because it was more relevant to the Federal job objective.

Federal Resume Builder

Federal Resume Template Part II
Federal Resume Help | Final Sample

Work Experience

Name: [   ]

email: [   ]

_____

Job No. 1

Please Type the following information into the field below. Follow
this format.

01/1999 to Present, 40 hours per week, EQUIPMENT SPECIALIST
TRAINEE, GS-1670-05, $26,000 annually. Norfolk Naval
Shipyard, Aircraft Maintenance Division, Avionics Maintenance
Squadron, Electrical Systems Branch, Norfolk, VA. Supervisor:
Jason Hamilton, 757-999-0001. Permission to contact.

Duties and Responsibilities

Work Experience Facts

✪ **Federal resumes must include compliance details for each job for the last ten years.** Compliance details include: supervisor's name and telephone; street address, including ZIP code; hours per week; and ending salary. This information is what the personnel staff require in the application forms.

✪ **Reverse chronology:** Typically, begin with your most recent position and work backwards, unless you need to highlight a position that is relevant and not the most recent.

✪ **Last ten years:** Develop an outline of positions with compliance details in order to plan the number of job-related positions held within the last ten years.

✪ **Prior to ten years:** If the positions are relevant, include the title of your job, organization, city, state, and dates. A short one-sentence description can be included. Prior to ten years, supervisor's name, telephone number, specific address, ZIP codes, and salaries may not be relevant, correct, or needed any longer.

✪ **Students:** Include relevant positions only.

✪ **Retired Military:** Combine early positions/ assignments.

✪ **Write your organization's name one time.** Do not repeat the names of your organizations if you have multiple jobs in the same place.

✪ **Unpaid volunteer experience is equal to paid work experience for Federal job qualifications.** You can write about volunteer and community service activities as though it is a job—if this will help you qualify for a position. If you are using unpaid work to qualify for a certain job, always include the number of hours per week in your description. If you have paid employment, then you can simply summarize your volunteer experience under Community Service.

✪ **Missing years of experience?** Just skip those years and write great descriptions about the positions you have held. You do not need to describe reasons for a gap in your dates. Be prepared to discuss it in an interview. Many people miss years of employment due to education, travel, and family responsibilities. The new Federal resume focuses on experience that is relevant, not every job you have held and every period of time in your life.

✪ **Returning to government after leaving?** Feature your GOVERNMENT EXPERIENCE first, then list your BUSINESS EXPERIENCE or OTHER EXPERIENCE second. Even if it is out of the reverse chronology, the personnelists will want to see your government positions first.

✪ **Many military assignments?** List the most recent ones first. Include many details on the last ten years. Before ten years, summarize and edit the text to include only the relevant experience.

Here is an example of a work experience outline for a Federal resume. This Federal resume is in the appendix of this book in its entirety.

EMPLOYMENT HISTORY:

EVENT MANAGER TRAINEE
Biddle Street Catering & Events
215 East Chase Street, Baltimore, MD 21202
Supervisor: Terry Dressin, you may contact at (410) 727-0000

March 2001 – Present
40 hours/week
Salary: $11/hour

CENTER MANAGER
LA Weight Loss Center
1810 York Road, Lutherville, MD 21093
Supervisor: Laura Krieger, (410) 304-0000

August 2000 – November 2000
50+ hours/week
Salary: $350/week + bonus

EXPEDITED PACKAGES SERVICE CONSULTANT
TIC Inc.
245 Hembree Park Drive, Roswell, GA 30076
Supervisor: William Reid, (877) 302-0000

March 2000 – August 2000
40 + hours/week
Salary: $2,000/month + commission
(Worked from home-based office)

ACCOUNT EXECUTIVE
PNE MEDIA
519 West Pratt Street, Baltimore, MD 21231
Supervisor: Thomas Parsons, (410) 625-0000

February 1999 – November 1999
40+ hours/week
Salary: $38,000/year

CUSTOMER CONSULTANT
PECO Energy
2301 Market Street, Philadelphia, PA 19101
Supervisor: Linda DeCowsky, (215) 841-0000

February 1996 – July 1998
40+ hours/week
Salary: $17.18/hour (hired at $14.28/hour)

REALTOR ASSOCIATE
Century 21 Roark
2042 Columbia Avenue, Lancaster, PA 17602
Supervisor: Hoyt Roark, (717) 295-0000

September 1994 – February 1996
50+ hours/week
Salary: Commission-based

LEGAL RESEARCHER
Haft Reports
Lancaster County Courthouse, Lancaster, PA 17601

December 1992 – March 1993
5–8 hours/week (PT)
Salary: $30–$50/week

ASSISTANT TO SITE COORDINATOR
ARC-PECO Energy
Peach Bottom Atomic Power Station, Delta, PA 17314
Supervisor: Lynne Ehret, (717) 456-7014

July 1991 – September 1992
35 hours/week
Salary: $10/hour

Lesson 5. Duties and Responsibilities

Writing your Work Experience Descriptions

The five sample Work Experience sections on the next pages were written with a basic outline in mind. First, the basic compliance details of the position; second, an introduction to the job; third, duties and responsibilities; and fourth, accomplishments or projects. This work experience description format does not have to be used, but components of this format can help you write about your work so that you will be qualified for Federal positions. Here is a Work Experience section broken down into the outline:

STEP 1
Start with your company and job information.

INDEPENDENT RESEARCH MANAGEMENT CONSULTANT 9914 Belhaven Road, Bethesda, MD 20817 Reference: Cheryl Morton, Director of Long-Range Research Institute American Chemical Council, you may contact at 703-741-5220	JANUARY 1999 – PRESENT 10–25 hours/week Fee: $100/hour

STEP 2
Write an introduction to your job.

Consult part-time with the American Chemical Council (formerly the Chemical Manufacturers Association) while pursuing and recently completing a masters degree in Public Health (Epidemiology) at Johns Hopkins University. Support the association's new efforts to explore how generic (non-chemical specific) research might be applied to new areas of study in addition to the existing endocrine research program (the effort I had previously developed and directed). Manage two of the ten new designated research areas: epidemiology and immunotoxicology. Total budget for these research programs: $800,000 in 2001.

STEP 3
Write three to seven bullets describing your skills and overall duties.

* Facilitate committees composed of industry, government, and academic scientists. Support committee efforts to develop research plans that are responsive to the sponsor's goals. Provide oversight of group activities to ensure consistency with the organization's principles and processes. Interfaced with both other internal teams and external groups to accomplish strategic objectives.

* Develop research agreements. These include contracts, gifts, and Cooperative Research and Development Agreements (CRADAs) in conjunction with legal counsel.

* Recruit expert scientists from government and academia to serve on peer review panels. Facilitate peer review panel meetings and document peer review decisions.

STEP 4
Write one to three accomplishments from your last (most recent) positions that will help the supervisor recognize your outstanding achievements on the job. Most resumes (and your competition) are written without accomplishments. You can read more about writing accomplishments in your resume in Lesson 6 of this chapter.

Work Experience Examples

The following five Work Experience sections are in both paper and electronic formats. You will see a combination of duties, accomplishments, and skills that will relate to the Federal vacancy announcements.

WORK EXPERIENCE FORMAT NO. 1 – Paper Federal Resume Format

This Federal job applicant was recently laid off from his private industry printer position. He is seeking a PRINTER position at Government Printing Office.

SHIFT MANAGER
COLORFAX
10776 Aurora Ave., Des Moines, Iowa 50322   June 2000 – February 2001
Salary: $52,000 annually   40 hours/week
Supervisor: Bill Balzer, you may contact at (515) 270-0402

Supervised pre-press, press, and bindery operations. Coordinated department and maintained production schedule. Met or exceeded quality expectations with help from 27 highly skilled subordinates. Reviewed work for quality assurance.

* **Planned budget.** Generated upcoming year's budgetary expenditure list, demonstrating equipment improvement for value added processes.

* **Developed staff.** Trained staff in policies, procedures, and customer service. Performed quantitative employee evaluations with written reviews.

* **Reviewed specifications.** Determined compatibility of ink, paper, art, and process color. Assisted with and/or approved intermediate or final productions. Approved/disapproved press sheets, plates, dies, negatives, and bindery stamps.

* **Solved problems.** Overcame pressroom and bindery difficulties involving ink, additives, fountain solutions, solvents, blankets, press rollers, and bookbinding materials including adhesives, stitching wire, thread and book cloths.

* **Made appropriate contributions to pre-planning stages.** Included specifications related to layout, color, size, and electronic preparations.

* **Operated and controlled inventories.** Included inks and ink-making materials, adhesives, and type metals. Established critical operating levels and reordered supplies. Initiated purchases of new rollers and the recovering of old rollers.

* **Performed ink and adhesive production functions.** Prepared standard and special inks. Modified purchased inks. Reprocessed surplus inks returned by pressrooms. Compounded adhesives used in binding and press operations. Inspected, stored and issued new and recovered rubber and plastic press rollers.

* **Performed production and procurement support functions.** Handled, stored, recycled, and prepared chemical and hazardous wastes for disposition according to applicable EPA regulations. Monitored isopropanol use in press division operations. Operated silver recovery equipment. Processed silver for disposition.

> *   **Equipment Supervised:**
>   *   Full service electronic pre-press and bindery departments
>   *   Heidelberg 8/color Speedmaster Perfector, 40"
>   *   Heidelberg 6/color Speedmaster, 40"
>   *   Heidelberg 6/color MOS, 25"
>   *   Heidelberg 2/color and 1/color, 36"
>   *   Harris M-1000A 6/color Web press
>   *   Heidelberg 8-page Web, 6/color

"Your point of 'more detail/specifics' is well taken."

WORK EXPERIENCE FORMAT NO. 2 – Electronic Format

This Federal job applicant is a recent AmeriCorps graduate applying for Public Affairs Specialist with U.S. Navy as a civilian. This is an electronic resume format.

8/1997-12/1998; 40 hours per week; AmeriCorps Leader, **MEETING PLANNER, RECRUITER, WRITER, EDITOR & PRODUCER**; $250 per week; AmeriCorps Leaders Program, Corporation for National Service, 1201 New York Ave., NW, Washington, DC 20525. Supervisor: Susan Wilson, 202/606-3111

Planned, facilitated and coordinated meetings and service activities for AmeriCorps Members. Served as liaison between Local Initiatives Support Corporation AmeriCorps Members, staff, and the Corporation for National Service. Assisted in volunteer recruitment for service projects. Communicated with members on a bi-monthly basis to give advice and support. Assisted the national Local Initiatives Support Corporation AmeriCorps Staff with the planning and coordination of national and regional training sessions. Developed, wrote and presented training programs for Local Initiatives Support Corporation AmeriCorps and other National AmeriCorps programs on the following topics: JOURNAL WRITING and reflection, PUBLIC SPEAKING and NATIONAL SERVICE HISTORY, etc.

WRITER and EDITOR of Local Initiatives Support Corporation AmeriCorps quarterly newsletter designed to keep workers informed of activities of the organization and matters affecting them. Edited and proofread all written documents.

PRODUCED and Co-directed the first Local Initiatives Support Corporation AmeriCorps video used for the support of the organization's recruitment and fundraising activities. Collected, prepared, and disseminated information to internal and external audiences both orally and in writing. Utilized interpersonal skills to maintain internal and external contacts. Team player with other New York AmeriCorps Leaders in starting the New York InterCorps Council for AmeriCorps programs throughout the state and City of New York. Skilled in audiovisual production and editing.

WORK EXPERIENCE FORMAT NO. 3 – Paper Federal Resume - Center Heading

This Federal job applicant is a Social Worker Program Director who is working on her Master of Science degree in Epidemiology. Since September 11, she has decided to start applying for positions in Bioterrorism with Centers for Disease Control now—even before she completes her graduate degree.

REVISIONS, INC.
390 Bloomsbury Avenue, Baltimore, MD 21228
May 1999 to Present

Program Director   40 hours per week
Full Time: 40 hours per week $39,000 per year
Supervisor: Tom Booth (Do not contact at this time)

Develop, design, and administer mental healthcare programs for agency clients. Responsibilities include management, supervision and evaluation of staff, assessment of existing programs, involvement in work of interdisciplinary teams, and recruitment and training of critical personnel. Requires in-depth knowledge of patient and family rights, resources and delivery systems, Federal, state and local laws and regulations, and treatment modalities and intervention techniques. Duties include:

- Managing & directing activities of 3 group homes with 24 residents.
- Supervising & evaluating performance of 3 Program Coordinators & 24 Direct Care Employees.
- Conducting in-depth research and producing reports related to health consequences for a wide range of REM clients.
- Developing/implementing required healthcare support programs based on results/conclusions of research studies.
- Maintaining critical database of information that includes analysis of patient/client behavioral effects utilized for quarterly psychotropic medication review.
- Planning & moderating key monthly & quarterly interdisciplinary team meetings to discuss client treatments, plan improved/enhanced care, and assess essential needs.

"When we surveyed 2,600 Federal supervisors, 82 percent said that job-related experience was 'very important' (the highest rating possible on the survey) when they were hiring people from outside the government."

"Filling Jobs – What do Supervisors Look For?"
Issues of Merit, Office of Policy and Evaluation,
U.S. Merit Systems Protection Board, May 1998, p. 28

WORK EXPERIENCE FORMAT NO. 4 – Paper Federal Resume: Internships and Leadership Activities from Law School

This recent law school graduate is applying for policy and public administration positions in many Federal agencies and congressional offices. This resume features volunteer positions that are presented like "real jobs."

Work and Volunteer History

CHAIRMAN, COMMENCEMENT COMMITTEE
Case Western Reserve University School of Law
11075 East Boulevard, Cleveland, OH 44106
Supervisor: Ms. Cheryl Lauderdale, you may contact at (216) 368-0000

September 2000 – May 2001
20 Hours/week
Salary: None

Provided substantial fund-raising support in 1999-2000 school year for 2000 commencement, generating record-breaking revenues. Assumed chairmanship role and responsibilities for planning a successful commencement for the 2000-2001 school year.

Improved pre-commencement programs. Sought competitive bids from area photographers. Engaged one to provide composite graduation photographs. Arranged successful social activities, including tickets to a professional baseball game.

SUMMER INTERN
New York State Assemblyman Robin L. Jones
3514 Delaware Avenue, Kenmore, NY 14217
Supervisor: Mr. Ken Berlinski, you may contact at (716) 873-0000

Summer 2000
40 hours/week
Salary: None

Assemblyman Jones served as the Chair of the Assembly Committee on Economic Development, one of the most powerful committees in New York state. Represented the Assemblyman at state conferences. Researched current and proposed legislation.

Wrote briefs. Interacted directly with constituents and state officials. Prepared 3–4 page briefs to describe each person met, concerns, goals, issues, questions, and needs.

Gained useful networking experience. Participated in closed-door conferences and saw first-hand the behind-the-scenes political process. Learned a great deal about the art of compromise and the interaction between people and politics. Observed that government and politics is all about dealing effectively with people and trying to find a common ground where you can meet their needs without sacrificing your own.

SUMMER INTERN
The Rutherford Institute, Legal Department
PO Box 7482, Charlottesville, VA 22906-7482
Supervisor: Mr. Steven H. Miller, you may contact at (804) 978-3888
Stipend: $2,500 paid by Case Western Reserve University School of Law

Summer 1999
40 hours/week
Salary: None

The Rutherford Institute is a "think tank" that focuses chiefly on civil rights and constitutional liberties. Conducted research for publication. Worked one-on-one with individuals who felt their constitutional rights had been violated.

Researched and wrote portions of law review article. Described ways that political employment can be affected by the exercise of gay and religious rights. Article citation:

Miller, Steven. "A Tale of Two Cities in the Gay Rights Kulturkamf; Are the Federal Courts Presiding Over the Cultural Balkanization of America?" *Wake Forest Law Review*, Issue 35, 2000. 295-342.

WORK EXPERIENCE FORMAT NO. 5 – Paper Federal Resume

This commercial television producer is seeking a Public Affairs Writer-Editor position at NIH and other Federal agencies.

WRITER/PRODUCER   August 2000 - Present
WJLA-TV   40 hours/week
3007 Tilden Street NW, Washington, DC 20008   Salary: $18.00/hour
Supervisor: Tom Davis, you may contact at (202) 555-5555

Wrote accurate, concise and interesting stories and matched video under extremely tight deadline pressure.
Edited on-air material. Identified and corrected errors before they appeared in broadcasts.
Often served as show producer.
Wrote print materials for electronic media. Prepared and uploaded reports for the station's website, www.wjla.com.
Re-wrote stories and wire copy. Rewrote and condensed materials for the 11 o'clock show that had run as longer packages in the earlier broadcast, often incorporating sound bytes and video attachments.

WRITER/PRODUCER   October 1997 – December 1998
WJLA-TV   40 hours/week
3007 Tilden Street NW, Washington, DC 20008   Salary: $18.00/hour
Supervisor: Jim Shaefer, you may contact at (202) 364-7715

Worked freelance for three day shifts and wrote a two-hour show on Saturday and Sunday mornings each week. Field-produced reports from the White House and other D.C. metro locations. Additional duties similar to those for WRITER/PRODUCER position with WJLA-TV from August 2000 to the present (see above). Left position to care for sick child.

MEDICAL SEGMENT PRODUCER   October 1987 – October 1997
WMAR-TV   40 hours/week
6400 York Road, Baltimore, MD 21212   Salary: $38,500/year
Supervisor: Drew Berry, you may contact at (410) 372-2300

Produced daily award-winning medical segment aired during major newscasts. Also produced longer pieces, including a half-hour program on men's health that generated more than 800 viewer requests for print information. Coached three physicians/neophyte reporters to develop friendly, authoritative on-air style. Attracted a vocal, involved and interactive viewing audience.

Lesson 6. Creating your Project List

Projects, Accomplishments, and Results

In addition to your duties and responsibilities, many people work on special projects in their jobs. Jobs such as engineering, architecture, information technology professionals, construction management, leasing, finance, contracts, and consulting are project-oriented. Employees work on one project or many projects at one time. These projects can be listed in addition to your duties. They will contain important keywords and skills for both human and automated recruiter reviews. In fact, sometimes the duties become less important after you have written your project list.

By creating your project list, you'll impress yourself, as well as your current and next supervisor! Your resume invariably builds upon what you have done, but effective resumes don't merely present duties—*they communicate results!* Effective public service resumes should present the applicant's ability to achieve those results if he or she is going to stand out among the competition.

Here is a list of measurable and quantifiable projects for a finance professional who saved her company lots of dollars through new processes, mergers, and calculations:

Federal Resume Builder

Federal Resume Template Part II
Federal Resume Help | Final Sample

Work Experience

Name: [   ]

email: [   ]

Job No. 1

Please Type the following information into the field below. Follow this format.

01/1999 to Present, 40 hours per week, EQUIPMENT SPECIALIST TRAINEE, GS-1670-05, $26,000 annually. Norfolk Naval Shipyard, Aircraft Maintenance Division, Avionics Maintenance Squadron, Electrical Systems Branch, Norfolk, VA. Supervisor: Jason Hamilton, 757-999-0001. Permission to contact.

Duties and Responsibilities

Project List

* Preparation of Internal Revenue Service Form 5500 - Annual Return/Report for Employee Benefit Plans for Retirement Income Plans. This could have been outsourced. By preparing in-house, created a savings of approximately $21,000 to $30,000.

* Coordinated merger of seven 401(k) plans into one plan at a single Trustee with a single Recordkeeper. This created savings of over $62,000 per year.

* Coordinated merger of three Defined Benefit Plans into one Defined Benefit Plan. Created savings of approximately $73,000 per year.

* Assumed responsibility of performing pension calculations based on actuarial formulas for three Defined Benefit Plans. Created a savings of approximately $48,000 per year by not outsourcing.

* Assumed responsibility of all recordkeeping for guaranteed investment contract associated with 401(k) plan. Created one-time savings of approximately $24,000 to $37,500.

* As a member of the parent Company's Benefits Committee, I am a named fiduciary. With that, I have the ability to exercise discretionary authority and control over the management and administration of the Company's Employee Benefit Plans. I also have the authority or control of any assets held under the plan and the disposition of those plan assets. Along with other committee members, I am responsible for the review and selection of investments for the 401(k), and all service providers who come into contact with the plan.

Develop a Project List with Results

You should develop and keep a list of accomplishments and projects so you can remember what you have achieved. You could give this list to your supervisor before evaluation time so that you can receive credit for accomplishments your supervisor may not remember. Create a project list so that you will be prepared for an interview. The project list could be excellent "talking points" for the interviewer.

Here is a basic outline for a Project List. With each item, describe the role you played in the project (leader, co-leader, member of team):

- ✪ Project/Program
- ✪ Title of Project/Program:
- ✪ Budget (if relevant):
- ✪ Role you played:
- ✪ Mission, objective, purpose of project:
- ✪ Customer/vendor:
- ✪ Who you communicated or worked with to complete project:
- ✪ Major challenge(s) or problem(s) during project:
- ✪ Results (i.e., cost savings, increased efficiency, improved service to customers):

Lesson 7. Highlighting Skills That Support the Announcement

Highlight skills that support the announcement and support your career change objectives. Focus your resume by using language from the vacancy announcements. Being truthful always, try to "mirror" the announcement and the new position's skills with your own skills. The closer the match from announcement to your resume, the easier it will be for the personnelist to find you qualified for the job.

The most important element of any work experience description is to make certain that the description you have written supports your objectives and the position for which you are applying. This is where the analysis of the vacancy announcement is most important. If the resume is a good fit for the position that you are seeking, it will reinforce your qualifications at every opportunity.

The best way to achieve this is to demonstrate that your previous activities include accomplishments and skills that relate to the potential employer's needs.

EXAMPLE #1

Sentence from Job Announcement:	Language you can use in your resume (if it's true):
Incumbent will conduct procurement planning and negotiation for blanket purchase agreements for information technology products.	Conduct contract plans and negotiate terms and conditions for purchase agreements for information technology products with Federal and commercial customers. Present product features and benefits, and manage contracting services through delivery of product.

EXAMPLE #2

Sentence from Job Announcement:

Incumbent will serve as Program Manager, Project Analyst managing resources, tracking employees, allocating awards and performance evaluations for staff.

Language you can use in your resume (if it's true):

PROGRAM MANAGER and PROJECT ANALYST for resource requirements, management and tracking of over 225 civilian employees, including budget inputs and projections; resource tracking and actions; employees, vacancies, dollars, workload alignment; Information Technology (IT); awards and department awards allocation; performance evaluations; special training courses; inventory evaluation and analysis; Student Aide coordinator and trainer; Cooperative Education (COOP), Coordinator; over-all problem-solver.

EXAMPLE #3

MAJOR DUTIES FOR A MANAGEMENT ANALYST WITH IMMIGRATION & NATURALIZATION SERVICE (INS) Team Leader in the conduct of field assessments of INS offices. The field assessment teams will be comprised of INS personnel detailed to the Office of Internal Audit for each review.

Leads a team comprised of staff temporarily assigned to the office to conduct each assessment.

The purpose of each review is to assess organizational compliance with established guidance effectiveness of administrative control systems, such as those designed to prevent waste, loss, unauthorized use, or misappropriation of funds and organizational performance against established measures.

Resume draft using keywords from the duties: (keywords are in italics)

Consultant
Independent Contractor:

February 2002 / Present
40 hours work/week
Salary: $26.00 per hour + all expenses

Supervisor: John Smith (301) 000-8888; Contact can be made

Team Leader for Choice Hotels International for *field audit and assessment* of performance and accounting controls at hotels throughout the U.S. Communicate with Franchisee and General Managers. *Assess organizational plans* with pre-openings, as well as ongoing operations. Coordinate pre-opening management *audits* and strategic plans, including sales/marketing plans, budgets, and construction management. Perform ongoing audits in order to discover *compliance, as well as waste, loss, and unauthorized use resulting in non-performance and income loss.*

Serve as *Team Leader* for salaried and *temporary audit team members* selected in local areas. *Assign tasks and analyze* corporate policies and procedures in compliance with management programs.

Ability to work in a *multi-task environment.* Travel extensively. Arrange for AAA inspections and rating. *Field Assignments* in Texas, Louisiana, Oklahoma, Kansas, and Arkansas. Requires 80% travel, Monday through Thursday.

Lesson 8. Including Recognitions in Job Descriptions

Most Federal announcements give instructions that you cannot attach letters of commendation to the application. Therefore, the best way to include a quote from an evaluation or letter is to quote the commendator in the Work Experience section of your resume. Emails or complimentary letters might be received from a supervisor, customer, or other important person that says you are an outstanding employee or supervisor. Collect and read the following letters you might have received. See if there are some good quotes in the text of your letters:

- Outstanding team reviews (as a member or leader of a team)
- Outstanding performance ratings
- Customer satisfaction awards or letters
- Write-ups in company newsletters
- Employee of the month recognitions
- Community or volunteer service recognitions
- Newspaper quotes

Honors from outside organizations, recognition for community service, achievements from your academic or civic background can also reinforce recognition of your skills.

Quoting Recognitions and Awards

The following are a few examples of how to use the quoted material in your resume:

- Received Letter of Commendation from the Chief of Naval Materiel, 2001.
- For planning, acquiring, and implementing a CAD/CAM system at 54 Navy sites, received a "Special Act Award" for all my accomplishments under this project.
- National Performance Review (NPR) Hammer Award for Acquisition Reform, 2000 Participation in the DoD EC/EDI Process Action Team.
- Received overall performance rating of "Outstanding" for accomplishments during this project. Also, received a letter of appreciation from NAWCWPNS, China Lake, CA, for my accomplishments in handling of "Past Performance."
- Organized 50th anniversary reunion of over 100 veterans from the 11th Air Force who fought in Hawaii during World War II. *Convention cited by Air Force Association Historical Society.*
- Developed and implemented budgetary requirements and procedures for media campaigns. Scheduled annual calendar for the Public Affairs Office. Devised and implemented components and timelines for strengthened general aviation safety component in FAA's Aviation Education program. *Campaign cited by AOPA for reducing general aviation accident rate during 2000.*

Accomplishments will help your resume to STAND OUT above your competition. You will look better than others who do not include accomplishments.

Here are Awards and Recognitions provided by Walt Schuette, author of *Finding a Job Just Got a Lot Easier!*
Impress your readers with awards and recognitions!

- ✪ Awarded Secretary of the Navy's Civilian Meritorious Service Award in recognition of Outstanding Performance of Duty as Director, Personnel Support Division, Base Housing Department, MCB, Camp Pendleton, California, September 14, 2000.

- ✪ Received Outstanding Workmanship Award from the Commanding General, Sacramento Army Depot, April 8, 2001.

- ✪ Analyzed work practices and requirements for Base Housing employees involved in maintenance of military housing, purchasing, acquisition, and requisitioning of parts, supplies, and equipment using MAXIMO software applications; significantly enhanced overall capabilities.

- ✪ Received Letter of Recommendation from Director, Maintenance and Operations Division, Oceanside Unified School District, January 18, 2000.

- ✪ Nominated for the Women of Merit Award, Chamber of Commerce, Vista, California, May 18, 2002.

- ✪ Acted as Project Manager for conversion of two 15,000 sq. ft. warehouses into an Administrative Headquarters and a Material and Parts Storage facility; oversaw project from concept to completion.

- ✪ Recipient, Navy and Marine Corps Commendation Award for Superior Performance of Duty from Commanding Officer.

- ✪ Initiated process improvements to facilitate maintenance of domestic housing and facilities by providing IT contractors and programmers proprietary requirements necessary for redesign and modification of MAXIMO applications designed for Base Housing employees.

Accomplishments can help with Interviews too! A success story for a private practice attorney who was hired into an Attorney-Advisor position.

First, before I went to the interviews, I thought about what I could offer to the prospective employer, with an emphasis on my strengths and accomplishments. I planned to use these as my themes for the interviews. I reviewed the strengths and accomplishments that were reflected in my resume. Bear in mind, my resume, which was prepared by The Resume Place, clearly set forth accomplishments in very specific terms.

Second, once I got into the interview, I tried to be sure to cover the themes when appropriate to the questions or discussion during the interviews. I planned to mention each accomplishment somehow in response to a question. Also, my referral to the themes included mentioning that I had covered them in my resume. I did this so that the interviewers could refer back to my resume.

Third, both before the interview and during it I tried to learn something about the interviewers and the work they were doing. Then I tried to show some commonality between us, either by something I had done that they had done also, or by someone I knew that they knew or an organization that we both belonged to.

Fourth, I tried to involve each of the interviewers in my response, by eye contact, body language, and asking them each at least one question when given the opportunity to do so.

Lesson 9. Skills and Talents for the Future Workforce

Core competencies are what rounds out a "value-added" public service employee! As discussed in Step 4, government agencies are seeking skills, education, experience, AND core competencies that will add elements of value to the employee. They are not just looking for "B.S. in Accounting." They want an accountant who is customer-focused, a problem-solver, creative, investigative, works well with others, and is an excellent team member. These are the core competencies that would be desirable in any employee. (See Step 4 for an excellent list of core competencies that can be included in your resume.)

Federal agencies have created lists of core competencies that they are seeking in their employees. The following paragraphs highlight a few of them.

The **Center for Medicare and Medicaid Services** wants their senior managers to have certain managerial core competencies in negotiating, political savvy, decision-making, flexibility, leadership, communications, and problem-solving. They also want the years of experience and education that are required for senior management positions.

The **Veteran's Administration Hospitals** want to hire Licensed Practical Nurses and other medical practitioners who have their licenses, but who are also empathetic to patients, flexible, hard-working, multi-tasked, able to work under pressure, and able to make decisions. These are the core competencies that are desired in the current workforce.

The **Office of Personnel Management** has a set of Executive Core Qualifications developed for Senior Executive Service candidates. Executives in government have to have five major competencies in the following areas: Leading Change, Leading People, Results Driven, Business Acumen, and Building Coalitions. Read more about the five core competencies and 27 sub-competencies on the CD-ROM and at www.opm.gov.

The skills that secured public sector jobs ten years ago (i.e. management, supervision, budget management, contract negotiations) are not enough for the current government workforce of the twenty-first century. In addition to the basic skills required to perform a job, public service employees should recognize and write about their core competencies: flexibility, creativity, innovation, empathy, customer service, communications skills, in addition to the basic management and supervisory skills.

Your perspective as you plan to write a resume must be to look back at your career and identify the skills and core competencies that will be useful to achieve your future career growth in public service.

Here is a Sample "Profile Statement" that can be used to feature core competencies and hard qualifications to catch the eye of the Federal hiring manager:

Profile:

Energetic, technically proficient and creative communications professional with extremely diverse experience in all aspects of **broadcast production**. More than 20 years of solid field experience in radio and television. **Ten years of experience in medical reporting**. Proven capabilities as a major-market television news producer and reporter. Significant **on-air radio and television experience**. Many years of **camera and editing** experience. Strong academic training with a **masters degree** in television and radio production.

Excellent writer. Award-winning storyteller dedicated to accuracy and maximizing audience impact. Stickler for grammar and spelling. Highly developed ability to write attention-getting stories. Skilled producer of video and audio segments.

Seasoned manager. Adept at managing all aspects of the broadcast newsgathering and presentation process. Have supervised diverse teams. Served for several years as the assignment manager for a large television news staff. Experienced teacher, coach, and mentor identifying and helping others actualize their potential.

Efficient organizer. Proven track record for planning and executing projects on time. Efficient, detail-conscious field producer able to get location stories.

Capable technician. Hands-on editor and videographer/photographer with a great deal of nonlinear, linear, and film editing experience. Proficient in Adobe Premiere, Panasonic Newsbyte, Microsoft Office, FrontPage, and Cool Edit.

Articulate speaker. Significant on-air radio and television experience, having served as a reporter, host, announcer, and anchor. Strong academic training in public speaking. Five years experience as a part-time pastor speaking regularly before large congregations. Have addressed community groups as representative of broadcast stations. Adept at running efficient meetings.

Strong team player. Can anticipate problems and questions. Highly developed people skills with ability to work extremely well with others.

"I inserted a Profile Statement (or Summary of Skills) category. The text was transferred almost verbatim from the Duties of 2 federal GS announcements. The Profile Statement gives my resume more attraction and focus. Thank you for this important improvement."

Lesson 10. Writing a Profile Statement

Summarize your entire career in one paragraph—your Profile Statement!

Create a new resume focus for every announcement by changing only about 10–15 lines! Very often in job interviews, an employer will open by saying, "Tell me about yourself." The "Profile" paragraph on page one of your resume provides an opportunity to develop a precise and targeted response with the keywords and skills from the "duties" section of the announcement.

For career change resumes, the profile or summary of skills is critical for featuring the skills and most relevant experience for the next career.

Samples

The following examples show two formats for writing the introductory paragraph. The Summary of Qualifications is a listing with bullets featuring experience that will match the announcement requirements. The Profile statement is a paragraph format.

Format 1- The Summary of Qualifications

OBJECTIVE:

Administrative Assistant, NIH, Announcement: NCI 02 1302, GS 0341-7

SUMMARY OF QUALIFICATIONS:

Experienced Office Assistant with 12 years diverse administrative experience including:

* Budget, payroll, and financial management
* Personnel coordination, travel, and schedule management
* Personnel action reviews
* Property and space management
* Travel order production, voucher review, funds checking
* Administrative office flow
* Type Correspondence, reports, financial tables, and personnel reports
* Database updating and management
* Forms design with Harvard Graphics and other software programs
* Keyboard 40 wpm

Format 2 - The Profile Statement

OBJECTIVE:

Logistics Program Specialist, Department of Health and Human Services (HHS),
OFC SEC Health and Human Services, Vacancy Announcement #OS-01-123

SKILLS & QUALIFICATIONS:

Experienced Logistics Chief and Emergency Response Coordinator with more than 27 months of experience
in numerous projects and deployments. Have served as Liaison, Facilities Officer, Logistics and Property
Management Officer, and Transportation Officer. Hands-on experience creating and implementing property
control databases. Able to evaluate and research new and rehabbed mechanical and medical equipment.
Expert in receiving, cataloging, and storing new and returned equipment. Meticulous record keeper who
maintains scrupulous inventory records. Adept at coordinating property control with other government
agencies and vendors.

* Current and up-to-date knowledge of logistics systems and regulations. Experienced in the
  development, coordination, and implementation of logistics functions for health and medical emergency
  response with Federal, State, and local emergency management authorities, also in problem resolution of
  logistics deficiencies relating to sufficiency of resources. Maintain logistics systems that relate to the
  procurement and tracking of emergency response supplies and equipment and developing and carrying
  out logistic policy and guidance.

* Technically proficient. Can update Management Support Team (MST) databases. Able to maintain
  a computer-based Federal property program and generate reports. Capable data communicator who
  uses Windows 95, Windows 98, Inventory Data Base for OEP Warehouse, Word, Excel, Access, and
  PowerPoint. Designed the Shipping/Receiving Data Base for OEP Warehouse. Designed Key Control
  Data Base for OEP Warehouse and Equipment. Adept at email systems.

* Strong communication skills. Concise, purposeful writer and speaker. Keeps communication on track.
  Can simplify complex or highly technical information.

Your profile is an abstract of your career as it applies to your career objective. Human resources recruiters and hiring supervisors appreciate the capsulized version.

Putting it all together

Now that you have reviewed the resume sections, headings, and information that can be written in your resume, you are ready to package, format, and organize your resume content.

The goal with the organizational presentation is to highlight the skills that will support your Federal job objective. You want to make it easy for the human resources staff to find the information needed to ensure that you are qualified for the job. Then you want the resume to STAND OUT so that the hiring official will want to speak with you by phone or in an interview.

The outstanding resumes keep the reader's attention longer, compelling the reader to move the resume to the "read again later" pile, then a few more minutes of reading, and then the "Best Qualified" list. Next the selecting official will go through the same process.

Step 1: Prioritize the information.

When organizing your resume, *prioritize the information*. Review the position announcement, and think in terms of two factors.

- ✪ First, what are my strongest skills?
- ✪ Second, what skills does the announcement emphasize?

Your resume is an advertisement of your candidacy for a particular position. Ideally, your qualifications will fit identically with the skills desired by the employer. *To make certain that the employer recognizes the fit, it can help to present the essential information up front, and save less vital details for later.*

Most people learned to write a resume in a college placement office when they were approaching graduation. Then, people were taught to list education first, because it is the leading qualification of a person who has little other experience. Fifteen years later, the education section may no longer be the strongest qualification on your resume. Your resume should convince potential employers that what you have done lately is more important for them (unless you've gone back to school for a new degree or certificate).

"I want a resume that will allow me to compete well for a job within this new structure or allow me to 'jump ship' if something attractive comes along. For the last 6 years, I've worked on a variety of programs as requirements and organizational needs have changed and as my responsibilities have grown."

Step 2. Select your resume focusing sections.

Many sections of the resume are optional. You can choose one of these headings or all of them.

- ✪ A **profile** can prepare the reader to look for the information that you want to emphasize. This section is highly recommended!

- ✪ **Critical skills** can be a list of your skills that support the position.

- ✪ Highlights of **key accomplishments** can be used to stress your successes that are relevant to the position.

Step 3. Modify the organization for various applications as needed.

To the best of your ability, arrange your information so that it sells you best for the position for which you are applying. If you believe the education should be listed before Work Experience, then you should feature your educational background. If you have Certifications that are critical to your work, list those before Work Experience. Remember that the human resources staff are very busy when reading many pages of resumes from applicants. Make it easy for them to find your relevant qualifications.

Step 4. Review the critical job elements.

Review the duties in the vacancy announcement against your resume AGAIN. Make sure the keywords in the Duties section are visible in your resume on the first two pages.

Step 5. Read your resume aloud and edit profusely!

Now that you have drafted your "everything" basic Federal resume, you will need to edit and decide what is relevant and most important for the position. Most public service resumes are two to five pages in length. Length is not the most important element of the resume—content is.

After you finish your paper "Federal" resume, you will want to read the next section of this chapter to learn how to convert this resume to an electronic format so that you are ready for automated human resources announcements.

"I believe that I possess all of the necessary skills, education, and experience for this position and would like to present my information more effectively."

TEN STEPS TO A FEDERAL JOB

RESUME PLACE FEDERAL RESUME BUILDER

"The Builders helped me write a lot of information that I would not have otherwise written."

The Federal Resume Builder can be found on the CD-ROM of this book. You will need Internet, a browser, and email so that you can fill in the information. Once you complete the form, you can hit SEND.
The content will come to you. It will not go into any database. You can then copy and paste your text into a Word processing software program and edit and format your resume. The Builders are designed to help you organize your content and build your resume. The Builders will not format, spellcheck, edit, or produce a final resume.

FEDERAL RESUME AND RESUMIX RESUME BUILDER

PERSONAL INFORMATION

KATHRYN KRAEMER TROUTMAN
2 Holmehurst Avenue
Baltimore, MD 21228
Home Telephone: (410) 777-7777
Office Telephone: (410) 744-4324
email: resume@resume-place.com

Social Security No: 000-00-0000
Federal Employment Status: Writer-Editor, GS-301-13, November 1995 to present
Veteran's Status: Honorably Discharged, U.S. Army, 1970-1975
Citizenship: United States

Please type the above information in this field.

OBJECTIVE

If you have a current announcement, insert the title of the position, grade, series, and vacancy announcement number. If you do not have an announcement at this time, write the type of position you are seeking and grade level.

Please type your job objective in this field.

EDUCATION

College Courses

List your colleges with the most recent first. There are five fields for college course information. Include College and Degree information, Relevant Courses, Awards and Honors, Special Projects and Activities. This section is for college courses, not training. The training section is later in this form.

Example #1:

B.S., English, University of Maryland, University College, College Park, MD 90909; June 1995. Relevant courses: Technical Writing, Web site Content Development, Editorial Process, Publication Planning, Project Management, Photojournalism, Internet Researching Skills. Awards and Honors: Magna cum laude, Dean's List 5 semesters, English Honors, Published in school newspaper (Eagle) 10 times. Significant course projects: Website Content Development: wrote content and created a Web site for the English program at the school which is now posted and updated by administrative staff. Activities: Member, Creative Writing Committee; Active in Poetry Guild.

Example #2:

Completed 25 credits, University of Maryland, University College, College Park, MD 90909; June 1995. Relevant Courses: Computer Sciences, Network Management, Project Management, and Public Speaking.

College #1
College #2
College #3
College #4

High School Information

Some Federal applications require high school background. If you are a recent high school graduate, you can write more information to support your high school experience, such as Relevant Courses, Honors and Awards, Activities, Projects. Please write the following information in this field:

Graduated Catonsville High School, Baltimore, MD 1975

Professional Training

Include your most recent (within the last five to ten years) and relevant training and conferences in your resume. Follow this format when writing your professional training.

TRAINING

Public Speaking, 3 credit hours, USDA Graduate School, 2001
Affirmative Action, 3 credits, Thompson Institute, 2001
Project Management, 24 hours, Management Concepts, Alexandria, VA 2001
Team Building, 8 hours, FPMI, Crystal City, VA, March 2001

CONFERENCES

Reinvention HR Conference, FPMI, Orlando, FL, Spring, 2001
Training in Automated Human Resources Systems, Recruitment and OPM Retention Plans for 2001.

Federal Manager's Association, Alexandria, VA, Spring 2000 Attended training in Commercial Activities, HR Planning and Workforce and Succession Planning

WORK EXPERIENCE

Name:
email:
Job No. 1

Please type the following information into the next field. Follow this format.

01/1999 to Present, 40 hours per week, EQUIPMENT SPECIALIST TRAINEE, GS-1670-05, $26,000 annually. Norfolk Naval Shipyard, Aircraft Maintenance Division, Avionics Maintenance Squadron, Electrical Systems Branch, Norfolk, VA. Supervisor: Jason Hamilton, 757-999-0001.
Permission to contact.

DUTIES AND RESPONSIBILITIES

Refer to the Instruction page for tips on completing the Responsibilities section.

ACCOMPLISHMENTS

COLLATERAL DUTIES, TEAMS, COMMITTEES, PROJECTS

OTHER QUALIFICATIONS

Name:
email:

LICENSES AND CERTIFICATIONS

HONORS AND RECOGNITIONS

PROFESSIONAL MEMBERSHIPS

CONFERENCES ATTENDED

PRESENTATIONS

PUBLICATIONS

INTERNATIONAL TRAVEL

LANGUAGES

SPECIAL INTERESTS OR ACTIVITIES

COMMUNITY OR VOLUNTEER SERVICES

OTHER

Focusing Your Resume

PROFILE

Often in job interviews, an employer will begin by saying, "Tell me about yourself." For this reason, the Federal ResumeWriter™ allows you to strengthen your application by summarizing your qualifications in an opening profile statement.

CRITICAL SKILLS

Identify the critical skills, expertise, and talents that will position you for the Federal workforce of the future.

Critical Skills 1:

Critical Skills 2:

Critical Skills 3:

MAJOR ACCOMPLISHMENTS

Summarize your key accomplishments to stress successes that are relevant to the position. Try to write these accomplishments in three to five lines here.

Accomplishment 1:

Accomplishment 2:

Accomplishment 3:

Remember . . .

Your potential employer is much less interested in what you have done than in what you can do to fill the need within another organization (or to demonstrate your abilities for the next promotion).

Helpful Tools for writing your Federal or Electronic Resume:

You can choose to use the Resume Builders on the CD-ROM to help you with your federal resume. Or you can use any resume on the CD as your template to write your resume. Just replace text.

"Today's public service resume focuses on:

ACCOMPLISHMENTS AND RESULTS —
Not merely a description of the duties and responsibilities that you performed. Include details of your projects or programs.

PROGRAMS AND POLICIES THAT SERVE —
Specific people (customers), not just a generalized public, or functions of job responsibilities.

DEVELOPING SKILLS AND CORE COMPETENCIES —
That will be required for your next career, whatever it might be.

DESCRIBING ACCOMPLISHMENTS —
In dynamic terms demonstrate that you have made a difference in your organization, not merely writing about job activities."

Edward J. Lynch, Ph.D.

WRITING AN ELECTRONIC RESUME

Four automated systems are being used in government: Resumix™ (a HotJobs software program), QuickHire™, AVUE™, and USA Staffing, which is managed by the Office of Personnel Management.
You will learn their various application formats as you read the announcement "how to apply" instructions.

As you begin your Federal job search and read vacancy announcements, you will see many announcements asking for RESUME ONLY. There are basically two kinds of electronic resume formats in government today. One is the paper Federal resume that was discussed in great length earlier in this chapter. The other is an electronic resume that is basically the same as the paper resume, only formatted differently. Step 8 will review in more detail the various "how to apply" instructions for using either a paper Federal resume or electronic resume.

Many Federal agencies have automated their recruitment and resume management systems. There are at least four automated systems in government right now: Resumix™, a HotJobs Software program used by Defense agencies; QuickHire™, used by EPA, USGS and many other non-defense agencies; AVUE, used by Library of Congress and other agencies; and USASTAFFING, an OPM personnel service provided to all Federal agencies for recruiting and selecting the best qualified candidates. All of these systems require "resume only."

Many other agencies are using in-house agency-developed systems to accept electronic resumes, questionnaires, and resume builders (for copying and pasting your resume into a field). When you see the government is hiring masses of employees, such as the FAA Security Screeners, Border Patrol Agents, and Firefighters, you will see automation being used to recruit and handle thousands of applicants. They also ask many personnel and security questions in their questionnaires and possibly other information that should be faxed. You have to read the HOW TO APPLY instructions to see what is required for each position. Some of the announcements are complex and long, but this is the way they are handling the recruitments. Be patient, read the directions, and keep applying.

One consistent element is that you use a resume to apply for all automated systems!

The one consistent element with the automated HR systems is that you use a resume to apply for the job. You write a resume the same way the instructions were given in the first part of this chapter (Federal resume writing), but you format the resume differently. You should format the resume very plainly, so that you can copy and paste it into a Resume Builder, or you can copy it into the textbox of an email. You can see the clear difference at the beginning of this chapter between the "paper" formatted resume and the electronic resume.

This part of the chapter introduces you to the electronic resume and how it is different from the "paper" Federal resume that was discussed earlier in this chapter. Here is the process we usually take for helping a client prepare an electronic resume.

1. We ask for announcements for jobs for three reasons:
   a.) read the directions on how to apply; b.) review the deadline—open continuous or real closing date for special announcement; and c.) to review and extract the keywords for the person's resume so that there will be a MATCH between resume and announcement.

2. We ask for basic resume information – same information as on the three Federal Resume Builders on the CD-ROM.

3. We ask for specifics and accomplishments (these will make your resume stand out).

4. We write the electronic resume, using available materials and as many skills from the announcements that are truthful in your case.

5. After we talk about the resume content, we discuss other important submission details.

6. We review resume length considerations (Army is three pages; Navy and AF are five pages, etc.).

7. We discuss submission procedures, including Resume Builder vs. email, supplemental statements, and self-nominations.

For an electronic resume submission to be successful, you have to get it ALL RIGHT—resume, keywords, submission, supplemental sheet, and timing. With effort and reading the directions, you can do it! If the application is not right, the personnel office will probably send it back. If the resume doesn't include good descriptions, you might not be considered for any positions.

Review the Resume Builder Requirements

A Resume Builder is an online form (that is not part of the automated HR system software) where you can either type your resume directly into the Builder fields, or you can copy and paste your resume into the fields. We prefer that you write your resume in your favorite word processing software, then copy it into the various Builders that you will find online at employment websites. The Builders are all different, so just be ready with your electronic resume.

Each Builder—whether Resumix, QuickHire, Commerce On Line, or other electronic application system—has particular requirements. Defense agencies have Job Kits that offer complete instructions on their application requirements. You must be familiar with the requirements of the Job Kit and the Resume Builder before entering your information into the particular system.

When you have a choice of using a Resume Builder vs. email submission (resume in the textbox), most agencies will prefer that you submit with the Resume Builder. It can go directly into a database faster with the Builder.

The Defense agency builders take time to submit, but once they are posted, you will be in a database waiting for job searches in your particular occupational series. Here are a few tips that can help you with these Builders:

1. Write your resume in your software, then copy and paste into the Builder.

2. Allow an hour at least. Get help if you are not quick at copy and paste.

3. Read the directions for how many characters you can fit into the Work Experience description sections.

Army allows 1,600 characters (without spaces) and three pages; Navy allows 6,000 characters (with spaces) and five pages.

The Resume Builders provide fields for the following sections:

Personal information

Work Experience—spaces for six jobs only! Focus on the last ten years, but also focus on the jobs that are most relevant to your career objectives.

Certificates & Licenses

Training

Education

Other Information

You can submit your resume by email instead of the Resume Builder if you prefer. But be sure to add the supplemental data sheet as a separate page at the end of the email.

Electronic Resume Is not a Mystery — It's Technical Writing

This part of the chapter will help take the mystery out of writing a resume for vacancies that require an electronic submission. Developing the materials you will need is essentially the same process as for preparing a Federal resume. The major differences are the electronic resume format, length requirements, and the importance of writing good, clear descriptions of your knowledge, skills, abilities, expertise, and equipment skills. This chapter will show you how to incorporate this writing style into your electronic resume so that you will be successful in Federal job databases. More information on the electronic resume (and samples) can be found in the 242-page *Electronic Federal Resume Guidebook & CD-ROM* written entirely for writing resumes for Defense civilian jobs by this author.

"I thought I understood Resumix since I used it to get my first civil service job. Boy, was I wrong. Thank you for your insight into how the system works and especially the project lists and buzzwords. I felt guilty using previous position descriptions to write my resume, but now I see that these buzzwords really help to bring out my skills in terminology the computer will pick up on. After using your *Electronic Federal Resume Guidebook*, I feel confident that this is a more accurate reflection of the work I did and am capable of."

Johanna M. Fielder

Finding Your Keywords

In order to focus your electronic resume, you should have a few vacancy announcements to refer to for key skills. Some announcements are better than others. You might find some announcements with the duties section being very short with almost no description. Therefore, these announcements will not be helpful for recognizing keywords and skills. Other announcements are lengthy and seem to describe a "real job." These are good announcements. Whenever possible, include keywords from vacancy announcements in your resumes.

Here are two announcements with different amounts and types of keywords that you could use in your resume. These are both taken from www.cpol.army.mil Web site. These announcements are found at the West Region Civilian Personnel Office Center (CPOC) office listings. You can find these by going to the above Web site; then to LINKS; then to Regional Offices; then to West; then to Employment; then to Open Continuous Announcements; and DEU Vacancy Announcements.

Resumix resumes and keyword lists are available in the *Electronic Federal Resume Guidebook* by Kathryn Troutman

Generic "Open Continuous, Database Building" announcement with few keywords:

SAMPLE 1

GENERAL ADMINISTRATION, CLERICAL OFFICE SERVICES (GS-0300)

COMMENTS:

THIS ANNOUNCEMENT COVERS ALL POSITIONS AND ALL GRADE LEVELS CLASSIFIED IN THE GS-0300 GENERAL ADMINISTRATION, CLERICAL, AND OFFICE SERVICES GROUP JOB FAMILY (GS-0300 THROUGH GS-0399), TO INCLUDE THE FOLLOWING JOB TYPES:
MISCELLANEOUS ADMINISTRATIVE AND PROGRAM MANAGEMENT
MESSENGER
MISCELLANEOUS CLERK/ASSISTANT
INFORMATION RECEPTIONIST
MAIL AND FILE/CORRESPONDENCE CLERK
SECRETARY/CLERK STENOGRAPHER/REPORTER
WORK UNIT SUPERVISOR
CLOSED MICROPHONE REPORTER
CLERK TYPIST
OFFICE AUTOMATION CLERK/ASSISTANT
COMPUTER OPERATOR/CLERK/ASSISTANT/SPECIALIST
PROGRAM MANAGEMENT
ADMINISTRATIVE OFFICER
SUPPORT SERVICES ADMINISTRATION
MANAGEMENT AND PROGRAM ANALYST/CLERK/ASSISTANT
LOGISTICS MANAGEMENT
EQUIPMENT OPERATOR

PRINTING CLERK
DATA TRANSCRIBER
ELECTRIC ACCOUNTING MACHINE OPERATION/PROJ PLANNING
EQUAL OPPORTUNITY COMPLIANCE
EQUAL OPPORTUNITY ASSISTANT
TELEPHONE OPERATOR
TELECOMMUNICATIONS
COMMUNICATIONS CLERK

HOW TO APPLY: A maximum three-page resume plus a one-page West CPOC supplemental data sheet that answers 32 employment questions in the Resumix format is required.

Duties:

The General Administrative, Clerical, and Office Services Group includes all classes of positions the duties of which are to administer, supervise, or perform work involved in management analysis; stenography, typing, correspondence, and secretarial work; mail and file work; the operation of office appliances; the operation of communications equipment, use of codes and ciphers, and procurement of the most effective and efficient communications services; the operation of microform equipment, peripheral equipment, mail processing equipment, duplicating equipment, and copier/duplicating equipment; and other work of a general clerical and administrative nature.

Good announcement with excellent description of the position and many keywords for your resume. This is a "real" announcement (not a database building announcement) with a closing date. This is a "DEU" announcement that means that anyone can apply for this position— either current Federal employees or anyone (who is a citizen) outside of government. Applicants for this position can see the keywords in the "duties" section easily. Keywords are underlined.

SAMPLE 2

Vacancy Announcement No.: 151-DEU-02

Opening Date: March 14, 2002

Initial Cut-off Date: March 27, 2002

Closing Date: April 15, 2002

Position Title (Pay Plan-Series): GENERAL EQUIPMENT MECHANIC LEADER (WL-4737)

Grade: 10

Duties:

Serves as a working leader of six or more employees in the accomplishment of trades and labor work. The highest level of nonsupervisory work lead is General Equipment Mechanic, WG-10. Uses well seasoned trade skills to independently perform a wide range of industrial and general maintenance tasks and major repair or renovation projects involved in the upkeep of differing types of machinery and equipment which incorporate mechanical, electromechanical, hydraulic, pneumatic, and electrical or electronic operating principles. Performs the full range of work involved in the <u>relocation</u>, <u>installation</u>, <u>repair</u>, <u>overhaul</u>, <u>modification</u>, <u>maintenance</u>, <u>servicing</u>, and <u>testing</u> of <u>special purpose high/low pressure compression systems</u> and <u>inert gas boosters</u> used in direct support of <u>atmospheric test operations</u> and <u>missile firings</u> conducted on the installation. <u>Diagnoses</u> and <u>locates malfunctions</u>; <u>disassembles</u>, <u>repairs</u>, <u>replaces</u>, and/or <u>adjusts high/low pressure air compressor systems</u> and <u>compressors</u> of <u>various horsepower</u> and <u>CFM ratings</u> with <u>reciprocating rotary vein</u>, <u>screw type full displacement compressors</u> and <u>vessel equipment</u> to include <u>receiver valves</u>, <u>regulator isolation valves</u>, <u>regulators</u>, <u>electrical switches</u>, <u>relays</u>, and other <u>automatic control devices</u>; <u>disassembles</u> and <u>repairs compressors</u> and <u>related components</u>; services and repairs <u>evaporators</u>, <u>condenser</u>, and <u>receivers</u>, <u>cilica gel type dryers</u> (particularly the units supplying <u>pneumatic pressure</u> for all types of cooling and heating controls and applications); <u>repacks valves</u>; <u>replaces electric motors</u>, <u>belts</u>, and <u>pulleys</u>; <u>lubricates moving parts</u>; repairs <u>electrical systems</u> and <u>wiring up to 115 volts</u>; replaces and/or <u>cleans filters</u>; <u>bleeds system</u>; <u>tests for leaks</u> and for <u>excessive load conditions</u>; <u>reconditions</u>, <u>modifies</u>, and <u>fabricates parts</u>. Operates a combination of <u>mobile, stationary, or portable industrial equipment</u>, <u>machinery</u> or <u>tools</u> such as <u>5-ton wrecker</u>, <u>10-ton tractors with trailer</u>, <u>forklifts up to 15,000 pound capacity</u>, and <u>mechanical or hydraulic lifts</u> in support of weight testing and installation, maintenance, repair, or movement of equipment.

Licenses, Certificates, and Military Service

Your licenses and certificates are important, too. If you have received a certification in your field of work, list it under the Certification category. Security Clearances can be listed in this section. As with job-related training, honors, awards, and recognitions should be prioritized by importance, and listed in reverse chronological order. And don't forget U.S. military service. Many individuals have valuable experience that should not be overlooked, and if job-related, can be treated as a work experience. Consider both active duty and reserve duty, leadership responsibilities, classified work, campaign medals, and be sure to list your type of discharge and any veterans preference eligibility.

Professional Memberships

Professional memberships can demonstrate how serious you are about your profession. You may also attend workshops, conventions, read newsletters, and follow current information in your profession. This is important information. If you attend the conventions, list them.

" I have been reading Kathryn's career advice for some time, first through her column in Government Executive Magazine and now through her weekly e-mails. Along the way, I purchased her book *The Federal Resume Guidebook* and recently, I bought *The Electronic Federal Resume Guidebook*. These books have been a big help to me in making the transition from the old SF-171 to the new Federal resume. I feel that the resume allows me more creative options in presenting myself on paper."

"Can I write a Profile on an electronic resume?" Maybe. You have to review the instructions and the desired format for an electronic resume. Some Resume Builders do not have a field for a Profile statement. But if you can submit by email or blend the summary into your work experience description, then maybe you can use a Profile in your electronic resume.

Other Information

Other information can be:

✪ A summary of your career with a clear list of important skills (found in the vacancy announcement if possible):

> EQUIPMENT MECHANIC LEADER with 20 years experience. Work leader with expertise in industrial and general maintenance projects. Skilled in mechanical, hydraulic, pneumatic industrial equipment operations, including use of gas boosters to support operations and missile firing operations. Experienced project manager with excellent interpersonal and customer management skills. Able to meet tight deadlines, ensure a safe work environment, and coordinate with other crafts.

✪ Computer/technical systems skills and expertise (in addition to what you write in Work Experience):

> COMPUTER SERVICES AND SUPPORT
>   Local area network installations and set-up
>   Support desktop systems with Windows NT/98/2000
>   ADP systems requirements, telecommunications
>   Desktop publishing software
>   Test new software applications
>   Knowledge of networking
>   Translate user needs into computer systems
>   Provide customer service and helpdesk support for computer systems

✪ Other positions summarized that you could not include in the Work Experience. "Other positions prior to 1985 have included: real estate agent, small business owner (in-home sales), and temporary worker as a clerical-secretary. Developed skills in communications, sales, business services and office operations."

✪ A reasonable length description of your core competencies (as in Step 4). "Critical skills include: working well under pressure, flexible, willingness to do whatever it takes to succeed on a project; excellent interpersonal and verbal communications skills; and resource in utilizing available sources."

✪ Community Service, Volunteer, and Interests that show leadership and can help you package yourself to stand out for the supervisor who is reviewing the 10 or 15 finalists for the position.

✪ Language Skills (also list this in Work experience if you use your language skills at work).

Focus your Electronic Resume — Avoid the "Shotgun" Approach

Determine your career objectives. Avoid the "shotgun" approach— that is, creating a resume that is so broad or general that it results in your being qualified for referrals, but not strong enough to make best-qualified lists. Rather, focus on a limited number—two or three— realistic, practical career objectives before getting started.

Barbara Wagner (sample in this chapter) is seeking GS-7 positions in the following occupational series:

1. Secretary (Office Automation)
2. Administrative Specialist
3. Program Assistant

Focus on your most recent ten years of work experience, and earlier only if the experience is especially critical for the target position. You may find opportunities to combine work experiences if the position(s) were short term and not related to the position. Barbara Wagner combined a couple of short-term positions working for the Air Force. Key in on the most important responsibilities of the position.

Basic Writing, Content, and Style

Writing your electronic resume is pretty much the same as writing any resume. But here are a few tips to maximize space, use more specific terms, nouns, and action verbs.

1. Use plain language. Write professionally and concisely.

2. Eliminate acronyms whenever possible. When you must use them, spell them out the first time used, and separate with commas or dashes.

3. Since your space is limited, drop words that do not add value such as "responsible for," "very,"and "duties include." Also, see how many times you can delete "the" without changing the meaning.

4. Avoid using the same descriptor twice in the same paragraph, such as "manage," "develop," and "coordinate," and minimize repeating words. Use a thesaurus to maximize descriptors that will bring out skills.

5. Start each sentence with an action verb, and not "I."

6. Active voice is more powerful than the passive voice.

7. Use present tense for present work experience, past tense for previous work experience, or for projects in the present work experience that have ended. Do not add "s" to your verbs, i.e. Plans, manages and leads. This is writing in the third person. Write in the first person, without the use of "I."

> "We are in the Resumix system. I reviewed 15 resumes last week referred through the database and only one of the resumes included accomplishments. The resume stood out far above the others. This person was hired."
>
> Hiring Supervisor, Corps of Engineers, Ft. Shafter, Hawaii

Power Plant Mechanic
Keywords / Skills List (partial)

Power Plant Electrician

Team Member

Customer Services

Safety

Quality Control

OSHA

Hydropower

Project Lead

Project Manager

Supervisor

8. Use ALL CAPS for official position titles. Also, this holds true for titles of roles in jobs, or unofficial, working job titles, such as PROJECT MANAGER, SENIOR STAFF ADVISOR, RECEPTIONIST, and so forth when you are describing these in your work experience summary. All caps can be used to identify major functional areas of work. Keep your paragraph length to 8 to 10 lines.

9. Use more nouns. Nouns are searchable terms in most databases. If you can use the phrase, "editor," rather than "responsible for compiling documents and preparing a publication," you will be more successful.

10. Include the proper names and generic descriptions of products, software, and equipment. It's difficult to know which words will be in a database. Write both to be sure.

Creating a Stand-Out Electronic Resume with Functional Working Titles, Accomplishments, and Projects

You need both duties and accomplishments in your electronic resume to be successful. You need the duties and responsibilities in your work experience to demonstrate that you can perform the job. You need accomplishments to keep the supervisor reading YOUR resume so you will be interviewed and selected. The goal is to stand out, get noticed, be remembered, receive a phone call, and be scheduled for an interview. You are going to have to brag, sell, market, and let the readers know that you are an excellent employee, highly-skilled, valued by supervisors and customers, and one who gets the job done! The following sections include a few more tips to improve your electronic resume.

Identifying Working Titles

You may have a "regular" job title, such as COMPUTER SPECIALIST. As a Computer Specialist, you wear several hats in your job. You are also a Webmaster, Graphic Designer, Customer Consultant, Desktop Publisher and Writer.

Here is an example of a before-and-after work experience description before the working titles (nouns) are clearly presented. The AFTER resume includes NOUNS and PROPER NAMES that are in ALL CAPS to improve the readability for the hiring supervisor. Since the electronic resume is not a formatted presentation, the use of ALL CAPS can help the reader find and understand the critical skills and experiences easily.

COMPUTER SPECIALIST, Naval Education and Training Professional Development and Technology Center

Before

Webmaster and developer for 5 sites: Naval Air Training Command, Naval Region South Texas, Marine Air Training Group 22, Mine Warfare Training Center. Software employed includes GoLive, FrontPage, Photoshop, and ImageReady. Web pages tweaked by direct HTML and Java coding.

Design and standardize both electronic and hardcopy presentation graphics and templates for Department Head and Command Level meetings. Major projects included the 1991, 93, and 95 BRAC rounds, airspace negotiations with USAF training units, change of command briefs and ceremonial materials for four Chiefs of Naval Air Training. Some of the BRAC materials developed percolated up to Congressional presentation.

Generate custom computer graphics for both presentation and training materials desktop publishing requirements. Communicate with customers concerning content, color, graphics, photos, maps, etc., in order to design unique presentations. Use strong background in statistical analysis to suggest optimal data presentation techniques to customers.

Management consultant to senior level managers concerning effective collaborative utilization of off-the-shelf software, including PowerPoint, Word, Excel, and various web browsers. Managers are striving to improve e-communication channels through new technology (most recently, Virtual Private Networks). My primary project in this area is the development and maintenance of web-based data sharing for the Naval Aviation Pilot Production Improvement Program.

Technical writer and subject matter expert on aviation training issues including technical content, wording and alternative explanations for training materials. Advise authors on plain-language writing techniques for training manuals, documentation, presentations, and reports. Major projects include primary flight training out-of-control flight procedures and airspace utilization illustrations for the staff Air Traffic Control Officer.

After

WEBMASTER AND DEVELOPER for 5 sites: Naval Air Training Command, Naval Region South Texas, Marine Air Training Group 22, Mine Warfare Training Center. Software employed includes GoLive, FrontPage, Photoshop and ImageReady. Web pages tweaked by direct HTML and Java coding.

GRAPHIC DESIGNER: Design and standardize both electronic and hardcopy presentation graphics and templates for Department Head and Command Level meetings. MAJOR PROJECTS: 1991, 1993, and 1995 Base Realignment and Closings, BRAC, rounds, airspace negotiations with United States Air Force, USAF, training units, change of command briefs and ceremonial materials for four Chiefs of Naval Air Training. Some of the BRAC materials developed percolated up to Congressional presentation.

DESKTOP PUBLISHER: Develop custom computer graphics for both presentation and training materials desktop publishing requirements. Communicate with customers concerning content, color, graphics, photos, maps, etc., in order to design unique presentations. Use strong background in statistical analysis to suggest optimal data presentation techniques to customers.

MANAGEMENT CONSULTANT to senior level managers on effective collaborative utilization of off-the-shelf software, including PowerPoint, Word, Excel, and various web browsers.

Managers are striving to improve e-communication channels through new technology, most recently, Virtual Private Networks. PRIMARY PROJECT: the development and maintenance of web-based data sharing for the Naval Aviation Pilot Production Improvement Program.

TECHNICAL WRITER AND SUBJECT MATTER EXPERT on aviation training issues. Technical content, wording, and alternative explanations for training materials. Advise authors on plain-language writing techniques for training manuals, documentation, presentations, and reports. MAJOR PROJECTS: primary flight training out-of-control flight procedures and airspace utilization illustrations for the staff Air Traffic Control Officer.

Identifying Major Functional Areas and Skills

Another way to break down your duties section is to identify major functional areas and skills with verbs, rather than titles and nouns. It's important that your electronic resume be clear and understandable to the computer and supervisor. This before-and-after example demonstrates writing style that is improved, skills that are identified and groupings of experiences described. The "before" is a mass of words clumped together – hard for the computer to understand (the Defense systems read skills "in context") and for the supervisor to read quickly and be impressed.

Lead Transportation Operations Specialist GS-2150, Department of Defense Dependents Schools

Before

Note that this is one paragraph and a mass of words.

Coordinate and supervise DoD school bus transportation services for American School system in Wiesbaden Germany. Interface with school administrators, community officials, parents, military and U.S. civilian customer base and contracted German national service providers. Manage and supervise a staff of three. Determine transportation requirements, order services and administer procedural and operational functions that ensure contractor compliance as the Contracting Officer's Technical Representative (COTR) and Blanket Purchase Agreement (BPA) Caller. Develop complex transportation plans that provide and enhance student transportation for daily commute requirements, as well as support both curricular trips and co-curricular activities. Certify and forward invoices for payment and maintain a detailed accounting of delivery order allocations to ensure availability of funds. Develop, implement, evaluate plans that affect Department of Defense Dependent student education across Europe. Administer a strict "Student Behavior Management" program and liaison with school administration on disciplinary consequences. Maintain continuous up-to-date status of the quality of Contractor performance, as well as monitor the maintenance/readiness status of all vehicles. Represent the District Transportation Division at applicable school, community, and installation level meetings.

After

Now the functional areas are clear and represented by smaller paragraphs.

PROGRAM OPERATIONS MANAGEMENT: Coordinate and manage DOD school bus transportation services for the American School System in Wiesbaden, Germany. Interface with school administrators, community officials, parents, military and U.S. civilian customer base and contracted German national service providers. Develop and execute complex transportation program and plans that provide and enhance student transportation for daily commute requirements, curricular trips, and extra-curricular activities.

Administer a strict Student Behavior Management program and serve as liaison with school administration on disciplinary matters. Represent the District Transportation Division at applicable school, community, and installation level meetings. Coordinate, prioritize, plan, and assign work for a staff of three. Direct work unit and assist in evaluation, coaching, developing, counseling, rewarding, and recognizing employee performance. Lead by proactive example in Equal Employment Opportunity and Civil Rights.

CONTRACT MANAGEMENT: Determine transportation requirements, order services and ensure contractor compliance as the COR and Blanket Purchase Agreement, BPA, Caller. Maintain continuous monitoring, evaluation, and enforcement of the quality of contractor performance against established standards, in accordance with the Quality Assurance Surveillance Plan (QASP).

Analyze trends and provide reports on contractor performance, including Contract Discrepancy Reports, according to the contract table of scheduled deductions. Focal point to receive and respond to queries; determine any shortfalls, reconcile disparities, and resolve problems. Monitor the maintenance services provided by contractor to assure readiness status of all vehicles.

CONTRACT ADMINISTRATION: Develop, implement, evaluate, and administer procedural and operational functions that affect DOD Dependent student education for the Weisbaden, Germany area. Verify, certify and forward contractor invoices for payment and maintain a detailed accounting of delivery order allocations to ensure availability of funds. Keep Contracting Officer and Contracting Specialist informed of the status of available funding.

Using Accomplishments and Project Details to Stand Out

Every electronic resume should include accomplishments or project details if possible. In order to STAND OUT when the hiring supervisor has 10 or 15 resumes to read, you should include accomplishments. If the resume is just a description of duties, you will look just like your competitors. To stand out, accomplishments are needed. How much money have you saved? Time have you saved by improving databases, information, customer services?

Both humans and databases read for keywords and skills.

FIRE PROTECTION INSPECTOR, GS-081-08

ACCOMPLISHMENT: Managed the updating and presenting staff training in Environment of Care Standards in Fire Prevention and Fire Extinguisher training. Developed and delivered training with two trainers, when previously it had involved three. RESULTS: Reduced training time to 16 classroom hours from 40 hours. Trained 629 staff members. Saved the Department of the Navy significant resources in overtime costs, as well as training hours for employees.

ELECTRONICS TECHNICIAN, GS-856-12, Maintenance and Reliability Engineer/ Logistics Manager, Naval Air Warfare Center

ACCOMPLISHMENT: Developed Engineering Change Proposal to resolve complex problems with MAVERICK program. Provided oversight of project between the Air Force and Raytheon Missile Systems to modify a Training Maverick and create a lightweight version of the Captive Air Training Missiles, CATM-65F. RESULTS: Project completed ahead of schedule and resulted in cost savings of $500,000 by reutilizing Air Force assets scheduled for demilitarization. Customer satisfaction of US Marine Corps is evidenced by their interest in procuring additional missile systems.

Example of Special Project

SPECIAL PROJECT: Member of the Data Services core work group. Identified, with Financial Management subject matter experts, legacy and Systems Applications Processes, SAP, data elements required in financial processes, Realization Phase. Team Leader for a review of the adequacy of data and interface requirements for 90+ financial process documents. RESULTS: highlighted gaps in data and provided process owners with additional interface requirement information.

Final Steps

Read the announcement and job kit instructions for how to apply and resume submissions. Research announcements and position descriptions to find keywords and skills for your resume for one or more occupational series. Fill out any additional questions and supplemental sheets correctly. Proofread carefully. Misspelled words, or words that are correctly spelled but the wrong word choice, do not score in the Resumix system. Your revised draft with keyword enhancements is now ready for submission to all of the Resume Builders!

Accomplishments are written primarily for the selecting official. But accomplishments could also have great keywords for the database.

KSAs are an opportunity, not a chore

WRITE YOUR KSAs AND COVER LETTER

A strong Federal resume that puts your best foot forward will be an extremely important part of your Federal government application package. However, the other equally important part of your application package is going to be your *KSA statements*. I cannot stress enough how important your KSAs are. In my experience, they have been the make or break point for many applicants in the job search process.

First off, what exactly are KSAs? When you get right down to it, KSA statements are just little essays, nothing more. KSA stands for **K**nowledge, **S**kills, and **A**bilities. Your KSAs will be a collection of half-page to full-page, highly-focused essays that you include in your application that speak about YOUR knowledge, skills, and abilities on topics assigned to you in the vacancy announcement.

For the highest-level positions, KSAs are usually written about specific and sometimes extremely technical knowledge, skills, and abilities. For example, I recently helped a computer specialist applying for a GS-13 job write a KSA statement about her "knowledge of advanced computer networking hardware, software, LAN operating systems, and LAN-based application software." I also helped a Foreign Affairs Officer applying at the GS-14 level write a KSA about her ability to "analyze commercial trade practices and independently develop and design projects and programs." Another client, a veterinarian applying for a position with the USDA, needed help writing a KSA that addressed his knowledge of and ability to "interpret and apply laws, regulations, and procedures pertaining to the inspection of domestic and imported meat, poultry, and/or egg products." These are extremely specific topics for applicants who have generally worked in their field for a long time and who have developed a high level of expertise.

***Laura Sachs**, the author of this section, is an expert, skilled KSA writer who advises and consults with clients who can't think of what to write in their KSAs.*

Your KSAs will demonstrate if you can perform the job.

Traditionally, candidate assessment has been focused on the extent to which individuals possessed the knowledge, skills, and abilities, and other factors, "KSAOs," but more often called only "KSAs" required to do the job. KSAs are the criteria determined through job analysis to be important to the job and to distinguish you among candidates.

At lower job levels (and even sometimes at higher ones) it is far more likely that you will encounter KSAs that ask you to address your more *basic* knowledge, skills, and abilities. For example, typical KSAs are ones that ask you to speak about your ability to:

✪ Communicate orally and/or in writing

✪ Plan and organize work (for yourself or for others)

✪ Independently plan and carry out multiple assignments

✪ Locate and assemble information for various reports, briefings, and conferences

✪ Analyze and solve problems, or

✪ Work well with others

Frankly, I have always found that KSAs such as these are the most fun to write. They provide a wonderful opportunity for you to breathe life into your application package. They give you a chance to show that you are thoughtful, articulate, and a very *human* human being. As well, the more basic KSA statements like those above are likely to come up again and again across many vacancy announcements. It is common, for example, to be asked about your ability to write and to communicate orally for practically any job in which communication is important. It is therefore an extremely good investment in your career to do an especially great job with these KSAs. You will be able to use them over and over again.

While a resume speaks of your past accomplishments, qualifications, and strengths, KSAs allow you to do that and so much more. For example, KSAs give you a chance to get into extensive details about specific projects and accomplishments. They provide a place for describing the context and the specific challenges you faced in a particular situation. They can be a platform for saying things like, "I have always found that" or "I believe that" as you explain your work philosophies and how you've applied them. They can also be a wonderful place to tell a good story or to brag about what someone else has said about you. They can focus much more heavily on what you have accomplished in just one or two meaningful experiences, including your volunteer work and schooling. And, they can give you a place to say flat out that you are really good at something.

KSAs also give you a fabulous opportunity to write with zing and to show your personality. When I write a KSA for a client, I want to do much more than convince the reader that the applicant is qualified for the job. A well-written Federal resume can usually do that. In addition, I also want the reader to LIKE the applicant represented in the KSA, to say, "Wow! This applicant sparkles! He/she is *exactly* the person we need in this job."

Remember, too, that KSAs are not only an elimination tool, but also a writing test. They require a highly developed ability to communicate well in writing, a skill that is so essential to many jobs for which you may apply. KSAs also enable you to demonstrate your ability to understand instructions, your skill in using a computer to produce the document, your ability to interpret the announcement, your knowledge of the agency's or organization's mission and purpose, and your ability to interpret the special needs of the hiring organization. This set of essays, whether done well or poorly, will speak volumes about you.

Are you intimidated? Don't be. Writing winning KSAs really is not as hard or as scary as it may sound, even if you don't think of yourself as a great writer. In this chapter, we explore everything you need to know about how KSAs work and show you, from soup to nuts, how to write winning ones. You will see lots of examples that can inspire you, that you can adapt, or that you can even use verbatim. Go ahead and take whatever you can use from my examples. That's why I've included them in this book.

As you read, you may be struck by the amount of time and effort necessary to follow the advice given. No matter how you slice it, KSAs do take time—sometimes, lots of it. Even a professional KSA writer like me who writes KSAs all the time still takes approximately one hour to write each KSA statement. A single vacancy announcement may require you to write a set of three, four, five, or even more KSAs. Recently, I helped a client prepare a set of *eight* KSA statements for a single application! Although KSA sets of this magnitude are rare, you should plan on spending several hours writing your KSA set. Don't cut too close to your deadline or rush the process. High quality KSAs definitely take time.

You may wonder whether it is really necessary to go through so much simply to apply for a job with the government. Let me tell you very clearly that the answer is a resounding YES. You can't write effective KSAs without investing significant effort and time. And, you absolutely need your KSAs to be effective if you are to be a competitive job applicant. Well-written KSA statements convince your readers that you have what it takes to succeed in the position for which you are applying. An excellent set of KSAs will put you in the final heat of the job race. Poorly written KSA statements are probably your best guarantee that you won't get the job.

With that said, let's roll up our sleeves and get to work. Don't worry – we'll take things one step at a time. Let's begin by exploring exactly what a KSA is and isn't, what will be expected of you, and how you will go about identifying KSAs in vacancy announcements.

"*B*asically I am completely confused about KSAs."

— Andrew Jacobs, Computer Specialist, TEK Systems

WELCOME TO THE WONDERFUL WORLD OF KSAS

"You helped me draft a resume and some KSAs a year ago. Thirty or so Federal applications later, and countless private sector applications, I did get a new job, an ideal position. It's a 12-13-14 position primarily to do marketing and communications."

KSAs are stories that accompany your employment application and give specific examples of paid and non-paid work experience, education, training, awards, and honors. They are specifically written as separate narratives (and usually on separate pages) to support each of the areas of knowledge, skill, and ability listed in the vacancy announcement. There are usually four to six KSAs required for each application, sometimes fewer, sometimes more. Unlike resumes, KSAs are usually written in the first person (*I did this or that*). They are typically one-half to one-full page each, single-spaced.

First-level Human Resources professionals grade or "rate" KSAs. They use a "rating and ranking" system for each KSA statement. Your statements can range from *Superior* to *Not Acceptable* or may be assigned a numerical score. There is no rule of thumb here because rating systems vary from one job opening to another and generally, from one agency to the next. You probably will not know which of the KSAs in your KSA set will be the ones hiring managers consider to be the most important. That's why you will want to do the best job possible on *all* of your KSAs.

It can be confusing at times to delineate clearly what is a skill, what is ability, and what is knowledge. To help, here is how the government defines each of these terms:

✪ **Knowledge:** An organized body of information, usually of a factual or procedural nature, which, if applied, makes adequate performance on the job possible.

✪ **Skills:** The proficient manual, verbal, or mental manipulation of data, people, or things. Observable, quantifiable, measurable.

✪ **Abilities:** The power to perform an activity at the present time. Implied is a lack of discernible barriers, either physical or mental, to performing the activity.

By these definitions, then, grammar and spelling are areas of *knowledge*—bodies of information you need to perform a job (such as writing or proofreading). Typing is a *skill*—measurable and quantifiable in terms of words per minute. On the other hand, being able to stay calm in tense situations is an *ability*—your personal power to manage stress and do your job well. For the sake of writing KSAs, however, it is *not* essential to distinguish an attribute as knowledge, skill, or ability. So don't get hung up on this point. You can talk about typing or spelling or keeping calm or really anything else you do well without worrying about labeling it as a *skill, ability,* or *knowledge.*

Agencies do not always call KSA statements "Knowledge, Skills, and Abilities," and here is where it can get tricky. Sometimes, agencies refer to KSAs as:

✪   Quality Ranking Factors

✪   Narrative Factors

✪   Supplemental Statements

✪   Statements of Qualifications

✪   Essays

You may even find some other designation for these statements. That's why it is essential that you read your vacancy announcement word for word carefully. And remember, a KSA by any other name is still a KSA. Follow the advice in this chapter UNLESS the vacancy announcement specifically tells you to do otherwise.

Some vacancy announcements will be clear about what they expect you to do. For example, an announcement may tell you to attach separate sheets of paper with a response to three or more elements, factors, or KSA statements. Occasionally, you may have a limitation about the length of your essays. However, other announcements may not be quite so clear. When that happens, you will have to rely upon common sense and the advice provided in this chapter to guide you through the KSA writing and submission process.

There is no standard for vacancy announcements. Each one will be different in content, instruction, detail, format, and font type. You will have to become accustomed to looking for the KSA requirements, and especially, to determining if they are mandatory or require a particular format for submission. To help you do this, let's look at some typical examples.

KSAs are actually graded by the personnel staff. They are "rated and ranked" with a point system. If you write good examples that really demonstrate you can perform this knowledge, skill or ability, you can get rated higher.

Finding KSAs in Vacancy Announcements: Three Examples

Let's look at the KSA portions of three typical Federal job announcements. As you read, look for the precise KSAs that are needed and whether there is any mention of the format for submission.

Ability to communicate orally and in writing are very popular KSAs. You can write these ahead of time for most announcements.

Job Announcement Example #1:
Executive Staff Assistant, Department of Health and Human Services

Knowledge Skills and Abilities Required:

* Demonstrated ability to coordinate work assignments.
* Ability to communicate in writing.
* Ability to communicate orally.
* Knowledge of the principles, methods, practices, and techniques of management and program analyses to function as a technical authority in the area of assignment.

Basis of Rating: The information provided in the KSA responses will be heavily relied upon in the rating process. Applicants must prepare a concise narrative addressing EACH of the KSAs listed. Show how your experience and/or education provided you with the KSA. Responses must be separate from the application form.

My comments: This is a very straightforward announcement that clearly states the KSAs, calls them KSAs, and provides only basic rating information. There is in fact no advice offered for submitting the KSAs— no format or other suggestions. However, do take note of the word concise, as in "concise narrative." This suggests to me that you'd want to be extra careful not to be too long-winded in your KSAs. You'll always want to make sure that every word in your KSAs counts, but perhaps even more so for this set. Also, notice that the applicant is required to write a separate narrative for EACH of the KSAs listed. This is always true. Do NOT lump KSAs together into one longer essay, but rather, treat them separately as shorter and separate narratives.

Job Announcement Example #2:
Administrative Coordinator, Office of Protective Operations

Presidential Protective Division

Knowledge, Skills, and Abilities Required: Candidates should submit a narrative statement on a separate page(s) with specific responses to the knowledge, skills, and abilities (KSAs) in this announcement. Failure to submit your narrative response to the KSAs for this job may negatively affect your eligibility and/or rating for this position.

* Knowledge of administrative and support functions, programs, policies, and procedures in order to independently perform and/or coordinate the full range of administrative functions.

* Ability to supervise, direct, advise, or instruct administrative and clerical support staff regarding operations and procedures.

* Ability to analyze and solve problems in order to identify problems, make conclusions or recommendations, and take appropriate action.

* Ability to communicate both orally and in writing in order to gather information and communicate findings.

Basis of Rating: Ratings will be based on an evaluation of your experience as it relates to the qualification requirements and on the knowledge, skills, and abilities (KSAs) listed. You should provide detailed evidence of the KSAs in your application in the form of clear, concise examples showing level of accomplishment and degree of responsibility. Qualified candidates will be assigned a score between 70 and 100 not including points that may be assigned for veteran's preference.

My comments: The part that screams to me in this announcement is toward the end where it calls for, "clear, concise examples showing level of accomplishment and degree of responsibility." In light of that, I'd focus these KSAs on the applicant's experiences in the **highest** responsibility levels and make very clear what those levels were. Also, notice the requirement to submit the KSAs on separate pages— a must.

Tricky "Knowledge of Policy" KSA?

If you do NOT have hands-on knowledge of an agency's administrative functions, programs and policies, then you should research these programs through the agency's website. Read press releases and agency program information. Your KSA should state that you have read about the agency's programs and policies, that you are a quick learner, able to study resources, and learn new information in order to perform effectively on the job.

Job Announcement Example #3:
Staff Assistant, Office of Volunteer Support,
Office of Medical Service (OMS)

Give examples of the types of writing, proofreading and editing you do. This could include correspondence, reports, newsletters, narratives, emailings, website content, and user tips.

The Peace Corps

Mandatory Qualifications: In order to be selected for this position, the applicant must be a U.S. citizen, must not have been employed in certain intelligence-related activities, and must submit an application that clearly documents how he/she meets each of the following mandatory requirements. Applicants must have at least one year of work experience equivalent to the next lower grade in the Federal service. The one year of specialized experience must include work performed in an administrative or management environment.

Desired Qualifications: The following qualifications are not mandatory for selection to this position. However, highly competitive applicants will have experience and/or education in all or most of the following:

* Demonstrated experience in written communication, including proofreading and editing documents.

* Demonstrated skill in verbal and interpersonal communications.

* Planning, organizing, and coordinating work assignments, and establishing priorities.

* Experience in using personal computers, specifically word processing, spread sheets, and data bases.

To receive maximum consideration, it is essential that applicants specifically address how they meet the Mandatory and Desired Qualifications.

My comments: Here we have a KSA by another name: Desired Qualifications. Nonetheless, these are KSAs—statements of knowledge, skills, and abilities. Note that the instructions say that statements are NOT mandatory. However, I believe it is unlikely that any applicant would land this job without them. My advice: Never pass up an optional opportunity to add to your application package. Someone else will submit optional components and if they do it well, will look a lot better than you do. Don't give anyone that edge. Show them what you've got, not only by submitting the optional KSAs, but by knocking their socks off. Write them extremely well.

Getting Great Ideas from Your Vacancy Announcement

Once you've identified the specific KSA statements you must write, your next step will be to comb the vacancy announcement very carefully for specific topics, ideas, or even terminology you might use in your KSA statements. A careful reading of the vacancy announcement, particularly the sections that describe the job responsibilities/duties (and the knowledge, skills, and abilities of the ideal applicant) may suggest appropriate KSA key words and examples and help trigger relevant memories. As you read the job duties or qualifications from your vacancy announcement, jot down any experiences and training you have had that would specifically qualify you for the job described.

For example, consider the wealth of information contained in this vacancy announcement for a position as a Staff Assistant with The Peace Corps. As you read the lengthy and very specific description of job duties, try to identify the many different areas of knowledge, skill, or ability an applicant might have in his/her background that speak directly to the job duties listed:

Duties: The incumbent has major responsibility for providing and coordinating a variety of administrative support and program activities, organizing and managing office systems, and serving as a trouble-shooter on various issues. Specific duties include: receiving telephone and personal callers; handling all administrative activities; maintaining Director's and Deputy Director's calendars; ensuring that pre-briefings are conducted by the appropriate personnel and that materials are distributed appropriately; providing program information to internal and external sources; maintaining a log record of incoming and outgoing correspondence and action documents and following up on work in progress to ensure deadline reply dates are met; receiving and reading incoming correspondence, reports, instructions, etc. and routing to the appropriate staff member; drafting letters; reviewing outgoing correspondence for procedural and grammatical accuracy, conformance to policy, and factual correctness; establishing and maintaining subject-matter files; assembling briefing materials; ordering supplies; making all travel arrangements; making arrangements for meetings and conferences; and typing a variety of correspondence and reports.

TIP

Fix Their Grammar

Proofread the KSAs listed in the vacancy announcement. Believe it or not, it is quite common to come across a KSA with a misspelling or that is ungrammatical. For instance, I have come across vacancy announcements that ask the applicant to speak of his/her judgement (when it should be spelled judgment) and that split infinitives (to effectively lead when it should be to lead effectively). Correct the announcement's grammar and spelling when you reproduce the required KSA topic in your KSA statement. Misspellings and misuse of the language will not reflect positively on you, even if the mistake is not originally yours.

Y ou have to analyze your job in terms of the knowledge, skills and abilities you have. The Federal personnelist wants you to prove that you can perform the job on the announcement based on your examples.

Three KSAs were required to apply for this position: 1) demonstrated experience in written communication, including proofreading and editing documents; 2) demonstrated skill in verbal and interpersonal communications; and 3) planning, organizing, and coordinating work assignments and establishing priorities. Each of these could be supported quite nicely with examples specifically mentioned in the duties list.

For example, here is a list of key words and phrases from the duties list above that could be used in each KSA:

1. Demonstrated experience in written communication, including proofreading and editing documents: drafting letters; receiving and reading incoming correspondence, reports, instructions, etc. and routing to the appropriate staff member; reviewing outgoing correspondence for procedural and grammatical accuracy, conformance to policy, and factual correctness; typing a variety of correspondence and reports.

2. Demonstrated skill in verbal and interpersonal communications: receiving business telephone and personal callers; providing program information to internal and external sources; making all travel arrangements; making arrangements for meetings and conferences.

3. Planning, organizing, and coordinating work assignments and establishing priorities: maintaining calendars; ensuring that pre-briefings are conducted by the appropriate personnel and that materials are distributed appropriately; maintaining a log record of incoming and outgoing correspondence and action documents; following up on work in progress to ensure deadline reply dates are met; establishing and maintaining subject-matter files; assembling briefing materials; and ordering supplies.

As you can see from this example, if you have done ANY of the things listed in the job duties section of your vacancy announcement in any of your previous positions (or even in volunteer work or as part of your education), it would be extremely prudent to say so in your KSA statement and when possible, to use the announcement's exact phrasing.

TIP

Use a marking pen to highlight key words and phrases in your vacancy announcement that you would like to address or use verbatim in your KSA.

The Ten Rules for Writing Winning KSAs

Now that you've identified the KSAs in your vacancy announcement and read it carefully, you're probably tempted to dive right in and start writing. However, I ask for your patience for just a little while longer. Before getting into the nitty gritty of KSA writing, it will help you start off on the right foot if you first learn and master the 10 basic rules for writing winning KSAs. These are the iron-clad rules of thumb you should follow EVERY TIME you write a KSA, that is, unless your vacancy announcement specifically tells you to do otherwise.

#1 Give at least one fantastic example per KSA.

Two is better. Three a dream. KSAs are no place to talk in generalities. Get very specific about what you did and your results. A good approach is to say you're great at something and then to prove it with a heavy dose of "For examples." Consider these examples:

- ✪ "I am particularly good at diffusing tense situations. For example, at one of our recent staff meetings, one participant took great offense at a comment made by another. I quickly diffused the tension by doing x, y, and z. The offended individual then saw that she had misunderstood her co-worker's comments and apologized for overreacting. Since then, the two have developed an excellent working relationship…."

- ✪ "I am an excellent proofreader and others have come to rely upon my exceptional spelling and grammar skills. For example, my supervisor recently asked me to proofread our quarterly report. I caught and corrected numerous errors that others had missed. Because of this, our quarterly report was greatly improved and represented our office more professionally to our shareholders. My supervisor commended my efforts, so much so, that he has asked me to proofread all future quarterly reports as well as our annual report…."

- ✪ "I enjoy writing tremendously and do a particularly good job of making complex information easy to understand. For example, I wrote the Standard Operating Procedures for our office's new telephone system, taking a complex and large volume of information and condensing it so it was concise, easy-to-follow, and user-friendly. More than 25 people in our organization currently use this manual. Many of them have commented to me that they find it extremely easy to understand and useful…."

"I took your Federal Resume and Managerial Core Competency KSA Writing Workshop last month. I'm in the process of writing KSAs for a Special Assistant job. My question is how long should KSAs be? I've been using your KSA builder, which has been very helpful, and using two examples. I'm coming up with about a page for each KSA (using single spaced Arial font 12). If it needs to be longer, should I just beef up the two examples or should I add an additional example or two? I would appreciate any insights."

"The new job (which has not been announced but is forthcoming) will probably have KSAs and I'm terrible at writing these. HELP!!"

– Denise Smith
Budget Technician
Naval Facilities Engineering

#2 Use different examples in each KSA statement in your set.

However, if the example is significant in your career, you can use it twice, but ONLY if you emphasize different aspects of the experience. For example, here are two KSA statements that could be drawn from a single example:

✪ "I am particularly good at making complex material easy for others to use. For example, when writing our Standard Operating Procedures for our new telephone system, I had to reduce and simplify the material in a 150-page technical manual into a 10-page document for our staff. To do this, I x, y, and z...."

✪ "I have excellent grammar and spelling skills and I am a meticulous proofreader. This has been proven time and again as I have tackled many written projects in my work. For example, when preparing our Standard Operating Procedures for our new telephone system, I had to ensure that sentences were complete and that the document was free of all spelling errors. As well, I ...."

#3 Use a consistent length and format.

Write each KSA statement so it fits between one-half and one full page, no more, no less. Write each KSA statement separately – do NOT lump all of your KSAs into a single longer essay. Use no smaller than 10-point type, no larger than 12. Ariel and New Times Roman are always good choices of typeface. However, it's usually best to use the same typeface and margins that you used in your resume, to make the two documents look like a matched set. Single-space your text. Write multiple concise paragraphs for each KSA statement—four or five is best. The most common mistake I see: KSAs that are too short—one measly paragraph. (I will share a typical example I received of one such KSA statement later in this chapter, along with my critique and specific recommendations for improvement.)

#4 Pack in the information.

Do not pad your KSAs with needless words and phrases and above all, don't repeat yourself. Think of it this way: You have only one page maximum per KSA to make your case. Use every single inch of that space to its absolute best advantage. Ask yourself what you would do if you had to pay for your KSA by the word, as you would in a classified ad. Then, make every word count.

TIP

I usually write MORE than one page per KSA and then whittle it down to fit. Almost always I can do this by chipping away a word here or there, removing the weak and unnecessary phrases, using a simpler word where I've used an unnecessarily long one. What happens: I keep every bit of the content and lose the fluff. Do your best every time to fill your KSAs so your reader feels that you have tons of knowledge, skills, and abilities AND that you're concise. Eliminate everything that doesn't contribute to making your KSA statement stronger.

Use the personal pronoun "I" 5 times per page at the most when writing KSAs.

#5 Write in the first person.

Do NOT talk about yourself as though you are someone else. Do NOT use the royal "we." Do NOT omit pronouns altogether (as you would in a resume). Rather, call yourself I, as in, "I serve as the point-of-contact for all inquiries that come to our office." Write in complete sentences and well-crafted paragraphs.

#6 Spell out ALL acronyms.

The government is well known for using acronym upon acronym to describe itself. Nonetheless, YOU are expected to define every acronym in your KSA statements. Therefore, spell out every name or phrase the first time you use it, even those that seem absolutely obvious to you. Then, introduce the acronym in parentheses. For example:

    National Institutes of Health (NIH)
    Food and Drug Administration (FDA)
    United States Postal Service (USPS)
    Computer Services Staff (CSS)

Exception: It is not necessary to explain the meaning of U.S. or acronyms that have commonly been used as words, such as scuba and radar.

Visual writing is interesting to the reader. Include numbers so that the reader can visualize your experience and results.

Example:

Before: Completed the project on-time.

After: Completed this $25 million project two months before deadline.

#7 Quantify your results/accomplishments.

It is better to say that you type 65 wpm than to say you type fast. It is better to say that you came in $12,000 below budget than that you saved your office money. It is better to say that you took 150 hours of training over a six-month period than that you took a course. Always, always put a dollar figure, time figure, or other measurement on what you accomplished or do, as long as it is a GOOD figure. Do NOT quantify only so-so results or abilities. In fact, don't even talk about them. Look for better material from which to draw.

Present your KSAs like a proposal with the agency's name centered at the top.

Your well-written accomplishments that demonstrate your knowledge, skills and abilities will be impressive and interesting to the HR recruiters.

#8 Draw material for your KSAs from all parts of your life.

Generally, the more basic the KSA statement, the wider you can cast your net. For the basic KSA statements—those about communication skills, people skills, organization skills, etc.—look for examples in your life from your volunteer work, school, or even in your personal life. Consider this final (and seventh) paragraph of a KSA statement I wrote for a client who needed to demonstrate her ability to communicate orally. The first six paragraphs of her KSA statement pulled examples of her oral communication skills from her professional work experience. Then:

> "Finally, I have had many wonderful opportunities to run meetings and speak both formally and informally while serving as the head of my church's Women's Ministry."

This brief addition to the applicant's KSA did two things extremely well. It added yet another great example of the applicant's oral communication skills. But more importantly, it demonstrated how diverse this applicant is and implied a great deal about her integrity.

#9 Use Resume Place's recommended setup for each KSA.

The following is our popular "proposal style" KSA setup for the top of each KSA. Type the agency name, office, position and announcement information. Use the same font, point size, and paper that you used for your Federal resume. This will give your application a polished, professional look.

Defense Intelligence Agency
Washington Metro Area, Washington, DC
Position: Staff Assistant-Officer GG-0301-07/09
Vacancy Announcement #01-002518-CPB
Candidate: Monica Daniels, SS#856-99-3948

KNOWLEDGE, SKILLS, AND ABILITIES

1. Ability to Communicate orally.
   Begin your paragraphs here.

#10 Proofread your KSA set. Then proofread it again. And again.

While spellcheck is a wonderful tool, it is *not* a substitute for proofreading. Only a human being would know that net is a typo for the word ten or that the Internet is not the same thing as the intranet. To proofread your KSA set most effectively:

- ✪ Print out a hard copy of your KSAs, go somewhere quiet, and proofread it. It is often easier to catch mistakes on the printed page than on the computer screen, and certainly easier to focus on your work when you don't have distractions.

- ✪ Force yourself to read your KSAs slowly. Consider every word and punctuation mark. Many proofreaders find it helpful to read the document forwards and then backwards. That slows them down and forces them to look at each word critically.

- ✪ Look for common typographical errors such as transposed letters, improper use of homonyms (using too instead of to), omitted words, and word repetitions.

- ✪ Let your KSAs incubate. Proofread the document and put it away. Then, take it out another time, preferably on another day when you're fresh, and proofread it again. If possible, have someone else also proofread your KSAs for you. Another pair of eyes may catch something you've missed.

Brainstorm about your KSAs with a friend or co-worker. Share with them the KSA and ask them to give you ideas for examples for the essay.

Brainstorm BEFORE You Write

Now that you've mastered the Ten Steps for Writing Winning KSAs, it's time to address your first KSA statement. As an exercise, let's imagine that you must write a KSA statement that speaks of your ability to communicate orally. The first thing I suggest you do is spend a few moments brainstorming ideas about what would make *anyone* a good oral communicator, and then specifically, what makes *you* so good at it.

Let's take these one at a time. What might make anyone a good oral communicator? How about these attributes?

- ✪ Clear, concise, to the point
- ✪ Pleasant, loud, and clear speaking voice in person, on the phone, etc.
- ✪ Training in speaking and an active member of Toastmasters
- ✪ Experience speaking before groups
- ✪ Articulate—can express complex ideas simply

- Ability to establish rapport with others—make them receptive to your message
- Good listening skills—can tailor and adapt messages as needed
- Natural teaching ability—good at motivating others to listen
- Extremely well organized and thinks sequentially (A, B, C)
- Tactful—knows how to make difficult situations easier to accept

Now, consider for a moment what makes YOU, particularly, a good oral communicator. What are your experiences, training, and accomplishments? Where have you done your speaking when it has really counted the most? For example, suppose that you:

- Took a public speaking course in college
- Run monthly staff meetings in your office
- Serve as the point-of-contact for all inquiries coming into your office
- Conduct employee performance appraisals
- Had to fire someone once who took it badly, but you made him feel better
- Give a formal presentation to your church women's club twice each year
- Served as a Tupperware representative years ago and conducted in-home parties
- Train new employees
- Represent your office at regional meetings

From this example, it is easy to see that brainstorming can help you generate lots of good ideas for material to include in your KSA. As you brainstorm, look to all areas of your life. Dig way into your past. Try to remember everything worthwhile that you have ever done that supports the KSA. Just keep a running list of ideas, without rejecting any during the brainstorming process.

Then, review your whole list of brainstormed ideas and choose the best three, four, or five. These can fuel a good first paragraph for your KSA statement.

The All-Important First Paragraph

In KSAs, as in life, first impressions are lasting impressions. The opening lines of your KSA statement will be extremely important in establishing an impression of you as a candidate for the job and as a person. The reader will decide quickly whether you are articulate, bright, interesting, clear, credible, and worthy of the job or whether you are tongue-tied, dull, muddled, ho-hum, prone to exaggeration, and worthy

KSA examples from your community service and volunteer work can help you change your career. If you want to demonstrate your teamwork experience, write about your non-profit leadership experiences. Trying to move up? Write about team leadership and supervisory experience from non-profit experiences.

of the reject pile. A strong opening paragraph is therefore essential to your success. Without it, you will be climbing an uphill battle throughout the rest of your KSA statement.

It can be tempting to dive in on the first sentence and start telling the reader about your many experiences that support your knowledge, skill, and abilities in the designated areas. Space in KSA statements is, after all, at a premium. However, a good and tightly edited opening paragraph is an excellent use of your limited space. You can use it to increase your reader's motivation and bolster his/her impression of you. As well, it will set the stage for all that follows in the remainder of your KSA statement.

In your opening paragraph, you might do any number of things, and we will explore some of the possibilities below. However, it's important to remember that you will be writing several KSA statements in your application set. Therefore, you will want to vary your opening paragraph from statement to statement to give the application package texture and variety. How tedious it would be if all five of the KSAs in a set of five began precisely the same way!

The possibilities for how you might structure your opening paragraph are virtually endless. To get you started, here are a few possibilities that I've used when writing for my clients (with concrete examples) that I know work particularly well:

✪ Take a philosophical approach.

Share some of the brainstorming and reflection you did about what makes anyone (and you in particular) good at the KSA or why it is important. For example, in response to the KSA, ability to plan and execute work, consider how this opening paragraph waxes just a tad bit philosophical: "My organizational skills come into play every day. As a computer specialist, it would be easy to become sidetracked or to get lost in minute details. There are always problems, often stressful ones with high stakes, and an incredible volume of work. I am constantly having to juggle competing demands and decide which project to tackle and in what order."

✪ Join their bandwagon.

Show that you understand why they might have asked for this KSA and why these kinds of knowledge, skills, and ability are so important. For example, for a KSA about communication skills, consider this example: "There are many good reasons that a logistics professional should be an excellent communicator. However, in my mind, one and only one reason stands out above all the rest. Simply put, it is the stakes. Every day, in everything we do, we must remember that careers are at stake. We must therefore

---

Your accomplishments will impress the personnelist!

Take time to write your accomplishments carefully!

do everything we can to work well individually and as a team, communicate effectively with one another, and do whatever it takes to avoid errors. For this reason, we must be absolutely precise in everything we say and write."

✪ Tell what you're going to talk about and why.

Give an overview of what you'll cover in the KSA statement. For example, "Three experiences have provided me with a broad base of knowledge about export marketing promotion, foreign trade practices, and government international trade programs and policies. First, I studied these subjects extensively while earning my International Marketing Certificate at Miami Date Community College. Second, I applied this knowledge in hands-on experiences in my internship at the U.S. Department of Commerce. And third, I continue to apply, hone, and increase my skills and knowledge of these subjects in my current position as the only Trade Information Specialist for the World Trade Center Miami." Use the remainder of the KSA statement to flesh out the ideas introduced in the first paragraph, perhaps devoting one paragraph to each topic.

✪ Blow your own horn.

Say flat out that you excel in the knowledge, skill, and ability they seek. For example: "I am upbeat and come across well. I am very good at reading people, working with them, establishing rapport and trust, and teaching. In addition, I have many years of practical career experience working through problems with others, sometimes difficult ones. As well, I have extensive knowledge of and formal training in counseling, which has served me well."

✪ Cite your experience.

Say that you have had a lot of experience with the specified KSA. For example, for the KSA on your ability to identify and analyze complex issues or problems and develop solutions or recommendations, you might write: "I work in environments that are fast-paced and that process a large volume of work. It would be easy to focus only on the details and to lose sight of the larger issues at play. Fortunately, I am particularly skilled at stepping out of the day-to-day concerns and seeing the big picture. Because of this, I have been able to identify and analyze large and complex problems and then develop effective solutions."

TIP

After you write your opening paragraph, read it very critically. Ask: Would I want to keep reading? Does this first paragraph capture my interest and build a strong case for my getting this job? Does it create a positive first impression of me?

The Body: Let "Context-Challenge-Action-Results" Drive Your Examples

The meat of your KSA statement will be the examples you use to illustrate your knowledge, skills, and abilities. Ideally, you will want to come up with several strong examples pulled from your work experience, volunteerism, or training that demonstrates, not tells, that you have the knowledge, skills, and abilities required or desired for the job. However, when writing about your examples, it is important that you give enough information so the reader knows what you did, why you did it, how you did it, and what you accomplished. This is what is known as the CCAR approach, which stands for **c**ontext, **c**hallenge, **a**ction, and **r**esults. Let's define these terms specifically:

- ✪ **Context:** The factors that contributed to the challenge you faced. Why did you do what you did in the first place? Budget limits? Staffing changes? Institutional reform? New goals handed down from on high?

- ✪ **Challenge:** The specific problem you had to address. For example, if the context is widespread institutional reform, what was the specific challenge you faced in your corner of the world that was caused by or answered that reform?

- ✪ **Action:** The specific steps you took to solve the problem, meet the goal, etc. Generally, it's best NOT to use ordinary examples. Just doing your basic job isn't all that remarkable. Instead, look for instances where you took action that went above and beyond the call of duty, applied particularly creative ideas, or put forth Herculean effort. Seek the extraordinary action in what you did.

- ✪ **Results:** The outcome—the difference you made. Quantify your results whenever you can possibly do so. For example, "My quick thinking saved our department $17,000." Again, ignore any examples with mediocre results. Talk only about the best of what you have done.

When writing your KSA statement, write in narrative paragraphs, rather than in bulleted style. Do not list "Context" or "Challenge" or "Action" as bulleted points. Rather, write a smooth-flowing paragraph that includes all of the information as a cohesive story. Exception: You can separate out your "Results" in your KSA statement (if you have particularly strong ones) and emphasize them graphically, such as with boldface type.

"Kathy's tips helped me get a position with a biotech company on my first try. The context-challenge-action-result format was just what I needed to add emphasis to my resume."

"I like using the CCAR model to write my KSAs. The formula helps me focus on specific examples. These KSA examples will help me with interviewing as well."

"I would like to create inspiring KSAs that will lead to career advancement opportunities and new challenges in Government IT."

— Ronald Hosten
Data Collector, USPS

Here is a great KSA paragraph that clearly illustrates proper use of CCAR formatting. A program manager at the Substance Abuse and Mental Health Service Administration (SAMHSA) wrote it. It might be possible to use or modify it for several KSA statements, such as "ability to plan, organize, and manage project," or "ability to communicate orally," or even "ability to negotiate and give presentations." Note that for the purposes of this book, I have separated out the Context, Challenge, Action, and Results, and labeled them for you. When submitted as a KSA statement, however, the text reads as a continuous paragraph without the CCAR headings.

- **Context:** "In January 1986 following the notification that SAMHSA would receive a dramatically reduced budget…"

- **Challenge:** "…I recognized that important programs would be discontinued, including a much-needed drug-abuse program for the Kickapoo Reservation Indians in the State of Texas."

- **Action:** "As the Federal program manager, I took the initiative to communicate the situation with the State of Texas to turn over funding to the state. I traveled to Texas on several occasions to negotiate directly with the State of Texas project officer to ensure that the state appreciated the severity of the situation and the change in Federal funding. I prepared a briefing booklet for state representatives giving them the data on the 1,300 eligible adults on the reservation and the fact that two-thirds of the total population participated in the program."

- **Results:** "I successfully achieved a cooperative agreement with the state with commitments of $500,000 per year. I also discovered an additional $400,000 from carry-over from the previous year. Additionally, I brought in four other state agencies to assist with service provision and additional funding and support."

End Your KSA Statement With a Bang — Three Rules

Just as the opening paragraph of a KSA creates an impression, so, too, does the last paragraph. End each of your KSA statements strongly by following three simple rules:

#1 Do NOT repeat what you've already said.

Space and the reader's time and attention are the precious commodities in KSA statements. Use them wisely. Make every word count by putting forward new ideas with each phrase and sentence, even those at the end.

#2 Give the piece oomph by making an unexpected turn.

If you've devoted the opening paragraph and meat of your KSA statement to work experiences, use the last paragraph to talk about something else: training, volunteerism, your philosophy, what other people think about you, etc. For example, this applicant discussed her work experiences operating and maintaining radio and broadcasting equipment for the bulk of her KSA. Then, the final paragraph said: "I believe that the radio listener must not be aware of the technology we use to prepare his or her broadcasts. I operate radio broadcasting equipment to provide my listener with coherent, smooth-flowing programs. Using radio broadcast equipment well enables me to produce really great sound and programs that seem effortless from the listener's point of view."

#3 Cue the ending.

One effective way to begin your last paragraph is to use the words "finally," or "as well." Or, write your final sentence as though it is the last line in a speech. Consider this final paragraph of a KSA on the applicant's ability to plan and execute work: "Finally, I have juggled a full-time career and schoolwork since 1984. At times, I have taken three or four college courses per semester, often requiring large-scale projects and extensive group work. Then, and now, I rely heavily on my organizational skills to ensure that I meet all of my responsibilities."

TIP

As you write your final paragraph, imagine that you are actually presenting your KSA statement as a speech. How would you end an oral KSA statement to motivate your audience's applause? What words could you use to let your audience know that it was indeed the end of the speech? Use those same ideas to end your written KSA statement.

How to Use Our Online KSA Builder

At The Resume Place, we have developed an excellent and popular online tool for our clients to help them gather and organize material for their KSA statements. Called the KSA Builder, this template-style tool leads our clients through a step-by-step process of identifying examples that support their knowledge, skills, and abilities in specified KSA statement areas. It then helps them organize their materials into Context-Challenge-Action-Result (CCAR) format. As well, The KSA Builder prompts the user to remember and list relevant training, awards, and supervisors' remarks that could support the KSA statement.

Because we are grateful to each of our readers for purchasing this book, we have decided to make our KSA Builder available to you as our gift, without charge. You may access The Resume Place KSA Builder at:

http://www.resume-place.com/ksa_builder/template/

Feel free to use the KSA Builder to help you organize your own materials as you prepare for writing your own KSA statements. Use it again and again, as many times as you like.

IMPORTANT: All that we ask in return is that you please **DO NOT** send your completed template to The Resume Place, **UNLESS** you would like to engage us to help you prepare or edit your KSA statements for a fee. Thank you. We hope you find this tool helpful.

Writing the Unwritable KSA

Every now and then you may come across a KSA in a vacancy announcement that you feel you just can't write. Before you give up, consider this.

Imagine that you've found a vacancy announcement for a dream job, one you'd love to have and for which you feel you are highly qualified. You need to write five KSAs, and the first four are a breeze. However, that last KSA stumps you. It asks you to speak about your knowledge, skill, or ability in a technical area where you know nothing. Should you fudge it? Try to talk about something else in the KSA? Abandon the application and your dream job altogether?

Obviously, you can't lie in a KSA. You can't manufacture knowledge, skills, and abilities that you don't have. And talking about *other* knowledge, skills, and abilities and avoiding the question won't work. You'll get nailed for it in your rating. But if you're otherwise an excellent fit for the vacancy announcement, I encourage you to apply for the job. Just make sure that you first take specific steps so you can write a truthful, on-target, and dynamite KSA for that stumper. How?

READ!!! You can always increase your knowledge of a subject by reading about it, especially when the KSA asks you to speak about your knowledge of technical information, regulations, procedures, etc. While you won't be an expert on a subject after only a little bit of reading, you can gain legitimate knowledge that you can talk about honestly.

For example, I recently worked with a client who was a perfect fit for a job as a Printing Specialist with the Government Printing Office. "Joe" had worked in printing in private industry since 1978, knew printing and bindery operations inside and out, was a great supervisor, and was extremely qualified for the job. However, he had to write a KSA explaining his "knowledge of Joint Committee on the Government Printing Office's Printing, Bindery Guidelines, and the Code of Federal Regulations." Having worked in private industry and not for the government, he knew nothing about the guidelines and codes.

Following my advice, Joe visited the Government Printing Office Web site and spent some time familiarizing himself with the material in the various chapters in the *GPO's Title 44 – Public Printing and Documents*. There, he learned a great deal about the Joint Committee on Printing, its printing and bindery guidelines, and the Code of Federal Regulations. After only a short while working on his homework assignment, Joe had something he could talk about and we had something we could write about in his KSA.

"**W**henever I try to answer KSAs, I have a hard time."

– Gwendolyn Goles
Lead Military Pay Technician, DoN

In Joe's case, and in all cases where the knowledge was obtained specifically for the employment application, I believe in coming clean about how the knowledge was gained and why. Here's how we explained it in Joe's KSA:

> "I have done extensive research to prepare myself for working for the Federal government. I have taken steps to learn more about JCP Printing, Bindery Guidelines, and the Code of Federal Regulations. Specifically, I have familiarized myself with the material in the various chapters of the GPO's *Title 44 – Public Printing and Documents*."

From there we wrote about specific examples of Joe's new-found knowledge. For instance, one paragraph begins: "For example, in Chapter 5, I learned a great deal about the production and procurement of printing and binding." We then elaborated on some of Joe's particular findings. Another paragraph begins: "I was particularly interested in many of the sections detailed in Title 44 that address procurement of printing, binding, and blank-book work by a public printer." Again, the remainder of the paragraph expands upon Joe's recently-gained knowledge.

Joe's KSA ended strongly, expressing his eagerness to learn more:

> "I have already learned a great deal about JCP Printing, Bindery Guidelines, and the Code of Federal Regulations through my work with Contract Officers Technical Representatives (COTRs) and on my own. I am eager to learn more and apply this knowledge to my work."

" I looked up the regulations on the GPO's website. That way I could write that I was familiar with their policies, procedures and regulations. "

TIP

In addition to or instead of *reading* to gain new knowledge for a KSA, you might also *interview* a person who has the knowledge you need and report your findings. Again, this is perfectly legitimate, as long as you acknowledge what you've done—who you interviewed, why, what you learned, and so forth.

If you are the best applicant for the position, and you've shown the initiative to learn what you needed to know to write the "unwritable" KSA, chances are reasonably good that you'll get the job. Just stick close to the question, do your homework, and always, always be truthful.

Weaving KSA Magic from Shreds: A KSA Critique

Now that we have considered the how-to's of writing winning KSAs, let's take a look at a typical KSA statement and how to improve it. Through this example, I hope to demonstrate many of the points I have made in this chapter.

The position was for secretary at the GS 05/06 level for HHS, and it required five KSA statements:

- ✪ Ability to organize effectively the flow of clerical processes in an office.
- ✪ Ability to organize and design a filing system.
- ✪ Ability to make arrangements for office procedures such as travel, conferences, and meetings.
- ✪ Ability to locate and assemble information for various reports, briefings, and conferences.
- ✪ Ability to compose non-technical correspondence using word-processing programs in a Windows environment on a personal computer.

These KSA topics are, like those for most secretarial types of positions, broad in their scope. Rather than demonstrating specific knowledge of particular information or mastery of a complex skill (as is often the case for the most technical positions), these KSAs look for the applicant's ability to do the basics—organize, write, file, arrange travel, and so on.

When faced with KSAs such as these, I approach them by asking, "What would it take for a person—any person—to be good at this knowledge, skill, or ability?" or "What does this knowledge, skill, or ability DO for someone?" After brainstorming a bit, and then narrowing myself to three, four, or five good ideas, I usually write an opening paragraph that speaks to that—before getting too much into the applicant's specific training and experience. Often, I come right out and plainly say that the client HAS the knowledge, skill, or ability. This sets up the KSA to be a complete essay in which the applicant first DEFINES what it takes to master the KSA (and says he/she has done so) and then DEMONSTRATES (using CCAR) that he/she, in fact, has done so.

For example, let's take a look at KSA #5, the ability to compose non-technical correspondence using a word processing program. When I began working with this client, here is what I received in writing for that KSA requirement:

"I would like my KSAs to be more streamlined and organized."

– Edward Waters
Recruiting Program Manager
SoloMio (Federal law enforcement)

As a *Purchasing Agent, Secretary* and *Clerical Assistant* for the Naval Facilities Engineering Command, Western Division, Engineering Field Activity, I created correspondence in WordPerfect and MS Word in a Windows environment in response to newspaper ads and Commerce Business Daily announcements. I additionally generated Selection Board Designation Letters and Source Selection Plans using various word-processing programs in a Windows environment. My proficiency in computer software includes but is not limited to MS Word 2000, Excel, Access, PowerPoint, Outlook, and Adobe Acrobat. My typing speed is 65 wpm.

KSAs should be one-half to two-thirds of a page in length.

A one-paragraph KSA will probably not achieve maximum points.

This example is typical of the KSA statements I see. It has some good information and no typographical or grammatical errors, which is great. However, it is too short, just a one-paragraph KSA that simply lists the applicant's experience without demonstrating much of a personality. It doesn't present experiences in the Context-Challenge-Action-Results format. And, most of all, it has no pizzazz, no sparkle. I imagine from the brevity of this KSA that the applicant didn't know what else to say. That happens a lot. With some KSA statements, it is not always easy to see how to elaborate upon limited experiences and knowledge/skill/ability bases.

In cases such as these, I find that it helps a lot to weave some magic in the opening paragraph and to talk more like a real person. Let me take a crack at it to demonstrate what I mean. Of course, to be complete, this KSA statement would need many more examples in CCAR format. In particular, it would need to stress the results more. However, I've tried to simplify things to give you an idea of what ELSE might go into a KSA other than the hard facts. Notice how much more HUMAN the applicant seems this time around:

Throughout my career, I have found word processing to be an extremely useful tool for composing non-technical correspondence. I have enjoyed writing in a Windows environment on a personal computer for more than 10 years, and through this experience, have found that I have become a better and more creative writer. Word processing enables the writer to try out ideas on the screen, to move blocks of text at will, and to delete unnecessary words and phrases easily. Because of these benefits, word processing has helped me improve my writing substantially, and today I write concisely and with great accuracy. As well, I have found that my spelling and grammar proficiency has shot through the roof, due to my regular use both of the spell-check and grammar functions of Windows programs. And interestingly, because I regularly exercise my writing skills using word processing, my typing skills have also increased tremendously. Today, I type at a proficient and accurate pace—65 words per minute.

KSAs are rated and ranked against a "Crediting Plan" that is set up by the selecting official. You will be graded on your KSAs, so try to get an "A" when you write your KSAs. The better your KSAs are, the higher your grade will be. The highest grades are "highly qualified" and could be considered for an interview.

In my current role as a Purchasing Agent, Secretary, and Clerical Assistant for the Naval Facilities Engineering Command, Western Division, Engineering Field Activity, I have daily opportunities to compose non-technical correspondence using word processing. For example, I compose letters about x, y, and z. As well, I generate Selection Board Designation Letters and Source Selection Plans using various word-processing programs in a Windows environment. In all of these projects, as well as in lengthier reports, I must ensure that each document generated is both professional and accurate and reflects favorably upon my office. Because of this, [list results].

I have taken extensive training to increase and hone my word processing skills. For example, I completed SPECTINTACT training with SRML for Windows. In this course, I learned x, y, and z. As well, I have learned a great deal about word processing by (working with a tutorial program, learning from a co-worker, another course, etc.). Because of my training and my varied work experiences, I have gained tremendous proficiency in several computer softwares. These include but are not limited to MS Windows 2000, Excel, Access, PowerPoint, Outlook, and Adobe Acrobat.

Finally, I have enjoyed numerous opportunities to exercise my word processing skills outside of work. I have a _____ computer at home and use it often to generate personal correspondence and other documents.

or

Finally, I am a quick learner and enjoy mastering new computer programs. In the past, I used WordPerfect and Windows 98, and found it easy to convert over to Windows 2000 when the opportunity to do so became available. I am enthusiastic about new technologies and embrace opportunities to learn them.

or

Finally, I feel I am particularly adept at using word processing to compose non-technical correspondence because I truly enjoy the process. I love to write and I feel I do my best work at the computer.

or

Finally, others have regarded me as an expert source of information about word processing technologies. I have tutored several co-workers on the use of Windows 2000 and make myself available to answer questions as they come up.

See the possibilities? I hope this example demonstrates for you how it is possible to embellish upon the little shreds of material from your past.

Remember, what I strive for in each KSA statement is not only to demonstrate that the applicant has the knowledge, skill, or ability that is required; I also want the reader to LIKE the applicant. I look at each KSA statement as a sort of platform for the applicant to demonstrate what a clear thinker he/she is, how rational, how articulate, how accomplished. Think of it as a persuasive speech on paper.

How to Use My Sample KSA Statements

Now, before you tackle your first KSAs, I strongly recommend that you spend some time reviewing the many KSA statements I have reproduced for you in this book. In so doing, look for examples of interesting opening paragraphs, supportive examples following the CCAR format, and strong endings. Look for proper use of the recommended KSA format. See how I have adhered to the 10 Rules for Writing Winning KSAs—defining acronyms, speaking in the first person, proofreading to eliminate errors, etc. Notice the use of fresh and breezy phrases to make the applicant seem HUMAN and down to earth, to make him/her sparkle. Ask yourself: Does this applicant possess the knowledge, skills, and abilities that are required? Do I like this applicant? Why?

Feel free to paraphrase material from my sample KSAs. Or, if you prefer, use relevant portions of them verbatim. Turn to my KSAs time and again to stimulate your thinking or as a source of inspiration. Or, once you read them, put them in the back of your mind and write KSA statements that are uniquely your own. Just be sure that whatever you write in YOUR KSA statements is a truthful reflection of you and YOUR knowledge, skills, and abilities. Be thoughtful, accurate, and meticulous with your KSAs both in their content and in their physical presentation. I promise you this: if you do a bang-up job with your KSAs and you are qualified for the job, you will greatly increase your chances of being invited for an interview.

So get going. Identify the KSAs in your vacancy announcement and any guidelines for submission. Highlight key words in the position description that you may be able to use. Read my sample KSA statements on related topics. Brainstorm. Write those strong first paragraphs. Pick your best examples from your past and put them into CCAR format. Weave your story with the building blocks of strong and grammatical sentences and paragraphs. Read critically. Make everything you write excellent. Proofread. Then proofread again. Be a ruthless self-editor.

Start today. Right now. Take the bull by the horns. Write dazzling, winning KSAs—KSAs that get results. And most of all, win yourself the job of your dreams!

Once you have a good KSA set, you can tweak the statements and use them for other KSAs that are similar. I save my KSAs and copy and paste my answers into the new application each time.

COVER LETTERS: YOUR GOODWILL AMBASSADOR, MAGICIAN, AND CHEERLEADER

Should you include a cover letter with a public service application?

Federal agencies rarely ask for cover letters as a required item in a job application. From a purely practical point of view, they don't need to. Both your Federal resume and your KSA set will prominently display the job announcement number and your name and social security number. With such clear labeling, there's little to no chance that anyone will confuse the components of your employment application with that of another applicant or with the mountains of other mail that pile into a personnel office every day. Each application component is self-explanatory and needs no introduction.

Or does it?

Essentially, the Federal government doesn't require you to submit a cover letter with your employment application. However, I believe that cover letters are absolutely essential. In fact, I am so convinced of the strength of cover letters that I recommend using them with every single Federal government employment application that is a "paper" application. You can't submit a cover letter with electronic applications.

This surprises many of my clients and seminar participants who work for the Federal government. However, Federal employees who have been recently hired into government know how important the cover letter is.

"Who's going to read my cover letter?" they ask. Will the personnel staff read my cover letter? What difference can the letter make? What could I possibly say in my letter that I haven't already said in my resume and KSA set? The answer is: PLENTY! Cover letters *do* get read, *do* make a difference, and *do* potentially play an important (and might I add unique) role in your application package. The cover letter could make a difference. Once you have one good cover letter written, you can change it slightly for each application.

However, to make anyone sit up and take notice of YOUR cover letter, you cannot write and send an ordinary or ho-hum letter. Your application package deserves something much better, a letter with interest (passion for the position, agency or mission), a summary of skills and qualifications, and a few logistical points that could help them make a decision for you.

You cannot use a cover letter with an automated application, but you can write a compelling letter with a "paper" application. The cover letter can explain special circumstances and sell your best skills and experiences.

What a Great Cover Letter Can Do

A great cover letter is simply one that creates an impression of you. It directs your reader's attention by showcasing your professionalism. It points out your best traits. As well, the letter can personalize your application package. It is a wonderful chance for you to speak directly to your reader, the hiring supervisor. It's your chance for you to say, "Hey, look at me! I'm the best-qualified, most interesting candidate. Call me!"

I like to think of the cover letter as the applicant's goodwill ambassador and cheerleader. Like a goodwill ambassador, a strong cover letter can greet the reader who picks up your application, casting a positive light on you at a critical point in the application process (when the supervisor has many applications to read and he is weeding through the piles of papers). And, like a cheerleader, the right cover letter will show you are the best for the job and serve as an enthusiastic voice for your qualifications. Specifically, an effective cover letter can put your best foot forward in so many ways. For example, you can use a cover letter to:

- ✪ Summarize the best you have to offer
- ✪ Write about your interests or passions in a particular field or job
- ✪ Highlight your expertise and qualifications that specifically fit the job
- ✪ Demonstrate your knowledge of the agency's mission
- ✪ Showcase your values as an employee
- ✪ Create a compelling rationale for why you are an outstanding candidate

All this in one page! The right cover letter can do wonders for your application and will take very little time to write. In this chapter, I'll show you how. It's easy...I promise.

The Cover Letter as a Sales Tool

If you're not fully convinced of the importance of using a cover letter with your application package, let me share one more idea to sway you over to my side. When you get right down to it, job-hunting is a sales effort. Your goal is to sell yourself (the job applicant) first to the individual(s) who reviews your application package, and later, to whoever interviews you.

Because job hunting is a form of sales, it can be helpful to consider effective sales strategies as you prepare your employment application. It just so happens that I have an excellent strategy to share with you. Actually, it comes from sales guru Tom Hopkins who offers this very useful advice to anyone selling anything:

> "I want to write a 'mindblowing' cover letter that will not only reflect my suitability for the position but will outshine all the others. Of course I want to use the same amazing resume. But where do I start?"

"You don't sell something by telling your customer what the features and benefits are ONE TIME. You repeat these items of interest several times in your sales pitch by introducing the product, reviewing the features and benefits, giving a demonstration, and telling the customer how the product will help achieve their business goals."

Repetition, as Hopkins tells us, is the key to sales success. In my experience, it is an effective strategy for any job applicant who is trying to sell himself or herself to a public service personnelist, hiring manager, or panel. I recommend using repetition, to your benefit, in your job application package as follows:

1. Explain in your cover letter what your strengths are.
2. Repeat this information and reinforce it with facts and information (features and benefits) in your Federal resume.
3. Demonstrate your strengths again and in a different way by showcasing your knowledge, skills, and abilities in your KSAs.

Think of your cover letter, then, as just one important part of your overall sales strategy. Use it to capitalize on a wonderful opportunity to repeat and highlight key information about yourself.

Tip: Your cover letter (and the rest of your application package) is also your personal "service proposal" to the organization. In it, you will explain what YOU can do for the organization, what services you have to offer, what goodies you bring to the table. Consider the weight of your service proposal carefully. If you earn $40,000 per year and you hope to be employed at least five more years, your proposal will be worth at least $200,000 to you, plus benefits! This is a serious proposal, one that deserves an excellent introduction in the form of a cover letter.

The Cover Letter: Your Letter of Interest

Universities and private industry employers that solicit job applications for higher-level positions often request a resume and "letter of interest." Such a letter is particularly meaningful and may serve as an excellent model for your Federal government application letter.

Consider the word *interest* very carefully. If you can't demonstrate your interest in a job in a one-page letter, then I think it's fair to ask why anyone would want to consider you seriously, let alone hire you.

Interest is the important word to remember. As you approach the task of writing your cover letter, keep in mind that you are writing a letter to express your interest in the job. In it, you must not only identify your strengths and qualifications, but also demonstrate your interest in the company, agency, mission, organization, or office.

Computer Professional:

"I would be an asset to your organization because I can bring expertise into play from the helpdesk technicians point of view. I have an upbeat and happy personality, and the ability to make others smile and feel good about the work environment."

Sometimes, it is not enough in an employment application simply to showcase your qualifications for a job. Personnel experts know that the applicant who wants a job a great deal is apt to do a better job than one who is less committed to it. Personally, I would hire an applicant who has the potential to learn what he or she needs to know for a job AND who is more highly motivated than one who is already qualified but who doesn't seem to care particularly about it. Wouldn't you?

Explain Special Circumstances in the Cover Letter

Hiring managers want to understand your application and what has motivated you to apply for the position. Job applicants sometimes have special situations and interests that should be explained early in the application. The cover letter is the perfect place to do this.

You reassure your readers and make them feel favorably toward your application by telling them everything they need to know to make sense of your application. For example, if you live in Baltimore and you are seeking a complete career change, geographic change, decrease in salary, and a move to Seattle, your application may not make sense to your reader. He or she may not take the time to figure out what is motivating you or bother to call you and ask for your rationale. Therefore, in cases such as these, it is best to *explain what you are doing* in a reasonable way. For instance:

- ✪ If you are relocating to be near family or parents, it's good to say so.

- ✪ If you have purchased a second home in a beautiful region of Tennessee and hope to move there and eventually retire in this area, explain what your goals are.

- ✪ If you want to leave the Washington, D.C., metro area and live and work in the West because it has been a dream of yours, say so.

- ✪ If you went to college in Colorado or Alaska and have always wanted to live there, say so.

- ✪ If you are currently in a job making $27,000 and you were making $35,000 in your previous job, explain what happened in the letter.

- ✪ If your current job is out of your original (and preferred) career path because of a corporate reorganization, not because of your choice, explain this change.

Whenever your circumstances are unusual or not obvious, tell the personnelists and managers why you are seeking the job you are seeking. Make yourself as clear as possible. Do not wait for the interview to explain the situation. You might not get the chance.

Customer Services:

"I would be an asset to your organization because I am a cooperative and energetic person. I strive to be the best that I can be. I will be productive."

Teacher:

"My relevant qualifications include: Two and a half years of experience with children from the ages of two years old through the fifth grade. I would like to get closer to the students and teachers by writing, and managing educational programs that will have an impact on environmental health though education."

Recommended Cover Letter Structure

Of course, it is possible to structure a cover letter any number of ways. However, in this section, I will share with you the structure that I have found to be both easy to write and particularly effective. Here's how it goes:

Paragraph 1: Explain your reason for submitting your letter/application.
For example: "I am submitting the enclosed resume and KSA set as my application for the position of Public Health Advisor with the National Safety Council." If you have special or unusual circumstances for seeking the job, explain them here.

Paragraph #2: My relevant qualifications include.... In this paragraph, present your qualifications either in narrative (paragraph) form or as bulleted points. For example, if you prefer to list bullets, you might say that you:

✪ Served as a Public Health Advisor at the National Institutes of Health, Centers for Disease Control and Prevention for 12 years. Managed projects and provided consultation to private organizations, educational institutions, and through the media to improve information on physical activity and nutrition.

✪ Are widely recognized as an expert in physical activity and nutrition issues. Authored curriculum, classroom text chapters, press releases, newsletter, grants, and training materials. Consulted with government, education, and non-profit organizations.

✪ Successfully directed the first public policy conference for public health graduate students and national forums on the importance of physical education on health and well-being.

✪ Have taken extensive training. Credentials include a master's degree in Health Promotion and Wellness from the American University and a bachelors degree in Exercise Science from the University of Virginia, concentrating on Health Education.

Paragraph #3: I would be an asset to your organization because.... Put yourself inside your reader's head and consider what in your background would make him or her sit up and take notice. For example:

"I am seeking new opportunities where I can use my knowledge of physical activity and nutrition issues gained from my years at the National Institutes of Health. I know that disseminating environmental and health information into the school systems is vital and challenging," or

"I would like to get closer to the students and teachers in schools by writing, creating and managing educational programs that will have an impact on environmental health through education," or

"I believe that with my research and government program knowledge I can contribute extensively to the mission of National Safety Council and the Council's focus on public education programs and environmental health."

Paragraph #4: Offer to come in for an interview.

For example:

"I am available to meet with you at your convenience to discuss your objectives and my background. You can contact me at either telephone number above. Thank you for your time and consideration. I look forward to your response."

Closing/signature. Use a standard business closing and signature. However, list all of the enclosures you are submitting with your application, including your Federal resume, KSA set, college transcripts, and anything else required in your application. For example:

Sincerely,

Helen R. Waters

Enclosures:

Explain Special Accommodations Needed for Disabilities

If you are a person with a disability, your letter will be essentially the same as any applicant's. First, you will focus on your skills, interests, objectives, and services you can provide to the organization to which you are applying. Then in a separate paragraph of your cover letter, you might choose to write about the special accommodations you will need to perform at the highest level of your capability. For instance:

Paragraph #1: Reason for submitting your application.

Paragraph #2: I would be an asset to your organization because….

Paragraph #3: My relevant qualifications include….

Medical Billings:

"My relevant qualifications include: one-and-a-half years of registration and admission experience in the admission department. While there, I have been able to develop several techniques to make recordkeeping more efficient, as well as making the department run more efficiently and becoming more organized."

Military IT Professional:

"My relevant qualifications include:

16 years of military experience computer repair and maintenance (mainframe, overseas packet switching network). Experienced in teamwork under heavy duress and able to get along with any personality with great results."

Paragraph #4: Special accommodations for disability.

For example:

"I am a person with a 90% visual disability. In order to perform effectively in my position, I would simply need special software on the computer so that I could listen to my email and other data. I have excellent health and hearing capabilities, so I am a high-performing employee with the exception of sight capability. I travel easily with a cane and learn new physical environments very quickly. I have a positive attitude and am willing to work hard and learn new policies, procedures and programs."

Paragraph #5: Offer to come in for interview.

Closing/signature.

It is your decision whether you will write about your disability and special accommodations in your initial application. Keep in mind, though, that agencies do have resources to help them with special software, hardware, and physical accommodations so that you can have a meaningful, well-paid position. Federal Government is hiring people with disabilities!

Discuss with your State Rehabilitation Specialist, job search counselor, and your family how you might communicate your particular strengths and your special needs. This is a personal decision, whether to tell the potential hiring manager about your disability or not. Nevertheless, the Federal government is mandated to hire thousands of employees with disabilities in the next few years.

Special Emphasis Officers—Human Resource Staff—are tasked with finding qualified, skilled people with disabilities to hire into positions that can accommodate special needs employees. So if you are working through a State Rehab Counselor, have a Schedule A letter stating that you have a disability. Then you can seek a position in government without going through the "competitive process" of writing KSAs and applying for announced positions. It could be important to tell the Special Emphasis Officer and Hiring Supervisor of your disability and your strengths, skills, and interest in working for the Federal government.

In my experience, public service agencies have excellent job opportunities for all people—those with and without disabilities. However, hiring managers and personnel staff need to know the special accommodations that you will require to determine if the job will work for your skills and abilities. I believe that if you are forthright, positive, informative, and honest about your capabilities, personnelists and panels will work with you to achieve a win-win job situation for you and the agency.

Draft your Cover Letter with our Online Template

It can be difficult to know where to start with a good cover letter. That blank computer screen can be awfully intimidating for many job applicants. That's why I have created an online cover letter template for my clients to guide them through the information gathering and writing process.

Thousands of job-seekers have used the Cover Letter Builder that is on the CD-ROM of this book. Use the Builder to write your cover letter.

You will see that the Cover Letter Builder is a step-by-step template that provides you with fields for writing your own cover letter. Using it, you will answer a series of prompts to create an excellent first draft of your cover letter. You can then edit and polish your letter yourself. Or, if you prefer, you can engage our editors to improve it for you for a fee.

Using The Resume Place Online Cover Letter Builder, you will be following a template that includes two sections for writing information. Let's discuss these one at a time:

1. My relevant qualifications include:

In this section, do your best to highlight your relevant experience and education. Make sure you pay attention to the vacancy announcement. If you have the qualifications required as stated in the announcement, repeat these qualifications here. You may even use language from the vacancy announcement verbatim if you like.

2. I would be an asset to your organization because:

Be persuasive here. You want a phone call inviting you to a job interview, right? Do your best to put yourself on the "best qualified" list. Tell your readers why you would be particularly well qualified to work in this organization. For instance, what do you know that will be useful? What special skills and training would be a particular benefit? Look for the extraordinary in what you know and do.

Teenage Librarian:

"I would be an asset to your organization because: I can find books on the shelves quickly and I am good at finding things that do not belong, such as books from other libraries."

THE RESUME PLACE COVER LETTER TEMPLATE

Our online cover letter template has been used more than 2,000 times in the last two years. This is a highly successful formula for writing your cover letter. The template inspires you to write about the best you have to offer. It gives you the structure you will need to complete your information and write compelling statements about what you want and what you believe. Access our template online or simply use the hard copy of our template below to gather and organize information for your cover letter.

Your Address:
State:
Home Phone:
Work Phone:
Email Address:
Date:
Person's Name:
Title:
Agency or Organization Name:
Street Address:
State:

Paragraph 1

Dear:

Please find enclosed my:

for the position of:

Paragraph 2

My relevant experience for the position includes:

1.

Paragraph 3

I believe that I would be an asset to your organization because

1.

Paragraph 4

Thank you for your time and consideration. I look forward to your response.

Sincerely,

Enclosures,

The cover letter builder is a fantastic tool to inspire you to write a great cover letter. Thousands have used the cover letter builder from www.resume-place.com

Sample Cover Letters Written with the Template

On the following pages are examples of excellent cover letters prepared using The Resume Place Online Cover Letter Builder. Feel free to use these for inspiration and to borrow good ideas. Just be sure, however, that YOUR cover letter accurately and truthfully reflects your assets and abilities and that it is also a reflection of your unique personality.

Remember, a strong cover letter is worth the extra time and attention. Do include one every time you apply for a job. Above all, don't rush through the writing. Do your best to make a positive first impression in your letter and never forget that it can be an extremely effective sales tool. Always write a cover letter that will serve your interests. Use it as your own personal goodwill ambassador, magician, and cheerleader. Let it introduce you positively, direct attention where you want it to go, and encourage you and your application.

You will find your efforts worthwhile. If you write your letter thoughtfully and well, you will greatly increase your chances of getting positive attention for your application package. Ultimately, an effective cover letter will give you a better shot at getting the job you want. Really.

Now, read some inspiring examples. Write your own cover letter following my guide. And whatever you do, don't forget to let your personality shine through.

Cover Letters and Electronic Applications

Cover letters require special consideration when using two types of electronic Resume Builders:

- ✪ Defense Department Resume Builder: Has specific fields for every piece of resume information. There is no place to write a cover letter. Therefore, you will not be able to submit one.

- ✪ QuickHire System: The EPA, USGS, Commerce, and other agencies use this system for automated selection and management of candidates. This Builder has one field where you can copy and paste your entire resume and a short introductory letter. Be aware, however, of the number of characters allowed in the field. It is 7,000 characters without spaces. Do not exceed that limit.

Cover Letters and "Paper" Applications

Any agency that tells you to send a resume, KSAs, and other paperwork to the agency implies that you can send a cover letter as well. Always include one.

Senior Executive's passion for a job in Homeland Security:

"The attraction to this job is not salary; I routinely get offers that exceed government wages. The attraction to the job is the opportunity to continue to serve my country and to make a difference in government. September 11 jolted us all into the realization that vast oceans no longer protect us from attackers. As we examine our vulnerabilities against the backdrop of this event, we now realize in glaring brilliance the challenges of homeland defense."

STAFF OPERATIONS OFFICER

DANIELLE MONTROTH
1403 Milling Drive
Occoquon, VA 22407
Work: (540) 777-7777
Home: (540) 777-7777
montroth@aol.com

Dear Human Resources Staff:

Please find enclosed my application for the position of Staff Operations Officer.

My relevant qualifications include:

- I am presently employed by the Federal Bureau of Prisons (BOP) as a Management Analyst in the Intelligence Section in Washington, DC. I have served in this post for approximately 18 months. As a requirement for this position, I have qualified for and presently maintain a "**Top Secret**" clearance.

- Prior to my work in Washington, I worked for the Bureau of Prisons at the Administrative Maximum Penitentiary in Florence, CO. My three years at that facility were spent entirely in the Special Investigative Office where I closely monitored, reviewed, and tracked the communication activities of such inmates. Further, I personally conducted multiple "debriefs" of high-ranking prison gang members (i.e. Aryan Brotherhood), interviewing potential inmate informants regarding weapons introductions, staff assault plots, etc. I also independently drafted weekly written intelligence reports containing information gathered through telephone, mail, and personal communication methods.

- Due to my expertise in the intelligence field, I regularly serve as an instructor during BOP Investigative Intelligence Training, a two-week course providing classes in crime scene management, interview skills, computer database operations, and current street and prison gang activities.

- I am currently pursuing a BS in Psychology and anticipate completion of my program within 18 months.

I would be an asset to your organization because:

- I am an extremely dedicated and hard-working individual. I have a great interest in the intelligence field that I feel may be better developed and satisfied by assuming a position with your agency.

- I have proven that I can function capably and adeptly within various intelligence circles under extreme pressure, as evidenced by my rapid promotion within the Bureau's intelligence section.

- I bring with me in-depth knowledge of prison gang activities as well as the ability to talk with and solicit information/intelligence from persons of varying backgrounds.

- I have worked closely with other federal and state law enforcement agencies to track and prosecute various federal crimes. Such agencies include the FBI, ATF, and NSA.

- I have strong public speaking and instructional skills, evidenced by my ongoing involvement in national BOP intelligence training sessions. I have also conducted "on site" gang training sessions for specific BOP facilities, as well as the Office of Enforcement Operations in Washington, DC.

Thank you for your time and consideration. I look forward to your response.

Sincerely,

INTERNATIONAL AFFAIRS ASSOCIATE

SARAH SADAT-FEHRAN, Ph.D.
5610 Wisconsin Avenue #1501
Chevy Chase, MD 20815
Home: (301) 718-8333

Dear Personnel Officer:

This letter transmits my application for the position as an International Affairs Associate. I believe that my education and experience provide an excellent understanding and background for the position.

My academic qualifications are extensive:

- I have just graduated in spring 2001 at the top of my class with a Ph.D. in International Affairs from the School of Foreign Service at The American University. This rigorous program prepared me well to work with individuals and organizations around the world.

- Prior to that, I completed an M.A. in International Affairs Summa Cum Laude from The Elliot School of International Affairs at The George Washington University.

- My Bachelors degree, Magna Cum Laude, is in English and I am an accomplished writer and public speaker in English as well as in other languages.

- My public school education was first-rate; I graduated with honors from an internationally renowned school in Geneva, Switzerland.

I would be an asset to your organization because:

- I speak, write, and read five languages fluently: English, French, Spanish, Farsi, and Arabic. I am an excellent translator and have substantive experience utilizing these languages to build and cement strong international client relationships.

- Throughout my graduate training, I was employed summers in international organizations where I had the opportunity to work with clients with diverse social and cultural orientations.

- I have traveled the world, and have either resided in or visited Europe, the United States, Canada, the Middle East, and South America.

- I find working in an international arena to be extremely stimulating. I have great sensitivity to and knowledge of international cultures, including customs, languages, foods, religions, and way of life. I derive tremendous pleasure from communicating with diverse individuals from different nations and cultures in their native languages.

- I am quick to establish rapport and trust and I pay meticulous attention to detail. I am diplomatic and can learn about people quickly.

I wish very much to apply my training, experience, and skills to new challenges and I am intrigued about opportunities at your agency. Thank you for your consideration for this position.

Sincerely,

SAMPLE COVER LETTER

SPEECH-LANGUAGE PATHOLOGIST

CELINA GARCIA

8209 Dallas Rd., #1091
Dallas, TX 75231
Home: (214) 999-9999
celina_ariel@yahoo.com

Dear Personnel Officer:

Please find enclosed my resume for the position of Speech-Language Pathologist.

My relevant qualifications include:

- Experience with assessment and intervention with all age groups.

- Proficiency in a wide variety of assessment procedures, particularly standardized testing.

- Ability to work extremely well with children who have sensory integrative dysfunctions.

- Strong skills in the diagnosis and remediation of swallowing disorders.

- Knowledge about working in diverse clinical, medical, and educational settings.

I would be an asset to your organization because I have:

- The ability to develop an excellent rapport quickly with my clients.

- Limited but effective Spanish-speaking skills.

- Excellent oral and written communication skills

- Experience working in multidisciplinary settings.

- A learning environment in which I can expand my skills.

Thank you for your time and consideration. I look forward to your response.

Sincerely,

Celina Garcia

Enclosures

CODE ENFORCEMENT OFFICER

JULIE ELLENBURG

3520 Palm Way
Sanford, FL 32773
Work: (407) 330-0693
Home: (407) 330-5697
wellenburgjr@cfl.rr.com

Dear Personnel Officer:

Please find enclosed my application for the position of Code Enforcement Officer.

My relevant qualifications are as follows:

- For the past ten years, I have worked in building, licensing, and code enforcement. Through extensive training and job experience, I have issued building permits and business licenses and have processed code enforcement paperwork and complaints.
- I have considerable knowledge of ordinances, codes, and zoning regulations.
- I have received outstanding feedback from the citizens and business owners in the community where I have worked.
- I have previous experience working with police, providing the necessary information on vehicle tows and proper identification.
- I am able to handle stressful situations and remain in control.
- I am currently studying for the Code Enforcement Level I Inspectors exam.

I would be an asset to your organization because:

- I know how to maintain strong relationships with local business owners and citizens.
- I have held several positions in community development and have a broad understanding of the issues at play.
- I have previously worked for your agency for approximately eight years.

Thank you for your time and consideration. I look forward to your response.

Sincerely,

Julie Ellenburg
Enclosures

SECRETARY/TRAVEL COORDINATOR

THERESA FLETCHER

6142 Marlboro Way
Orange Heights, CA 95610
Home: (916) 888-8888
fletch@aol.com

March 15, 2003

Human Resources Office
Microsoft, Inc.
2001 Microsoft Drive
Seattle, Washington 90090

Dear Human Resources Staff:

Please find enclosed my resume for the position of Secretary/Travel Coordinator.

My relevant qualifications are as follows:

- I have a six-year record of strong customer service.
- I have worked successfully within specific time frames. I know how to prioritize and manage busy workloads and complete my work.
- I can type 60+ wpm. I know how to manage multi-line telephone systems and perform filing, data entry, and clerical duties. As well, I operate all office equipment including fax machines and copiers.
- I have excellent communication skills with strong abilities in spelling, grammar, punctuation, and writing. I have technical/computer skills with emphasis on Windows, Excel, Word, Access and Lotus Notes, which I use daily. I also have people skills.
- I have successfully completed courses in Accounting/Bookkeeping, Business Communications, and Business English.

I would be an asset to your organization because:

- I am excited about new learning opportunities and wish to apply the many skills I have acquired throughout my career.
- I would like to learn more about how the court systems operate.
- I believe that with my past experience and willingness to learn I can contribute extensively to the Microsoft Human Resources needs.

Thank you for your time and consideration. I look forward to your response.

Sincerely,

Theresa Fletcher

Enclosures

Part iv summary

Writing your Federal resume, electronic resume, KSAs, and cover letters will take time—obviously. Applying for and landing a Federal job is a major undertaking. If you succeed, you should be extremely proud of yourself for getting in. Every time I meet someone in my workshops who has recently entered government from private industry, I congratulate them for landing a Federal job. They tell stories of how it took them six months to a year; persevering with sending in 10 or 20 or 30 resumes and KSAs, wondering what's going on all the time. But they stick with it and then they are in. Then they come to my workshops to learn how to get a promotion, change job series, write KSAs better, and write the best Federal resume possible in order to manage their career inside of government. It's never easy. Never. I wish that it were easier. For now, you need a good resume and KSAs and the know-how to use your network to get your government job.

Step 8 is almost as complicated as Steps 4 through 7. Luckily, it's a lot different. Step 8 will teach you how to understand vacancy announcement "how to apply" instructions better. You need to know when to use which resume format. When do you use an electronic resume? When do you use your paper Federal resume? When do you need to write separate KSAs? When should you combine your KSAs and skills into your resume? Since each agency requires a different resume format and application process, we have to study several major application processes. You will succeed much faster if you know there are five major ways to apply for jobs in government. Keep reading, consider this a major career challenge, and good luck.

"After 18 years as a temporary employee with the Bureau of Land Management as a Fire Fighter, I have finally landed a permanent position – thanks to your book, workshops and advice. Now I can begin my retirement investment and continue my career with benefits! "

APPLY FOR JOBS

APPLY FOR JOBS AND SUBMIT YOUR RESUME

If you think that writing your Federal resume, electronic resume, and KSAs was challenging, wait until you read this chapter. The Federal job application process is complex, to say the least, because each agency has its own way of recruiting, selecting, and requesting application formats. I have made every attempt to make the application processes as simple to understand as possible.

-Kathryn Troutman

Now that you have your Federal and electronic resume prepared, you are ready to start applying for jobs! If you are a serious and determined Federal job searcher, finding, reading and interpreting announcements is going to feel like a part-time job because there are so many announcements and they are all so different. Hopefully, this chapter will help you understand the instructions and you will be able to apply correctly for each position.

STRATEGIES FOR APPLICATION SUCCESS

The best thing you can do is focus on particular agencies, no more than three. Then you will become familiar with their hiring processes. If you look at all agencies, you will get overwhelmed and confused with the varying application requirements. If you have environmental interests, then you should look at the Environmental Protection Agency (Quickhire), Department of Energy (Quickhire), and U.S. Army Corps of Engineers (Resumix). You will learn to recognize the agency's hiring format as you study the announcements and after you read this step a couple of times. You have to take your time and do the application right, or you may not be successful.

Remember that the more applications you submit, the higher your odds will be for landing a job. You should prepare many applications and keep applying. Step 9 tells you how to manage the follow-up on your applications so that you can find out the status if it's been four weeks or more with no notice.

> "I'm amazed at the variety of application instructions as I read the job announcements."

> "It's best to focus on particular agencies, learn their recruit process and mission, then apply for jobs more successfully."

PERSONNEL REVIEW STEPS FOR YOUR APPLICATION

The Federal application process involves the following:

1. **Do you have the Status to apply for a particular announcement?** Is the announcement "Open to Anyone"? Or is it an internal announcement, which could also be called a Merit Promotion Announcement? Do you have any Status that can be used so that you can apply for jobs as though you were a current Federal employee? You can see the types of Status in Step Two: Sources of Eligibles.

2. **Do you have the basic qualifications for the job?** Your resume is reviewed for **the basic qualifications** for the job (education and years of generalized or specialized experience).

3. **Will your resume rate high enough to get referred to the supervisor?** Your application is **rated and ranked** through assessment tools, including Qualifications (self-rating) Questionnaires, Application Questions, Keywords, and KSAs.

4. **SUCCESS!** If you are referred, you have made the first cut! Then if you are qualified and ranked high enough, your resume will be **referred** to the hiring supervisor for consideration and hopefully an interview.

INTERVIEW! If you stand out among the referred applications, you will get a telephone or in-person interview for the position.

The number of resumes referred to the selecting official can range from 3 to 30, depending on the system. You want your resume to STAND OUT for the selecting official so that you can be considered for an interview or discussion on your experiences.

Who can apply for federal jobs

The OPM Web site and other Federal employment Web sites ask certain questions before you are considered for a Federal job. We discussed Federal Status in Step 2 of this book. Some Federal jobs are OPEN TO ANYONE and some Federal jobs require Status. More and more Federal jobs are open to anyone because of the large number of Federal employees who are retiring. The government needs new people in the system.

The Status Question displayed here to the right is on the www.usajobs.opm.gov website on the first screen before you can look at job announcements. This is a good qualifying question. You will have to click YES or NO before the site will search for jobs for you. If you click NO, then the site will automatically return with jobs that are open to anyone. If you do have status, you will have many more jobs to choose from. Approximately 60 percent of all Federal jobs are Open to Anyone.

Remember to check "Who can apply" on the announcements to see if the position is Open to Anyone before you apply for the jobs. These are the jobs that are open to anyone. Sometimes the announcement number will have a "DE" or "DEU" in it. That means the job is open to anyone. DEU stands for Delegated Examining Unit. This is a special personnel office that is "delegated" to handle recruiting and selection of first-time Federal employees.

You could have Status if you are a Veteran, an Outstanding Scholar (3.5 GPA overall or in your major), disabled, married to a military person, have worked for the government before, or been laid off by the government.

A full list of hiring authorities and ways you can have status is included in the appendix.

Let's look at a couple of sample vacancy announcements at the "who can apply" sections:

> **Status Employee**
>
> Are you a current Federal employee, a former Federal employee with reinstatement eligibility, or a person with special appointment eligibility?
>
> YES
>
> NO

SAMPLES: WHO CAN APPLY —
All Qualified Persons

SAMPLE 1

www.hcfa.gov - Center for Medicare and Medicaid Services

Area of Consideration (who may apply): All Qualified Persons.

Persons who are eligible under special hiring/ appointment authorities (e.g., 30% compensable veterans, severely handicapped individuals, former Peace Corps, and VISTA Volunteers, etc.) are also encouraged to apply. Applicants eligible under these special placement programs must indicate on the front of their application the program under which they are applying and MUST submit proof of eligibility. Applicants who wish to be considered under a special hiring authority as well as under the competitive examining process MUST submit two applications. When only one application is received, it will be considered for the appropriate special hiring authority.

Applicant MUST be a U.S. citizen.

"I spend 10 hours per week poring over announcements, qualifications, and duties. I hope that I land a Federal job soon. Maybe I haven't really cracked the code."

SAMPLE 2

www.justice.gov - Drug Enforcement Agency

DEPARTMENT OF JUSTICE

DRUG ENFORCEMENT ADMINISTRATION (DEA)

Vacancy Announcement Number: 02-FN-0001

Opening Date: 02/25/2002

Closing Date: 03/18/2002

Position: ACCOUNTANT

GS-0510-09/13

Salary: $38,406 - $86,095 per year

Duty Location: 2 vacancies at ARLINGTON, VA

WHO MAY APPLY: Open to all qualified persons.

Every vacancy announcement will be clear about Who Can Apply. Be sure to look at this item before you go to the trouble of applying for the position.

APPLICATION FORMATS AND PROCESSES

There are at least six ways to apply for a Federal job. The vacancy announcements are different in their instructions for "how to apply."

Here's a review of the various "how to apply" instructions, application formats, and rating and ranking processes. The first cut applicants are those who are qualified to apply (have the correct status), have the correct number of years of experience and/or education, and are rated and ranked high enough to go to the second cut. The second cut or final step is where the hiring supervisor or panel will review your resume among the top candidates.

Application Formats and Rating and Ranking Processes

Since application formats are different, the rating and ranking of applications is different. You will notice this as you review Federal vacancy announcements. There are AT LEAST six ways to apply for a Federal job:

1. **Paper Application — Federal Resume & KSAs.** Manual paper application. Replaces the SF-171 and OF-612. The personnel specialists will rate and rank candidates by giving grades to KSA applications. The Federal resume is reviewed to determine if you meet the basic qualifications of the job.

2. **Resumix + Supplemental Data Sheet.** Resumix™, HotJobs Software Resumes are placed in a database with a supplemental data sheet which provides specific job title, geographic and salary information. All Defense agencies use this system. The human resources recruiter searches for best candidates (rates and ranks) by searching for keywords/skills in your resume.

3. **Electronic Resume and Occupational and Task Questions.** Quickhire™, Avue and USA Staffing, an OPM-automated recruitment system. These formats require an electronic resume and answers to questions. You will rate yourself from 1 to 5 on many of the questions (Rating level 1: you know nothing about this subject; Rating level 5: you are the office expert). Rating and ranking of applications is done by your answers to the questions. Some of the questions could be a short narrative as well.

4. **Resume Only with Application Questions.** Internal agency databases.
    The HR professionals rate and rank various ways—answers to questions and resume information. The FAA, CIA, FBI and other agencies have various on-line applications, questionnaires, tests and systems to obtain applicant information.

5. **Optional Form OF-612.** The OF-612 was designed in 1995 to take the place of the SF-171. All of the information that you will write in your Federal resume will also be listed in the OF-612. The problem with the OF-612 is that the form is rigid for the applicant. It is a "personnel form." If you have a choice to use a resume, rather than the OF-612, please use the Federal-style resume as shown in this book.

6. **SF-171.** The SF-171 was eliminated in 1995 by the Office of Personnel Management and has not been renewed by the Office of Management and Budget. BUT some agencies still list the SF-171 as an acceptable form of application for a Federal job. This author recommends that you should not use the SF-171 now for a job application. You should try first to submit the Federal-style resume. A second-best choice would be the OF-612. Many agencies still state in their instructions that you can submit an OF-612, SF-171 or resume. The best format is the resume.

The reason the application formats and instructions are so different for each agency is that the agency's human resources offices choose different ways to manage recruitment, selection, rating, and ranking of applications. Some still use paper applications (fedres + KSA) and many use electronic resumes (a larger percent are automated now). The move is toward more electronic resumes, but you have to be prepared for all instructions and application formats at this point.

SOME FEDERAL AGENCIES AND THEIR REQUIRED APPLICATION FORMATS

AGENCY	FORMAT
Defense Agencies	Resumix
Army	Resumix
Navy	Resumix
Air Force	Resumix
NASA	Resumix
U.S. Army Corps of Engineers	Resumix – Internal applicants
U.S. Army Corps of Engineers	Fedres (or OF-612, SF-171) & KSAs – external applicants (or without any "status")
National Institutes of Health	Online resume + KSAs faxed or mailed
Center for Medicare and Medicaid Services	Fedres (or OF-612, SF-171) & KSAs
Most Dept. of Health and Human Agencies	Fedres (or OF-612, SF-171) & KSAs
Dept. of Justice	Fedres (or OF-612, SF-171) & KSAs
Some Justice Agencies	Automated various methods
Federal Drug Administration	Quickhire
Environmental Protection Agency	Quickhire
U.S. Geological Survey	Quickhire
Department of Energy	Quickhire
Department of Interior	Quickhire
All Commerce Dept. Agencies	COOL system – e-resume & questions
Federal Aviation Administration	Online resume and Fedres & KSAs,
Library of Congress	Avue
U.S. Forest Service	Avue
Any Federal Agency	USA Staffing
US Agency for International Development	SF-171 or OF-612 + KSAs for Personal Services Contracts (PSC) (overseas contracts); resumes + KSAs accepted for domestic positions

INSTRUCTIONS AND INTERPRETATION OF HOW TO APPLY FORMATS

This chapter is going to give you insights into applying for jobs successfully with manual paper review processes, Resumix, Quickhire, USA Staffing, and other processes that require online resumes and questions. Some agencies still ask for the OF-612 and SF-171. Get ready to READ THE INSTRUCTIONS to determine the correct way to apply for a Federal job.

Federal Resume and KSA — The Paper Application

Many agencies are still requesting paper applications and KSAs from candidates. How can you tell if the agency is automated or non-automated?

Any announcement with "how to apply" requesting the OF-612 as an application format will NOT be automated. The OF-612 is an employment form (replaced the SF-171) that cannot be submitted electronically. You can also tell the agency is still a manual paper reviewing agency because they ask for written KSAs.

Another sign is that they will give you a street address showing where to send the package and lengthy instructions on how to mail the package. In the Washington area, you should not mail your package to an office, but instead either fax, hand deliver or send by another mailing service (because of the anthrax problems with mail).

A Personnel Staffing Specialist will receive your envelope, review the resume for basic qualifications and status, and then rate and rank your KSAs manually by reading for keywords and content. The top candidates will be referred to the hiring supervisor.

Here's how you apply to a non-automated HR office:

1. Focus your Federal resume (with formatting) on the announcement, picking up some of the keywords from the duties section.

2. Add the job title, grade, series, and announcement number to the top of the resume and KSAs.

3. Write your KSAs for the position.

4. Mail, fax, or email your application to the address (follow their directions).

5. Send other information that they may request such as last performance evaluation (if you have one—not mandatory), transcripts, and DD-214.

Don't send any attachments if they don't ask for any.

> "I always go to "how to apply" in an announcement. I can't wait to see what creative application formats, questions and instructions the HR folks come up with."
>
> K. Troutman

> Always submit a resume, if possible. If the instructions request an OF-612, SF-171, or resume, your best choice will be the Federal-style resume.

Sample "Paper Application" Announcement Instructions

The following announcement instructions come from the Department of the Interior, Office of the Secretary of the Interior.

Vacancy Announcement Number: NBC-JA-DO-02-07

Opening Date:	02/22/2002
Closing Date:	03/14/2002
Position:	ACCOUNTANT
	GS-0510-07/09
Salary:	$31,921 - $50,757 per year
Promotion Potential:	GS-12
Duty Location:	1 vacancy at LAKEWOOD, CO
WHO MAY APPLY:	Open to All Sources.

You can tell this is a "paper" application because the OF-612 is in the list of forms accepted. The OF-612 cannot be sent electronically.

This announcement listed many items to send for the position, but it did not ask for the Knowledge, Skills, and Abilities in the list of "what to submit." You would have to read that instruction in the KSA section. Even if KSAs are not in the list of what to include, submit them anyway; they are mandatory.

HOW TO APPLY:

Please submit the following:

**Application/Resume: You may apply using a resume, OF-612 (Optional Application for Federal Employment), or any other written application form.

The OF-612 is available in any Federal personnel office or on the OPM website at www.opm.gov/ forms. Although a standard application form is not required, we do need certain information to evaluate your qualifications and determine if you meet the legal requirements for Federal employment. If your resume or application does not provide all the information requested in this vacancy announcement, you may lose consideration for the job.

This announcement mentions the OF-612, but you do not have to use it. You can use the Federal resume style from this book.

KNOWLEDGE, SKILLS, AND ABILITIES REQUIRED

If you meet the basic eligibility requirements for this position, you will be rated and ranked relative to the knowledge, skills, and abilities required to perform the duties of the position. The following KSAs have been identified as being important to the performance of this position. You should submit a narrative statement on a separate page(s) with specific responses and examples of each of the knowledge, skills, and abilities in this announcement. Include in your narrative the work experience(s) that provided you with the specific knowledge, skill, and ability that relates to this position, including work objectives, work accomplishments/evidence of success, awards, etc.

Note: You will receive credit for unpaid experience related to the position duties (i.e., community work/service, cultural, social service, and professional association activities) on the same basis as for paid experience. Your final score will be determined from the information you provide in your application and the narrative KSA statement(s). Failure to submit your narrative response to the KSAs may negatively affect your eligibility and/or rating for this position.

"Failure to submit" means that you should write these KSAs as part of the application.

1. Knowledge of generally-accepted accounting principles and of the laws, regulations and guidance applicable to governmental accounting.
2. Ability to identify accounting events and to enter transactions into an automated accounting system, and the ability to understand how the systems process the data.
3. Skill in interpreting, explaining and applying tax laws, directives, policies, and regulations.
4. Ability to effectively interact with employees and customers from various organizations and functional areas and to communicate effectively about financial matters.
5. Ability to plan and organize work to meet the goals and objectives of the organization.

Resumix and Supplemental Data Sheet

You are going to see many of these announcements in any of the Federal job search databases. The Defense Department is doing most of the hiring now and there will be an increase in the next years, according to the current White House.

The Defense agencies (Navy, Army, Air Force, Marines, other DOD agencies) are using Resumix to manage their recruitment and selection of qualified employees. Resumix is a keyword resume system similar to private industry online applications such as HotJobs.com or Monster.com. Resumix is the system that www.disney.com uses to recruit and hire all of the employees at Disneyland as well.

The HR recruiters search the job databases (that you will select in your supplemental data sheet) with key skills for the position. This is why we emphasize analyzing vacancy announcements for key skills for your resume throughout this book.

"If I put my resume into a database, how can I include keywords from a vacancy announcement?"

"Is it really worth my while to submit my resume to an announcement that has a closing date two years away?"

Two Kinds of Resumix Vacancy Announcements

Open Continuously – Inventory Building – Database Building Announcements.
These announcements have very short "duty" descriptions and list multiple job titles in an occupational series. These are databases where HR professionals will search for qualified candidates when positions become available. These are valuable and real announcements. If you are qualified for these positions in a particular region of the country, you should submit your resume to these databases.

Here is a sample of Open Continuously (resume database building) instructions:

U.S. Army, West CPOC Announcement for Merit Promotion candidates or applicants with Status:

Announcement No: WCPOC-DCIPS-2200

Opening Date: January 01, 2002

Closing Date: December 31, 2003

Position Title (Pay Plan-Series): Information Technology (IT) Specialist (-2210)
Grade: 05

Comments: THIS ANNOUNCEMENT COVERS: The position you selected as well as those positions within the following occupational series:

    POLICY PLANNING INFORMATION SECURITY

    SYSTEMS ANALYSIS

    APPLICATION SOFTWARE

    OPERATING SYSTEMS

    NETWORK SERVICES

    DATA MANAGEMENT

    INTERNET

    SYSTEMS ADMINISTRATION

    CUSTOMER SUPPORT

OPEN UNTIL FILLED: Referrals from this announcement may be issued at anytime as vacancies materialize.

HOW TO APPLY: All positions filled through merit promotion procedures by the West Civilian Personnel Operations Center are filled under RESUMIX, an automated ranking and referral system. Only one resume and supplemental data sheet is required for ALL occupational series and locations for which you indicate interest. West CPOC Resumix application procedures must be followed to receive consideration. Application procedures can be obtained on the West Region Web site at: http://www.wcpoc.army.mil, then click on Employment Opportunities

How to apply for positions in the US Army Military Intelligence Community.

To apply, you will be instructed to:

    1. Prepare a maximum 3-page resume using the Resumix format.

    2. Complete the Supplemental Data Sheet (basically this is your Job Profile).

    3. Submit the resume and supp sheet by email or regular mail.

This particular announcement is only open to applicants with status. "All positions filled through merit promotion procedures…" This means internal employees or people with status only. There would be another announcement recruiting IT applicants without status. If you have been in the military, you can apply under this announcement. You should submit your resume by email preferably.

Special Announcements – Actual position – with closing dates that are usually within about 4 weeks. These are specific job announcements where they are looking for new candidates from all sources—internal and external, with or without status. The "Open Inventory" database may not have enough qualified people in it, so they are announcing the position to find more candidates. Follow the announcement instructions for how to apply.

Here is a sample of instructions for a real position. This is a **HOT JOB** from the U.S. Army Corps of Engineer's West CPOC Region (http://cpolrhp.belvoir.army.mil/west/).

Some announcements are "open continuously". They are real announcements for jobs that may come open at any time. This is basically a database building announcement

ANNOUNCEMENT NUMBER: WCPOC-3500

TITLE: Laborer, WG-3502-03

SALARY RANGE: $9.91 TO $11.56

LOCATION OF POSITION: Corps of Engineers, Lucky Peak Project Office, Boise, ID

DUTIES: Performs duties necessary for the beautification of the area. Cuts and trims grass, cuts weeds, rakes leaves and grass cuttings, and disposes of debris and leaves. Does clean up, trash collection, tree watering and cleaning and supplying public comfort facilities.

HOW TO APPLY:

IF YOU ARE INTERESTED IN APPLYING FOR THIS VACANCY, PLEASE ACCESS OUR WEB PAGE AT WWW.WCPOC.ARMY.MIL . COMPLETE INSTRUCTIONS FOR APPLYING FOR THIS POSITION, AND ANY OTHERS YOU MAY BE INTERESTED IN, CAN BE OBTAINED BY SELECTING EMPLOYMENT OPPORTUNITIES AND FOLLOWING INSTRUCTIONS ON HOW TO APPLY THROUGH RESUMIX AT THIS SITE.

APPLY NOW, REFERRALS MAY BE ISSUED AT ANY TIME!

If you are willing to move to Lucky Peak in Boise, Idaho, you could be considered for this HOT JOB with the Corps of Engineers.

Self-Nomination Process

If your resume is already in the database, you can simply "self-nominate" for a special position that is interesting to you. The Navy uses both Open Continuously announcements and special announcements with closing dates. You will not need to resend or re-submit your resume to the particular database. Make sure your resume is in the right database.

Here's How You Apply to Resumix Jobs

1. Read the announcement to see if it is an "Open to Anyone" announcement or requires Status (or is called Merit Promotion).

2. Write the correct length resume
   (Army – 3 pages; Navy, Marines, AF – 5 pages).

3. The announcement will lead you to the correct region where you can find the correct email to submit your resume or use the online Resume Builder.

4. Find the Job Kit for the region so that you can find the correct Supplemental Data Sheet.

5. Copy the Supplemental Data Sheet questions in a word processing file, if you are sending your resume by email. Send your 3- or 5-page resume, plus supplemental data sheet (separate page).

6. If you send by email, copy and paste your resume and supplemental data sheet in the textbox of the email. Do not attach any files.

7. If you submit through a Resume Builder, the Supplemental Sheet will be part of the Builder.

"Sixty percent of all jobs are Defense positions—with the Resumix resume."

Better have your electronic resume ready!

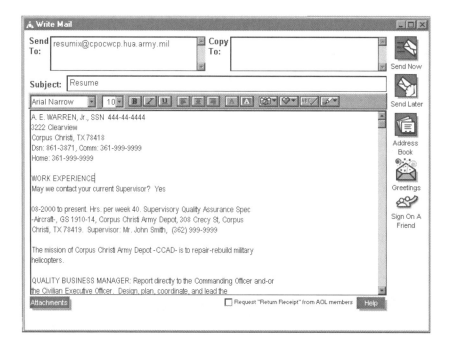

Completing the Supplemental Data Sheet

The supplemental data sheets (supp sheet) are a very important part of your application. The supp sheets are basically your Job Profile (that's what private industry companies call this same information). The personnelists will search on items of information from the supp sheets to determine your status and qualifications for consideration of the job. You can find the various region's supplemental data sheets in their Job Kits on the Web sites.

Each region has a different supplemental data sheet. Don't try to use one supp sheet for all Army or Navy regions. The geographic region preferences are different and some of the questions are different. The blue text describes the questions somewhat. For more details, please refer to the actual West CPOC Job Kit that is included on the CD-ROM for this book. It could be updated anytime, however, so you should refer to the online Job Kit on the Internet. It won't be long before there will be fewer supp sheets. The Army will have only two supp sheets and the Navy might have only one.

This supp sheet and Resumix resume can be used for internal employees and anyone with status. Applicants without status will apply with the electronic resume and KSAs—read the announcement instructions.

To submit this supp sheet and Resumix to the West, follow these instructions:

1. Complete your Resumix in your favorite word processing software.

2. Type your supp sheet in your word processing software also.

3. Copy and paste your resume (three pages max) and your supp sheet (as a fourth page) into the textbox of the email.

4. Send it to: Resumix@cpoc.wcp.hua.army.mil

5. Subject line: resume

6. You can check on the status of your resume and if there is any activity on your resume in the databases by going to ROAR— an excellent feature on the West CPOC's Web site. (More about ROAR in Step 9)

7. Web site address: www.cpolrhp.belvoir.army.mil/west

" I like the Resumix resume and emailing it to the agency, but the supplemental data sheet is difficult to understand."

Sample Supplemental Data Sheet

West Civilian Personnel Office, Army Format

SUPPLEMENTAL DATA SHEET
1. Name and SSN: LIEBERMAN, BRIAN L. 333-33-3333
2. U.S. Citizen? YES
3. Employment category: INSERVICE

You should read the actual job kit to get definitions on your Employment Category. Inservice means that you currently work in the West Region and you are served by the West CPOC.

4. Veterans' Preference: none
5. Current Federal Civilian Pay Plan, Series & Grade, and Months held:
   GS 1101-11, 4/22/01 to present
6. Current permanent Federal civilian employee? YES

Items number 5 and 6 are important so that the system will recognize your current pay plan, series, grade, and months.

7. Period of Military Service: 8/14/66 to 8/15/72
8. Retired Military? No
9. LOWEST acceptable grade you will accept? GS-11

This is important. You will not be considered for any position lower than a GS-11.

10. TEMPORARY employment? No
11. PART-TIME employment? No
12. INTERMITTENT employment? No
13. SHIFT work? No
14. HIGHEST civilian permanent pay plan? GS-11

This is important also. You are telling the personnelist your highest grade in your past or current work history.

15. Words per minute you can TYPE: 40
16. Words per minute you can take dictation: None
17. Federal appointment/position you hold today: PERMANENT
18. Currently on Leave Without Pay? No
19. Geographical availability: Corpus Christi, TX

There is a drop-down box for geographic locations serviced by the West CPOC. You can choose any of those locations. See the Job Kit.

20. List OCCUPATIONAL SERIES of position(s) for which you wish to be considered:
    1101, 1670

You are actually selecting your Job Occupational Series Databases with this question. You can choose as many as you like, but be reasonable with this. You can only cover so many occupations with one resume. We recommend that you focus on no more than three occupational series because it is difficult to cover keywords for more than three series in a 3- to 5-page resume.

21. Indicate your eligibility for any of the following priority consideration programs. If not applicable, enter "not applicable."
    a. Repromotion eligible   NA
    b. Re-employment Priority List   NA
    c. ICTAP   NA
    d. Restoration of a separated employee   NA
22. Have you received a Separation Incentive? No
23. If current Federal employee, include last performance rating and date: March 1, 2001
24. Willing to travel? Less than 25%
25. What is the LOWEST grade you will accept with PROMOTION POTENTIAL: GS-11

This question is different from question no. 9. If you are interested in taking a lower grade so that you can change occupational series, you should write the lowest grade you will accept with promotion potential. You will see some announcements with grade levels ranging from GS 7 through 12. That means you may go down in the grade initially, but you will go up within a reasonable number of years toward the GS-12.

26. Term appointment?   No
27. Competitive term?   Yes
28. Competitive temporary promotion?   Yes
29. Competitive detail?   No

Definitions of these are in the West Job Kit.

OPTIONAL INFORMATION
    30. Birthdate: 8/31/44
    31. Race/Origin Designation Caucasian
    32. Indicate Male or Female: Male

These 32 questions are very important in your Resumix applications. They will qualify you for positions based on your answers. This supp sheet is the Army West CPOC format. If you apply for jobs with the North Central or Southwest Regions, the supp sheet will be slightly different. At some point Army and Navy will provide the same supp sheet for all regions.

Need more help with the Resumix and Defense hiring system? Consider the *Electronic Federal Resume Guidebook & CD-ROM* published by The Resume Place, Inc. You can read more instructions on how the system works, what happens to your resume, and how to write a great Resumix skills-based resume.

The Electronic Federal Resume Guidebook can help you further with your Resumix resume.

Wishful thinking for applicants: Maybe in two to three years there will be one database for all Resumix Defense civilian jobs. Maybe there will be only one supp sheet for all Civilian Personnel regions. Maybe a person could submit his or her resume one time and be considered for all Defense civilian jobs in particular occupational series. The "one database approach" is not here yet. Good luck with your Resumix and your applications!

Quickhire

Many Federal agencies have chosen to use the Quickhire system for their recruitment and management of applicants. The Quickhire system can be recognized for instructions that refer to Resume and Application Questions. The agency will also have the Quickhire logo on the announcement.

Distinguishing Features of Quickhire Announcements

If you have found a Quickhire agency that you would like to work for, you should begin the application process ahead of time by setting up your account and submitting your initial resume. You can go to the log-in page, get registered, answer 30 basic Federal personnel questions (similar to the Supplemental Data Sheet in the Resumix system), submit your resume (you can focus the resume toward the announcement later), and be ready to apply for jobs. When you find an announcement, you will have to answer 20 to 40 MORE job-related questions, so it's best to get your resume in ahead of time.

It's easy to post your resume in the Resume Builder—just copy and paste the resume into one Resume Builder field. You can have 16,000 characters (five pages) in your resume. Be sure to use your electronic resume format for the builder. You cannot copy and paste a resume with formatting (bold type, bullets, indentations, etc.) into a builder. The resume will possibly be unreadable and will be rejected.

The Second Application Phase — Answering the Application Questions

The Quickhire system is a combination of personnel questions, posting your resume, and then answering job-related questions by rating yourself.

When you have the opportunity to look at announcements, you find a rating scheme based on your level of competency for each question. Don't be bashful, if you are a 4 or 5, rate yourself that way. Be honest. The personnel staff will verify your answers with your resume.

Rating Scale for Application Questions

Here are some example questions. You will have to select the most relevant skill level for each question.

Performed administrative duties relating to purchasing supplies and services for an office.

1. I have not had education, training, or experience in performing this task.
2. I have had education or training in performing this task, but have not yet performed it on the job.
3. I have performed this task on the job, with close supervision from supervisor or senior employee.
4. I have performed this task as a regular part of the job, independently and usually without review by supervisor or senior employee.
5. I have supervised performance of this task and/or I have trained others in performance and/or am normally consulted by others as an expert for assistance in performing this task.

> "It feels like I'm stretching to rate myself as a '5' to the questions, but I know that I am the office expert for many of the questions."

Quickhire Sample No. 1—Environmental Protection Agency

HOW TO APPLY FOR THIS VACANCY ANNOUNCEMENT:

Resume and application questions for this vacancy MUST be received online via the EZHire@EPA website BEFORE midnight Eastern Standard Time on the closing date of this announcement. If you fail to submit a COMPLETE online resume, you WILL NOT be considered for this position. Paper applications WILL NOT be accepted and requests for extensions WILL NOT be granted. Unless otherwise stated in this announcement, all required supplemental application materials must be received by the closing date of the announcement (including Saturdays, Sundays, or government holidays). If you have accessed this announcement from an alternate website, please visit www.epa.gov/ezhire to apply for this position.

Here's how you apply:

1. Write and format an electronic resume.
2. Log-in and answer preliminary job interest questions.
3. Obtain password and log-in name and get ready to apply for jobs.
4. Open the vacancy announcement and begin the process of applying.
5. Rate yourself to each of the questions.
6. Print out the questions so you can study them on paper to prepare your answers.
7. Submit.

Job-Specific Questions

Here are the job-specific questions for a Secretary GS-7 or 9. These questions are the basis of the rating and ranking of your application. Answer them carefully and honestly. You will also see two Essays requested within these questions (similar to KSAs). This questionnaire is very important to your candidacy for this position. Be sure to include some of these skills (and keywords) in your resume. You can go back to your resume and edit it to include some of these skills before you officially apply for this job.

Grade: 09

1. GS-09: You must have one year of specialized experience equivalent to the next lower grade in the Federal service that has equipped you with the knowledge, skills, and abilities to perform successfully the duties of the position. Select the choice that best describes your experience.

    1. I have one full year of specialized experience equivalent in responsibility and scope to the GS-08 level as described in the vacancy announcement under specialized experience requirements.

    2. I do not meet requirements as described above.

2. Do you possess a typing skill of at least 40 wpm?

    Yes   No

Grade: 07

1. GS-07: You must have one year of specialized experience equivalent to the next lower grade in the Federal service that has equipped you with the knowledge, skills, and abilities to perform successfully the duties of the position. Select the choice that best describes your experience.

   1. I have one full year of specialized experience equivalent in responsibility and scope to the GS-06 level as described in the vacancy announcement under specialized experience requirements.

   2. I do not meet the requirement as described above.

2. Do you possess a typing skill of at least 40 wpm?
   Yes   No

All Grades

1. GS-07: Select the choice that best describes your specialized experience and/or education.

   1. I have completed major study in safety or occupational health fields, or I have a degree in other related fields that included or was supplemented by at least 24 semester hours in the following (or closely related) disciplines: safety, occupational health, industrial hygiene, occupational medicine, toxicology, public health, mathematics, physics, chemistry, biological sciences, engineering, and industrial psychology.

   2. I have one full year of specialized experience equivalent in responsibility and scope to the GS-05 level as described in the vacancy announcement under specialized experience requirements.

   3. I possess a combination of post-high school education and experience that together meet the qualification requirements for this position.

   4. I do not meet any of the requirements as described above.

2. GS-08: You must have one year of specialized experience equivalent to the next lower grade in the Federal service that has equipped you with the knowledge, skills, and abilities to perform successfully the duties of the position. Select the choice that best describes your experience.

   1. I have one full year of specialized experience equivalent in responsibility and scope to the GS-07 level as described in the vacancy announcement under specialized experience requirements.

   2. I do not meet the requirement as described above.

3. GS-09: You must have one year of specialized experience equivalent to the next lower grade in the Federal service that has equipped you with the knowledge, skills, and abilities to perform successfully the duties of the position. Select the choice that best describes your experience.

   1. I have one full year of specialized experience equivalent in responsibility and scope to the GS-08 level as described in the vacancy announcement under specialized experience requirements.

   2. I do not meet requirements as described above.

4. Do you possess a typing skill of at least 40 wpm?
   Yes   No

5. Have you received recognition or other awards for performance of secretarial and/or administrative type duties? Respond yes or no. If yes, please complete the type received in the next question.
   Yes   No

6. Performed administrative duties relating to purchasing supplies and services for an office.
   1. I have not had education, training, or experience in performing this task.
   2. I have had education or training in performing this task, but have not yet performed it on the job.
   3. I have performed this task on the job, with close supervision from supervisor or senior employee.
   4. I have performed this task as a regular part of the job, independently and usually without review by supervisor or senior employee.
   5. I have supervised performance of this task and/or I have trained others in performance and/or am normally consulted by others as an expert for assistance in performing this task.

All the following questions require that you rate yourself from 1 to 5 as the previous question. Most of the questions have the 5 same choices for rating. A few of the questions have specific answers related to the skills.

7. Prepare requisitions for office supplies, maintenance, and equipment.

8. Perform word processing, typing of official correspondence, and various forms and reports.

9. Review and edit technical and/or non-technical materials, identifying inadequacies in format, grammar, or construction in accordance with accepted standards.

10. Coordinate and prioritize supervisor's appointment calendar.

11. Plan, coordinate, and establish work tracking systems to monitor action items and office deadlines.

12. Organize and maintain office organizational charts, telephone directories, and routine information.

13. Search files, documents, or other sources for informational materials to prepare responses to inquiries, briefing packages, or background for meetings or conferences.

14. Maintain office filing system.

15. Serve as custodian of division/office personal property records to include tracking of personal property issued to employees.

16. In the text box below, provide a summary of your degree of responsibility as it relates to preparing, reviewing, and finalizing memoranda, reports, and other documents. Include any training you may have that improved your skills in verifying documents for proper grammar and punctuation.

(Essay Question)

This question appears to be similar to writing a KSA statement as described in this step.

17. From the list below, select the choice that most closely represents your experience in managing and organizing files and records systems.

1. I independently maintain records and files for my assigned organization. This includes applying policies and procedures for protection of classified documents, insuring for proper document markings, and insuring records/files checked out are accounted for and returned accordingly.

2. I independently maintain records and files for my assigned organization. Records and files are typically routine memos, administrative documents, and other records that may be subject to certain privacy act requirements.

3. I independently maintain records and files for my assigned organization that typically include routine administrative information. Files and records are not regarded as sensitive and are readily available for distribution to employees or the general public.

4. I do not have any experience as described in the choices above.

18. From the list below, select the choice that most closely represents your experience in administrative support functions.

1. I have served as a principal office assistant in a Federal organization (as a Federal employee or contractor providing secretarial support) and have prepared responses to routine correspondence and phone calls on my supervisor's behalf.

2. I have served as a principal office assistant to an entire division/department or equivalent organization.

3. I have served as a principal office assistant in a Federal organization (as a Federal employee or contractor providing secretarial support).

4. I have provided general clerical and administrative support to one or more individuals.

19. From the list below, select the choice that most closely represents your experience in travel arrangements and time and attendance reporting.

1. I have made travel arrangements and managed time and attendance reporting for a small office staff.

2. I have made travel arrangements and managed time and attendance reporting for staff in a division/department or equivalent in a Federal agency and its subordinate organizations.

3. I have made travel arrangements and managed time and attendance reporting for staff in a division/department or equivalent and its subordinate organizations.

4. I have limited experience in these areas.

20. Select all software applications with which you have experience.

    1. Lotus Notes
    2. WordPerfect
    3. Lotus 1-2-3
    4. Word

21. In the text box below, provide a summary of your experience in arranging high-level meetings, conferences, or workshops. Indicate what you were expected to perform independently in coordinating and planning such meetings, the extent of interaction with attendees, your interaction with hotels/conference centers, and what type of follow-up action was required. Also, describe the level of such meetings, e.g., with headquarters, corporate offices, etc. (Essay Question)

22. Contact others orally to obtain information.

23. Communicate effectively with administrative officials and peers on a variety of non-controversial topics.

24. Interact with groups/individuals of all levels, both within and outside the agency/organization, U.S. and foreign.

25. Do you have experience in arranging meetings, conferences, or workshops?

    Yes   No

26. Performed administrative duties related to domestic and international travel.

27. Work effectively with co-workers, supervisors, and higher management.

Congratulations, you have completed the Questionnaire that will provide the information for rating and ranking of your application. If you are well qualified for this position, you should be referred to the supervisor.

When you rate yourself from 1 through 5, you are basically "self-certifying" your skill level. If you are a 4 or 5, please take credit for your experience.

Over 95% of USGS applicants apply online, and there has been an increase of 400-500% in the number of applications received per typical vacancy. The agency's managers now can have the Job Certificate usually in 4 days of the job close date down from 30 to 60 days in the past.

OPM Announcements with the many questions are also called "Form C." Sometimes you will see up to 158 questions where you have to rate yourself. This is a long application. Be careful with your answers. OPM is working on eliminating this long form, but you might see this format as you search for Federal jobs.

Quickhire Sample No. 2—U.S. Geological Survey

The U.S. Geological Survey has successfully cut down the hiring time from three months to seven days with the use of the Quickhire/OARS system of electronic resume and the answers to questions. This system works!

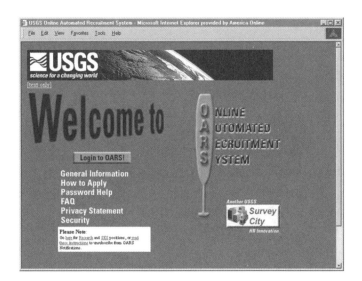

USA Staffing

USA Staffing is an automated recruitment service by OPM Servicing Centers located throughout the United States. The Office of Personnel Management provides recruitment and selection services for various agencies. You might see an announcement for a job with the U.S. Immigration & Naturalization Service; Bureau of Alcohol, Tobacco & Firearms; or many other agencies with an OPM address. Don't be confused by seeing two agencies on one announcement. OPM is the recruitment service bureau for the actual agency that is hiring. The OPM personnel specialists receive large volumes of applications, rate and rank candidates, and refer the best qualified "certified" candidates to the hiring agency customer.

Here's How You Apply for OPM Announcements

1. Follow the directions to submit your electronic or Federal resume. It could be by mail or email, or you could complete your resume in the www.usajobs.opm.gov Resume Builder.

2. Answer the Occupational Questionnaire online if you can.

3. Fax other information that they might request—last evaluation, DD-214 (veterans), and transcripts, for example.

Here's an example of an announcement managed by OPM's USA Staffing Service:

USAJOBS   CONTROL NO VW1041

ALCOHOL TOBACCO AND FIREARMS SPECIALIST

SERIES/GRADE: GS-1854-05/07

SALARY: $ 25,347.00 TO $ 40,818.00, ANNUAL PROMOTION POTENTIAL: GS-09

ANNOUNCEMENT NUMBER: WA134540WR

HIRING AGENCY: TREASURY, Bur of Alcohol, Tobacco & Firearms

DUTY LOCATIONS: 0002 Vacancies WASHINGTON, DC

PHONE: (478) 757-3000

WASHINGTON SERVICE CENTER

1900 E STREET NW ROOM 2469, WASHINGTON, DC 20415

HOW TO APPLY:

Your application will consist of three components. The first component consists of the occupational questionnaire that you must complete. The second component is your resume. The final component of your application consists of "other" application materials. Examples of these other materials include your college transcripts (if required) and documentation of veteran status (if applicable). Instructions on completing and submitting these items follow.

STEP ONE:

Complete and Submit the Occupational Questionnaire.

Submit your answers online via the USAJOBS web site by clicking on the following link: http://www.usajobs.opm.gov .

You may also follow the instructions below to get to the questions.

1. Connect to the USAJOBS web site at http://www.usajobs.opm.gov
2. Click on the *Online Application* menu option (under the USAJOBS logo)
3. Scroll down the online application screen until the "Enter Vacancy ID" box appears
4. Enter Vacancy ID 134540 and click on "Submit" to begin the online application. We highly encourage you to complete the Occupational Questionnaire using the online method since it is the most efficient way for us to process your responses. If you are unable to submit your responses online, refer to the alternatives described under Alternative Methods for Completing Occupational Questionnaire at the end of this announcement.

Instructions for answering the questions in the Occupational Questionnaire:

Please use the following step-by-step instructions as a guide to filling out the required questionnaire. You will need to print the vacancy announcement and refer to it as you answer the questions. You may omit any optional information; however, you must provide responses to all required questions. Be sure to double-check your application before submission. You must submit your online questionnaire by midnight, Eastern Time, on the closing date of the application.

Be sure to answer the questions, send your resume, and respond to other required application requests. Since this is both a paper (faxing or mailing resume and other information) and electronic process (questionnaire), you have to remember both to be successful.

Sample Occupational Questionnaire

Social Security Number
Enter your Social Security Number in the space indicated. (Providing your Social Security Number is voluntary, however, we cannot process your application without it.)

Vacancy Identification Number
Enter the Vacancy Identification Number: 134540

1. Title of Job
Position Title: Alcohol, Tobacco and Firearms Specialist

2. Biographic Data
All biographic information is required, except for your telephone number and the contact time.

3. E-Mail Address
If you would like to be notified by E-mail, please enter your E-mail address in the space provided.

4. Work Information

5. Employment Availability
Questions A through D are required.

The Occupational Questionnaire involved 30 questions. Some of the questions had to do with occupational knowledge, skills and abilities; other questions had to do with your Status for the position and the grade level. Again, this is similar to a Profile that most private industry databases require.

" Take time to research jobs and write an outstanding resume.

Be prepared to write a good resume.

Don't wait until the last day to write your resume.

Do not use acronyms if possible."

Director of Human Resources, U.S. Army Corps of Engineers
Great Lakes and Ohio River Division

OPM'S *Resume Builder*

You can write your resume and hold it on OPM's Resume Builder database. You can update it as often as you like. The disadvantage to your final resume is that it is in HTML, rather than a word processing software. The USAJobs Resume Builder resume is also rigid in format. You have to use their format. If you wanted to list education before experience, you could not do that. But the Builder is handy for writing and submitting to USAStaffing announcements. Here are the instructions for using the Resume Builder at USAJOBS Resume Builder:

You can submit your resume online through the Resume Builder at www.usajobs.opm.gov.

Submit Resume Online: To submit an online resume for this announcement, click on the link to our online Resume Builder above. You can use the Resume Builder to create a resume on the system or to edit and submit a resume that you already have on file.

NOTE: Submission of a resume from the USAJOBS website may not be a complete application. Many positions require the completion of additional forms and/or the submission of supplemental materials. Please carefully review the vacancy announcement that follows for full "How to Apply" instructions. Failure to provide the required information and/or materials may result in your not being considered for employment.

The NOTE above is saying that when you write your resume and submit it to the USAJOBS Web site, you are not actually applying for a job. You are simply getting the resume set up. You will have to answer Questions and possibly fax other information to complete the application.

About 30,000 people have their resumes in the OPM Resume Builder. You have to update every 6 months. The OPM Resume Builder is useful to build your resume, but you cannot email it to anyone, because it is in HTML, not Word or Word Perfect.

One Federal Manager said that the best way for anybody to get into Government is to apply for a job that nobody wants, in a place where nobody wants to live, and at a grade level lower than you are really qualified. After that, you can move to another job.

SF-171 or OF-612 — Employment Forms

Some agencies are still requesting the SF-171 and OF-612 applications, as well as KSAs from candidates. If the list includes resume, please use the resume instead of the form because of the flexibility of the information. But if you have to prepare one of these forms, you can find the forms online. You can open them with Adobe Acrobat Reader and type in the fields directly on the form. The form is not flexible with length and you will have to use continuation sheets, but it is online. You can find both of the forms in Microsoft Word and Adobe Acrobat PDF on this page: http://www.usaid.gov/procurement_bus_opp/procurement/forms/. (Better do a test if you're going to use the forms; I couldn't save my content.) You can print the forms and email.

A Personnel Staffing Specialist will receive your envelope, review the form for basic qualifications and status, and then rate and rank your KSAs manually by reading for keywords and content. The top candidates will be referred to the hiring supervisor.

Here's how you apply to a non-automated HR office:

1. Focus your SF-171 or OF-612 on the announcement, picking up some of the keywords from the duties section.

2. Add the job title, grade, series, and announcement number to the top of the each page of the form and the KSAs.

3. Write your KSAs for the position.

4. Mail, fax, or email your application to the address (follow their directions).

5. Send other information that they may request such as last performance evaluation (if you have one— not mandatory), transcripts, and DD-214.

Don't send any attachments if they don't ask for any.

OMB No. 3206-0

OPTIONAL APPLICATION FOR FEDERAL EMPLOYMENT - OF 612

You may apply for most jobs with a resume, this form, or other written format. If your resume or application does not provide all the information requested on this form and in the job vacancy announcement, you may lose consideration for a job.

1. Job title in announcement	2. Grade(s) applying for	3. Announcement number
4. Last name	First and middle names:	**5.** Social security number

6. Mailing address:		7. Phone numbers (include area code)
City	State Zip Code	DAYTIME EVENING

WORK EXPERIENCE
8. Describe your paid and nonpaid work experience related to the job for which you are applying. Do not attach job descriptions.

1) Job title (If Federal, include series and grade)			
From (MM/YY)	To (MM/YY)	Salary per	Hours per week:
Employer's name and address			Supervisor's name and phone

Describe your duties and accomplishments

Application for Federal Employment--SF 171

Read the instructions before you complete this application. *Type or print clearly in dark ink.*

Form Approved:
OMB No. 3206-0012

GENERAL INFORMATION

1 What kind of job are you applying for? *Give title and announcement no. (if any)*

Epidemiology Prog. Spec. (GS-301-12), NCI-01-1703

2 Social Security Number: 999-99-9999

3 Sex: ☐ Male ☑ Female

4 Birth date *(Month, Day, Year)*: 09/09/57

5 Birthplace *(City and State or Country)*: Baltimore, MD

6 Name *(Last, First, Middle)*: SUSAN J. ERICKSON

Mailing address *(include apartment number, if any)*: 2334 Kensington Road

City: Bethesda State: MD ZIP Code: 20817

7 Other names ever used *(e.g., maiden name, nickname, etc.)*: n/a

8 Home Phone: Area Code Number (301) 999-9999

9 Work Phone: Area Code Number (202) 333-3333 Extension 122

10 Were you ever employed as a civilian by the Federal Government? If "NO", go to Item 11. If "YES", mark each type of job you held with an "X".

☒ Temporary ☐ Career-Conditional ☐ Career ☐ Excepted

What is your highest grade, classification series and job title?
GS-11

Dates at highest grade: FROM 09/95/ TO 09/97

FOR USE OF EXAMINING OFFICE ONLY

Date entered register: //
Form reviewed: / Form approved:

Option	Grade	Earned Rating	Veteran Preference	Augmented Rating
			☐ No Preference Claimed	
			☐ 5 Points (Tentative)	
			☐ 10 Pts. (30% Or More Comp. Dis.)	
			☐ 10 Pts. (Less Than 30% Comp. Dis.)	
			☐ Other 10 Points	

Initials and Date: // ☐ Disallowed ☐ Being Investigated

FOR USE OF APPOINTING OFFICE ONLY

Preference has been verified through proof that the separation was under honorable conditions, and other proof as required.

☐ 5-Point ☐ 10-Point--30% or More Compensable Disability ☐ 10-Point--Less Than 30% Compensable Disability ☐ 10-Point--Other

Signature and Title
Agency Date

AVAILABILITY

11 When can you start work? *(Month and Year)*: 2 weeks notice

12 What is the lowest pay you will accept? *(You will not be considered for jobs which pay less than you indicate.)* Pay $ 42,000.00 per year OR Grade 12

13 In what geographic area(s) are you willing to work? Washington DC metropolitan area

14 Are you willing to work:

	YES	NO
A. 40 hours per week *(full-time)*?	☑	
B. 25-32 hours per week *(part-time)*?		☑
C. 17-24 hours per week *(part-time)*?		☑
D. 16 or fewer hours per week *(part-time)*?		☑
E. An intermittent job *(on-call/seasonal)*?		☑
F. Weekends, shifts, or rotating shifts?		☑

15 Are you willing to take a temporary job lasting:

	YES	NO
A. 5 to 12 months *(sometimes longer)*?	☑	
B. 1 to 4 months?		
C. Less than 1 month?		

16 Are you willing to travel away from home for:

	YES	NO
A. 1 to 5 nights each month?		☑
B. 6 to 10 nights each month?		☑
C. 11 or more nights each month?	☑	

MILITARY SERVICE AND VETERAN PREFERENCE

17 Have you served in the United States Military Service? *If your only active duty was training in the Reserves or National Guard, answer "NO".* If "NO", go to item 22. YES ☐ NO ☑

18 Did you or will you retire at or above the rank of major or lieutenant commander?

MILITARY SERVICE AND VETERAN PREFERENCE (Cont.)

19 Were you discharged from the military service under honorable conditions? *(If your discharge was changed to "honorable" or "general" by a Discharge Review Board, answer "YES". If you received a clemency discharge, answer "NO".)* If "NO", provide below the date and type of discharge you received. YES ☐ NO ☐

Discharge Date *(Month, Day, Year)*	Type of Discharge

20 List the dates *(Month, Day, Year)*, and branch for all active duty military service.

From	To	Branch of Service

21 If all your active military duty was after October 14, 1976, list the full names and dates of all campaign badges or expeditionary medals you received or were entitled to receive.

22 Read the instructions that came with this form before completing this item. When you have determined your eligibility for veteran preference from the instructions, place an "X" in the box next to your veteran preference claim.

☐ NO PREFERENCE

☐ 5-POINT PREFERENCE -- You must show proof when you are hired.

10-POINT PREFERENCE -- If you claim 10-point preference, place an "X" in the box below next to the basis for your claim. To receive 10-point preference you must also complete a Standard Form 15, Application for 10-Point Veteran Preference, which is available from any Federal Job Information Center. ATTACH THE COMPLETED SF 15 AND REQUESTED PROOF TO THIS APPLICATION.

☐ Non-compensably disabled or Purple Heart recipient.
☐ Compensably disabled, less than 30 percent.
☐ Spouse, widow(er), or mother of a deceased or disabled veteran.
☐ Compensably disabled, 30 percent or more.

THE FEDERAL GOVERNMENT IS AN EQUAL OPPORTUNITY EMPLOYER
PREVIOUS EDITION USABLE UNTIL 12-31-90

Standard Form 171 (Rev. 6-88)
NSN 7540-00-935-7150 171-110 U.S. Office of Personnel Management FPM Chapter 295

Page 1

Submit your resume to each government database. The databases are not shared by all agencies. You can submit through a Resume Builder or sending it by email. Read the specific agency's job announcement instructions for "how to apply."

GOVERNMENT AGENCY RESUME DATABASES

As of the writing of this book, there are many resume databases for Federal agencies in government. It is hoped that someday the Federal government will have one database where all resumes will be stored. Maybe the next edition of this book will write about one database in government. But at this writing, here are your databases. For example, if you submit your resume to the Army West Region database, and then apply for a job in Maine, you will have to send your resume and the correct supplemental data sheet to the NE Civilian Personnel Office Center (CPOC).

- ✪ The Army has six or seven databases and hiring regions.
- ✪ The Navy has eight databases and hiring regions.
- ✪ The Air Force has only one database.
- ✪ The Commerce Department's database is a stand-alone database.
- ✪ The EPA and USGS databases are completely separate.
- ✪ OPM's database is shared with USA Staffing clients.
- ✪ Every agency has its own database.

Please remember that you will need to submit your resume for each announcement and agency. For the Defense agencies, if the resume is in the database, you can just self-nominate by email or a special form.

SUMMARY

Even though this chapter is a complex one, it is better that you understand the vacancy announcement "how to apply" instructions. Today there is great need for people to understand how to apply for Federal jobs NOW—even if it is complex. The only way to be successful is to understand the instructions. The more you read the announcement instructions, the more familiar you will become with the system.

TRACK AND FOLLOW UP ON APPLICATIONS

So far in this book you've learned how to figure out the right job titles, grade, and appropriate agencies; how to write a correct Federal or electronic resume; how to write KSAs that will get the maximum points. We've also learned lots about reading and interpreting vacancy announcements for qualifications, duties, keywords, competencies, closing dates, how to apply, and application formats. If you know all of this, then you should have applied for the jobs correctly for the right job at the right grade level with the correct application.

But what if you have done all of this, submitted the package on time, and have heard nothing in four weeks? What then? Here's what you can do to continue your Federal job search. You have to take action— be patient, but persevering—in order to get information from personnel about what happened to your application and the announcement. Was it filled? Were you qualified? If not, why not?

What's going on?

In order to be successful, you need to track and follow-up with your applications. This chapter is intended to give you tips and information about communicating with Federal Human Resources professionals— how you can call and write to the personnel person listed on the announcement about the status of your application.

Submit many packages, keep track of your applications and follow-up. Something will eventually "hit" and you will be qualified and land an interview.

"To get satisfactory responses from HR office, applicants must know the announcement number, title, and job location of the job they applied for. If you know the announcement number, I can usually have an answer for an applicant in about 30 seconds. I get many, many calls from applicants saying they are calling about 'the job' or a job that begins with 'GS.' Some offices keep very complete databases of every applicant and can look you up by SS# and see what you applied for. We don't; our only system of record is the job folder."

—Personnel Officer

Here are the various things that can happen to the position openings:

- ✪ The position can actually be filled. If you are one of the finalists, you will be contacted for a telephone or personal interview. The supervisor will SELECT one of the applicants.

- ✪ The announcement closing date can be EXTENDED because they did not receive enough applications.

- ✪ The recruitment can go through certain steps (review of applications, qualified persons "certified," interviews), and then the position can be CANCELLED.

- ✪ The announcement can be CANCELLED due to budget cuts or the announcement was written incorrectly. The announcement may come out again corrected. You will have to apply again. The old applicant materials will be thrown out.

It is hard to believe all of the trouble the supervisors and personnelists go through to hire someone, then to postpone the hiring or cancel the position or announcement, but it happens. Often. That's why this chapter is in the book. You need to know that even if the position seems solid when you read the announcement and the job seems sincere, it may not actually happen. Be ready. You may spend hours on your package and it could go nowhere.

Most of what is written in this chapter has not been written before. There are so many Federal announcements and applicants that the personnel staff don't have time to communicate with applicants much. But you can talk or send an email to the name of the person on the announcement. Their mandate is to provide excellent customer services to applicants.

The Federal Job Search Game

Play it! Be ready! You need to keep your resumes and KSAs ready so that you can apply for positions within a reasonable amount of time, so that if the announcement or position is cancelled, or you are not hired, you have not wasted too many hours.

Personnelists' Insight

Customer service is not what it should be in many HR offices—we just don't have enough people. If you have not sent your application by some method that gets you a receipt, I would call the agency and make sure they have your application. I have seen applications get misfiled, put in wrong folders, and otherwise mishandled. If you are calling four weeks later and the agency did not get your application, it is too late to do anything about it. Also (and most readers of this book won't make this mistake), if you are calling by the last date, you can make sure that the HR office has everything it needs (DD214, SF-50, performance appraisal, and so forth) to consider you. In our office, if you don't submit necessary paperwork (say DD214 for VEOA jobs), you're out—we're not going to call you and ask for it. I have seen applicants attach their own self-addressed, stamped postcard with boxes to check acknowledging receipt of application.

If you are told by the HR office that you were not rated "qualified" and you feel you really were, you can ask for a reconsideration. Agencies have different procedures for this, but it's probably best to ask in writing to the attention of the Personnel officer. Your rating (or non-selection) is unfortunate, but mistakes do happen. The office will not be able to consider any new information, only what you submitted with your application.

WHAT HAPPENED TO YOUR APPLICATION?

"How long does the process take? It depends on many factors. One is whether the job is considered a priority and another is the workload of the human resources staff who is responsible for the vacancy. If the HR staff has a heavy workload, then it may take some time; if not, it should take no time at all. Then again, you have to consider the time after the selecting official receives the list of referred candidates. Some selecting officials act quickly while others don't. But if you want to know what's going on, I would advise calling HR 30 days after the announcement has closed."

Call the Personnel Specialist Listed on the Announcement

Sometimes a person's name is listed on the announcement with perhaps a telephone number or email address. This is the person who has produced the announcement working with the hiring supervisor. The personnel staff is busy with many recruitments, selections, and consulting tasks with supervisors. But it is also their job to answer questions from applicants. If you call and get voicemail (as you most likely will), you should leave an informed message. Here is a script you can use to leave an efficient voicemail for personnel.

"Normally I do not call HR to follow up unless it is a job I am especially interested in or feel I'm well qualified for. But I have found HR people to be helpful, if you are polite and thank them for their time."

—Job Applicant

What happened to my resume?
Recommended telephone message script

"Hello, I'm Kathryn Troutman. I'm calling regarding my application submitted for announcement number 10505 for Writer-Editor, GS-12. The closing date was 3/31 and I'm checking on the status of the recruitment. I can be reached at 410-744-4324 from 9 until 5, Monday through Friday, eastern standard time. If you get voicemail, you can leave a message regarding the position. Thank you for your time. I look forward to your information."

The Human Resources staff would like to help you, but they may not be able to talk to you on the phone.
Be patient and follow the directions here to obtain information on your application.

Sometimes there is no name or number on the announcement. However, the Office of Personnel Management currently is writing memoranda to Human Resources offices recommending that all vacancy announcements include a contact name and number to answer questions, which means this situation should improve in the near future.

Investigating to find a contact name

If there is no name and number, you can investigate to find someone to talk to from personnel regarding your announcement. Here's what you can do to track down Human Resources for this agency and office.

1. Go to www.usajobs.opm.gov.

2. Search under agency for the agency you have applied to.

3. Find another announcement from that agency and office— preferably a position similar to the one you submitted for (computer, executive, clerical, trades). Sometimes the personnel staff specialize in particular types of employees.

4. See if there is a name and phone number on any vacancy announcement for that agency and office.

5. Call that person and ask who is the HR specialist for your particular announcement. The personnel people usually work together (if it is the same agency). If you can get ANYONE on the phone, you can probably find the person who is managing your recruitment.

6. Ask for the name and phone number of the proper contact person; better yet, ask if that person is available so you can ask a quick question.

7. If you get him or her on the phone, ask about the status of vacancy announcement 09000, Secretary (Office Automation). Be ready to give the announcement number, or they won't be able to research the answer quickly.

Christmas Eve investigation

I actually did this one time when an announcement closing date was December 25. I did not believe that the announcement really closed on Christmas Day. My client was anxious about this closing date and I wanted to confirm if this was real or an error. The person named on our announcement was out because of the holiday. I went to www.usajobs.opm.gov and found another announcement for this agency and got the name and number of the person on the announcement. I called and this person actually answered the phone. I said I was checking on announcement 10501 and was looking for John Jones. She confirmed that John Jones was out on leave. I told her that the closing date was 12/25 and I thought that the closing date had to be an error. This personnel specialist told me that the closing dates are set automatically by a computer when the announcement is posted on www.usajobs.opm.gov and that the date was an error. The applicant could submit the resume the next working day by midnight. I felt so clever! I was a successful investigator and my client had a better holiday for it.

Customer Services and the Massive HR Downsizing

People will often tell you that customer services is almost non-existent in government. There is a reason for this. In 1995–1996 about 30 percent of the personnel staff were let go…believe it or not! Because of more automation in Human Resources, senior managers decided that the government didn't need so many personnelists. Since then it has become more difficult for applicants to get answers to their questions. This was particularly bad because at the same time the agencies switched from the standard SF-171 to the multitude of application formats and processes that are covered in Step 8.

Nonetheless, we have to deal with it as it is. The fact is this: The government has jobs and is hiring. If you can understand the announcements, continue to apply for jobs, and try to follow-up when you don't hear a word for more than four weeks, you are a successful, enduring person—and the government truly needs you.

Closing Dates Change Regularly

If you have found a great announcement and the closing date is too close for your submission, you should attempt to call the office to see if the date is still the same. Many announcements are set back because of the lack of applications. It's worth the effort to check on the closing date.

> "What I have experienced is the HR folks do NOT want any calls. Now what I've seen recently (although I haven't applied for more than about 5 or 6 jobs), is that the announcements have been cancelled. Sometimes the job cancelled for budget reasons and expected to be re-advertised in the future, so I know I'll apply again."

Emailing the HR Representative

If there is an email address on the announcement, you could try contacting the personnelist by email. I recommend this letter:

Subject line: Status of announcement 10101

Dear Ms. Jones,

I submitted my Federal resume, KSAs, and evaluation for the position of Writer-Editor, announcement no. 10101 on Dec. 22 by USPS. I'd like to check the status of my application and the recruitment please.

Is it still open and was I found qualified? Thank you very much for your time.

Sincerely,

Kathryn Troutman, SSN: 000-00-0000

Daytime phone: 410-744-4324 (M-F EST) messages okay

"If you really want the information and HR is playing hard to get, request it under the Privacy Act. Ask HR who and where to send your request. (Remember though that this may cost you—If the HR staff knows that you have written for Freedom of Information Act (FOIA) information, they may not be as considerate with your application in the future.)"

Faxing the HR Representative

If there is a phone, but the voicemail seems really distant or the mailbox is totally full, why don't you try a fax? Here's a recommended fax format. Type your fax in 24 to 28 point type—bold!

4/01/02

Re: Position of Writer-Editor, Announcement, 20202

Closing date of 12/23/02

Applicant: Kathryn Troutman, SSN 222-22-2222

Attention: Rita Chambers, Personnel Staffing Specialist

Dear Ms. Chambers:

I'd like to know the status of the above announcement. Could you please call me and leave a voicemail message or speak with me? I am available at 410-744-4324, Mon-Fri, EST.

I'd like to know if I was found qualified and if the recruitment is still being considered. Thank you for your time. I am very interested in this position and I believe I am well qualified.

Thanks, Kathryn Troutman

WRITING A CONGRESSIONAL LETTER UNDER THE FREEDOM OF INFORMATION ACT

If all else fails, write a Congressional letter or find the Freedom of Information Act Office in the agency. Write for the information you want. The government offices call these letters *Congressionals*. Government offices have a special staff who answer Congressionals on a timely basis.

Here's a suggested letter to your Congressperson or Senator:

Kathryn Troutman
89 Mellor Ave.
Baltimore, MD 21228
(410) 744-4324

Sept. 20, 2002

Re: Job application submission, July 20, 2002
Federal Aviation Administration, Transportation Security Office
Announcement No. 20202, Writer-Editor, GS-301-12

Honorable _____
Hart Office Building, Room _____
Washington, DC 20006

Dear Honorable _____,

I would like your assistance in gaining information concerning my application for the position of Writer-Editor with the FAA, TSO listed above.

There is no name or telephone number listed on the job announcement, so I did not know who to contact. It has been four months since I submitted my application. I have not heard one word from the hiring agency. I would have contacted personnel, but there was no number or name to contact.

I believe that I am qualified for the position. I would like to know if the position is still being considered and if I was found qualified. If I was not found qualified, I would like to find out why.

I would like to work for the Federal government where I can be part of providing service to the American public in the area of communications and public affairs/public relations.

I can be reached at the above address or at 410-744-4324, M-F 9 to 5 EST. I appreciate your assistance. I am working hard to obtain a Federal position. Thank you for your help.

Sincerely,

Kathryn Troutman
Currently unemployed, seeking a Federal job

PEOPLE WITH STATUS AND SPECIAL HIRING AUTHORITIES — MAKE YOUR LETTERS STAND OUT!

If you have special hiring authority, when you are writing to the personnel office or your Congressional office, be sure to tell them that you have some kind of special status. This can help them find your information and respond more quickly.

> PERSON WITH A DISABILITY – SCHEDULE A
>
> VETERAN WITH VRA PREFERENCE
>
> OUTSTANDING SCHOLAR

List this information in ALL CAPS right under your name. When you write letters or faxes, make the type as large as you an on the sheet. The congressional and government offices are busy and they appreciate BIG TYPE.

OPM has a new website for People with Disabilities. Learn about how to obtain a Schedule A Certificate, apply for jobs non-competitively through the Selective Placement Officials (a list of Federal employees' names and emails is on this page), and special accommodations services are on this page:

http://www.opm.gov/disability/

Personnel Myths and Truths

Myth: Personnel do not want phone calls from applicants.

Truth: The personnel staff don't mind phone calls; they're just very busy.

Myth: Personnel staff do not want to answer questions about announcements that have been cancelled or closed.

Truth: The personnel staff do not mind answering these questions about announcements, but closing an announcement is not their decision. It is out of their control.

Myth: Personnel staff can't understand most resumes and applications because they do not have subject-matter expertise in your area.

Truth: The personnel staff can understand the subject of the application if you write your resume so that it includes language from the announcement. They do need for you to make it readable and understandable to a non-technical person so that they can determine if you are basically qualified for the position.

Not selected? What's next?

If you received a letter saying you were found "qualified," that is all that you will get from the agency. More than likely, your consideration for the job stops here. To move into the next phase of the hiring process, that is, to get an interview, you must have been rated "best qualified" for the job. Meaning that, based on the review of your knowledge, skills, and abilities, you were rated one of the best from among the group of applicants who were found qualified for the job.

Again, you need to talk to the personnel staffing specialist who reviewed your resume and KSAs. You need to know why you were not qualified (or not "best qualified"). If you don't find out, how will you know what to change for the next announcement? It is difficult to get the personnelist on the phone looking at your announcement, but if you can persevere to get someone on the phone, it would help you tremendously. They are very informative and it could be a simple explanation. Here are a few of the basic reasons your application could be found "not qualified" when in fact you are qualified:

> "I received a letter saying I am 'qualified' for a job I applied for. Now what?"

✪   They could not see your qualifications quickly in your resume.

✪   They could not see specific qualifications, such as one year of specialized experience.

✪   They could not see keywords from the announcement in your work experience descriptions.

Again, here is a telephone script you can use to call the personnel staff who handled the recruitment:

"Hello, I'm Kathryn Troutman. I received my letter that I was found not qualified for the position Writer-Editor, GS 301-12, Announcement No. 10101. I would like to request a few moments of your time so that I can know what I did not have in my application so that I would have been qualified for the position. I am intent on obtaining a Federal position as a Writer-Editor. I have the education and experience needed for the position. Please help me to understand why I was not selected. I appreciate your time very much. Thanks. I am available at 410-744-4324 during the days, Monday through Friday, 9-5, EST."

AUTOMATION AND KNOWING THE RESULTS OF YOUR APPLICATIONS

When a computer rates and ranks your application, it's going to be difficult to get human feedback on what's wrong with your resume when you are not found qualified for a position for which you are qualified. There's going to be some mystery.

The U.S. Army has an excellent system where you can find out what activity has occurred with your online resume in the database. You can go to a program called ROARS (http://cpolrhp.army.mil/swr/swhome/ResumixROAR/ewRes.asp) and SOARS (https://pacific-cpoc.ak.pac.army.mil/resumix/soars.pl) and see your resume online. You can also see how many times your resume has been "pulled" for an announcement. You can also see if your resume has not been touched in a long time. And you may know that there were jobs (for which you may have "self-nominated") that you should have been "pulled" for. The ROARS and SOARS systems are excellent. But if your resume is not working and is not being found in the database, you should know that either your resume does not have the right skills and keywords, or the supplemental data sheet has errors in it so that you are not being considered for the right occupational series or grade.

The U.S. Navy has their resume tracker system.

The Air Force has a new system as well—check out their Web site.

The U.S. EPA is using automation for their recruitment and selection, but these announcements have a contact person and phone. So you could call them and find out the results of particular announcements.

The USA Staffing (OPM) announcements might have a contact person, but they might not. According to Richard W. Whitford, Acting Associate Director of Employment Information, they are striving to add a contact name and telephone to all announcements. So these OPM announcements will probably have a contact very soon.

All of the agencies are different in terms of their application management.

Most automated systems include an application tracking system for applicants to check the status of their applications.

Resumix Job Search and Follow-up Applicant Challenge:

"The problem occurring right now with Federal employment is
that the only job for which you may apply (in many cases) is an
"Open Continuous" position in your field. This means that there are not
necessarily any vacancies; rather, they are accumulating resumes so that
when a vacancy does occur, they already have a pool from which to
generate a list. Consequently, when you apply on an "Open
Continuous" position, you receive a postcard (or email notification)
stating your resume was received by whatever personnel office is
handling that region. For example, I am applying on GS-1101 and
GS-1102 positions in the Corpus Christi area. That means if I am
interested in working for the Army, I had to apply to the West CPOC,
or for the Navy, I had to apply to the HRSC Southwest, and for some
other job, to a personnel office in the Southeast (even though my intent
is to go to Corpus Christi). It's confusing at best. I have applied both
electronically and hard copy and I'm not sure if that's going to confuse
things or not, but I just wanted to make sure they have it on file!

Regarding follow-up, I don't think there is any...at least with these
"Open Continuous" announcements. Rarely is a point of contact listed
and, if so, they have been of little help. For example, I was told that
Navy jobs in Corpus Christi in my field (contracting) are hired by
personnelists at Great Lakes in Chicago. I tried five different numbers
and couldn't get a human voice. Other times I've called and the
personnelists can't comprehend what I'm talking about (they are
especially unfamiliar with job announcements under USA Jobs). In my
experience over the last 6 months or so, only a Dept. of Agriculture
personnelist was helpful in answering questions. But follow-up?
Again, I don't know how it's possible."

"Some Resumix sites, such as the Defense Logistics
Agency (www.dla.gov) site, allow you to check on
the status of the announcement online. See if this
is available, as you can check as often as you like
without having to contact HR. Just remember the
announcement number and the site will tell you if it is
still open, if a selection has been made, if it has been
cancelled, and so forth."

PART V SUMMARY

Helping you understand the vacancy announcement "how to apply" instructions is the complex task of Step 8. The more you read the announcement instructions, the more familiar you will become with the system, and the more the Federal government needs an employee like you!

The question posed by Step 9 is: Is there hope for customer services and follow-up? Yes, there's hope. Every time I have reached a Human Resources representative by phone, he or she has been helpful and efficient. The big challenge is to find the names and phone numbers of these contacts. Follow the instructions in this chapter and you should find some success with your follow-up. Again, be patient and keep applying for jobs. You will come to understand it better after a few applications. Good luck with your applications.

INTERVIEW

INTERVIEW

INTERVIEW SUCCESS STORY:

"I was hired into a new GS-14 position recently, and my experience with a Federal hiring panel was intense and surprising. First, I learned that I made it into the top 12 out of 150 applicants by my Federal resume alone! I was scheduled for a panel interview consisting of six people. Five weeks later, I learned that I was one of four contenders for the position, and another panel interview was scheduled consisting of two people. I subsequently learned that I was one of two contenders for the position, and luckily I was selected! I was hired into an exciting GS-14 position with supervisory responsibilities in my field. Tips: (1) Prepare by brushing up on interviewing techniques to successfully win the job. (2) Be yourself during the interview; you cannot be someone you are not. (3) If you don't know the answer to a question, admit it; don't try to bluff your way through. (4) If you find you are working too hard in the interview, perhaps the job was not intended for you, so relax and enjoy the experience!"

The entire application and selection process is tedious enough without having to worry about yet another hurdle to make it through before you are made a job offer. But there is another hurdle, and it is called "The Interview."

After your package has been rated against the other applicants' packages and you are determined eligible based on your work experience and education, you are then ranked against other eligible applicants to assess whether you are "best qualified." Only those applicants who make the best qualified list are forwarded on to the Selecting Official, who then selects the individual for the job. Interviews are coordinated and often conducted by the Selecting Official, but interviews are optional. Many agencies do, however, opt to conduct interviews, because in addition to the paperwork that has been submitted, interviews enable the Selecting Official, and others involved with the open position, to get to know the candidates and determine who will be the person best suited for the job. An interview is an opportunity for the department to learn more about your background, competencies, knowledge, skills, and abilities (KSAs), interests, and personality. It is also a time for you to learn more about the organization you may work for, the position you may be in, and the individuals you may work with. It is your only chance to truly assess whether this is the work you want to do, if it is a culture you can acclimate nicely to, and if the job aligns well with your values and professional goals.

INTERVIEW

FOR A

FEDERAL JOB

In the Federal environment, interviews can vary from agency to agency and department to department. There is no official "interview process." Because of this, it is often difficult to know what to anticipate. The only thing we know for sure is that if you are selected for an interview, you will do better if you are prepared and if you have practiced.

Over the years, interviews have taken many different forms—in both who conducts the interview (the type of interview) and how the interview is conducted (the interview format). The Federal government, as well as private industry, has adopted various interview fads, only to drop them and do something else that is currently "the best way to interview." Regardless, there have been several trends that have been incorporated into common interview practice. That is what we will focus on in this step.

"How do I improve my interviewing skills? I've made it through the interview, and not been selected. Help!"

- GS-9 Clerk

Before we discuss the types of interviews you may encounter, or the different interview formats, it is important to realize how much the interviews can vary from job to job.

First, the experience and preparation of the interviewer can affect your interviewing experience. Few interviewers have been through formal interview training. Many of them are handed a sheet of questions to ask without much time to prepare. Some have had little time to look at your application materials before you arrive. This is not to say that there aren't good interviewers out there. There are. There are some individuals who have helped design the interview questions, who have conducted numerous interviews prior to yours, and who are keenly familiar with the requirements or competencies that the candidate must possess. However, the majority of interviewers do not fall into that category.

While it may be unnerving to feel as though you are about to be assessed by someone who has not had much experience making such important (to you) decisions, it should also be helpful to know that the interviewer is often as nervous about the interview as you are. It puts you on more equal ground. As we stated earlier, the interview is an opportunity for you to interview them as much as it is for them to interview you.

Now you can go into the interview feeling a bit more confident that you will not be the only person who is anxious. This should enable you to take a couple of deep breaths and be more relaxed. The more relaxed you are, in addition to being prepared, the better you will do during the interview.

Another way interviews can vary from job to job has to do with whether the supervisor or Selecting Official already has a candidate in mind for the position. There is often no way of knowing if this is the case. Agencies must post open positions, even when they have someone they want to fill it. The best way to handle situations such as these is to consider yourself successful when you make the best-qualified list and are asked in for an interview. Always presume that you have a shot at the job because according to Issues of Merit (August 2001, U.S. Merit Systems Protection Board), "even when supervisors initially have someone else in mind for the job, many do consider other applicants. In fact, (according to our survey) 20 percent of the time supervisors ended up selecting someone other than the person they initially had in mind."

Regardless of what the outcome may be, use every interview as an opportunity to gain more experience—practice makes perfect—and always feel confident in your ability to have gotten so far along in the process. Keep in mind that making it to the interview stage for one position is a good sign that you will be selected for interviews for other positions in the future.

Now that we know there is no such thing as an across-the-board interview, let's look at the different types of interviews you can encounter.

TELEPHONE INTERVIEW

The telephone interview typically falls under the category of a pre-screening interview. If the best-qualified pool is large, calls are often made to those candidates in an effort to determine who should be selected to be invited for an onsite or more formal interview. This may also be called a pre-employment interview. An appointment is usually made for this sort of an interview, so you should have time to be prepared. The questions asked are more general in nature, relating to your experience and qualifications listed in your application package.

During a telephone interview, you can have notes in front of you to help you with your responses. Just do not rely too heavily on the notes— you do not want to sound as though you are reading from a script.

Remember, the Selecting Official is mainly interested in determining whether you should be invited to further participate in the process.

The Challenge of the Telephone Interview

When faced with a screening telephone interview, what's the best way to make it to the next interview level? I asked this question of Nick Corcodilos, author of *Ask the Headhunter: Reinventing the Interview to Win the Job* (Plume, 1997) and www.asktheheadhunter.com. His answer follows:

Don't wait for the screening call—strike first. Remember that all the clever telephone repartee in the world is irrelevant if you can't suggest how you're going to make the employer more successful when he hires you. So, you need to be armed. While you should do your own research, you can also gather crucial information from the employer directly. Once your screening call is scheduled, call the office in advance and speak to an administrative staff person or other office professional. Here's what to say: "I will be doing a telephone screening with Ms. Jones by phone next Monday and I'd like to ask a few questions, if you have a couple of minutes. I have researched your agency and office through your website so I am familiar with your mission, but can you tell me what specific problems and challenges are in your office? Are there new programs or initiatives that I should be aware of? Who are your customers that you work with most? Thanks so much for your time, I hope to have a very successful telephone interview.

Get dressed nicely for the Telephone Interview; be prepared, relaxed and confident. Have your resume and the announcement in front of you. Create your skills and accomplishments list. Be seated at a big table. No noise in the room. Feel good about yourself. Get ready to talk.

Is that aggressive? No, it's assertive and it's pure common sense. Without this crucial information, all you know is the title and the basic functions of the job. What does the manager need you to pull off if he or she hires you? Remember you're competing with other candidates who could have the answer! While you're going into the phone screening interview blind, another candidate will know all the details about what the manager needs.

Once you know the problems and challenges behind the job, sit down and prepare a short "business plan" to show how you will tackle those problems and meet the challenges. A good manager will recognize you as an exceptional candidate who takes his or her work seriously. A phone screening need not be a dopey chat; it can be a compelling business discussion that instantly makes you the leading candidate for the job.

"I have done one-on-one, behavioral, and a variety of panel interviews—including only one speaker and two observers that did not say anything. Several where there was a panel that made the first cut, and if you were one of the three finalists, the second was a one-on-one."

- Federal employee who went through 23–25 interviews when applying for GS-14 promotional opportunities

INDIVIDUAL/ONE-ON-ONE INTERVIEW

If you are still in the running after the telephone interview, you will most likely be invited in for a face-to-face interview with the Selecting Official and/or other members of the staff or Selection Panel. In a few cases, especially when a candidate or an interviewer is unable to attend the face-to-face interview, a more formal interview can be conducted by telephone. If there has been no pre-screening interview, the face-to-face interview will be the first step in your interview process. The face-to-face interview can either be individual/one-on-one or group/panel. Often, you may be called in for a preliminary interview (either individual or group), then be invited back for another (or multiple) interviews with the Selecting Official, staff members, and/or members of the Selection Committee who will then meet and make a decision regarding your qualifications.

An individual/one-on-one interview occurs when you meet directly with the Selecting Official or another individual in the position to help make a hiring decision. This type of interview intimidates some candidates. It is often an across-the-desk, question-and-answer format. However, in recent years more interviewers have opted to make the experience more comfortable and may have each of you sit in chairs on the same side of the desk and make the dialogue more conversational. This all will depend on who is conducting the interview.

GROUP/PANEL INTERVIEW

The third type of interview is the group/panel interview. Here, you are interviewed by two or more interviewers who are either directly related to the position (supervisor, co-workers, subordinates), members of the department, and/or members of the Selection Committee. Usually each member of the panel has questions to ask, but there have been interviews where only one person has done the asking, and the others involved are there simply to observe. One suggestion in this type of interview is, if given a choice, try to get a seat at the end of the table so you can make eye contact with more of the panel members.

Informational Interview

One type of interview that hasn't been mentioned, and that you may have heard of, is the informational interview. This interview does not have much to do with the hiring process, which is why it has not been addressed until now. The informational interview is one that you can conduct in preparation for your job search to determine what agency, department, or position may be best for you.

INTERVIEW FORMATS

In addition to different types of interviews, the interviews themselves can have various formats. The way an interview is conducted can be different from interview to interview. Some interviewers use traditional questions, some prefer behavior-based questions or situational interview questions, others opt for difficult and negative questions, while still more like to use competency-based questions. Again, the format, like everything else we've learned so far, depends on who is conducting the interview. Most likely, each interview you have will contain some of each of the question formats that follow:

✪ **Traditional Questions.** The standard interview questions that ask what you may do in a given situation. These questions are more hypothetical and allow you to give best-case answers; they concentrate little on your actual experience.

✪ **Behavior-Based Questions.** These questions are based on the assumption that past experience and performance can predict future experience and performance. Questions are designed to have you respond to how you have handled situations in the past. These questions require you to draw on your experiences and give examples.

The most common way managers gain additional information about job candidates is through interviews, which may be either structured or unstructured.

E xcerpt from a recent Federal job posting:

"File your application by the vacancy announcement closing date and meet all the application criteria and conditions of employment (e.g., submit all required documentation, **Pre-employment Interview, Panel Interview**, Physical, Reference Checking, etc.)."

✪ **Situational Interview Questions.** Similar to the behavior-based questions, these questions are not so much questions as they are scenarios or situations you could encounter in the new job. The interviewer is looking for how you would react and respond to these situations.

✪ **Difficult/Negative Questions.** These questions put you on the spot. They can be designed to increase your level of stress to see how you will respond. The questions themselves should be answered by giving the most positive responses you can and by showing ways you are trying to improve.

✪ **Competency-Based Questions.** Many agencies have made their entire application and selection process competency-based. This means that certain competencies have been determined necessary for a candidate to possess if he/she is to be deemed qualified for the position. In the interview, questions are designed based on these competencies to determine whether the candidate's competencies match those required for the job.

✪ **Illegal Questions.** Not mentioned as a possible format, these are questions that should not be asked and do not need to be answered. Interviewers should not ask any questions regarding race, gender, religion, marital status, sexual orientation, or national origin.

A couple of other things to expect when you go on an interview include:

✪ EEO (Equal Employment Opportunity) involvement

✪ Rating systems

In order to keep everything running smoothly and fairly, and to decrease the possibility of any grievances, an EEO representative is usually, but not always, present during an interview. The EEO representative ensures there is consistency with the questions asked and the length of the interview. The EEO representative also ensures that no illegal questions are asked. The presence of a third-party observer is to try to make sure each candidate is treated equally throughout the interview process.

Many agencies also use rating systems during the interview process. A rating system is a means for the Selection Committee to measure one candidate against another based upon pre-formulated measures or scales. When rating systems are used, interviewers typically have a sheet, or scorecard, to use during the interview to rate the candidates' responses to the questions asked. At the end, the candidates can be compared, based upon their scores.

Preparing for an interview

Now that we have a better idea of what to expect going into the process, let's focus on how you can become prepared to be successful during the interview. As we mentioned before, and will again and again, preparation and practice are the keys to success. The best way to go into the interview prepared is to:

1. Know the paperwork.
2. Research.
3. Practice.
4. Make a sales pitch.

To **know the paperwork** means more than simply being familiar with the announcement and having your package together. It means knowing and understanding the Position Description (PD), the critical elements of the position, and the KSAs. It also means being familiar with the paperwork you have submitted detailing your professional experience and background. You may recall that we mentioned earlier how not all interviewers have had a chance to read through all of your application materials. It will be up to you to be familiar enough with what is in your package to bring certain items to the interviewer's attention if it is necessary. Finally, knowing the paperwork means knowing why you are the person for the job, and being able to sell yourself.

After reviewing all of the paperwork, it is essential that you **do the necessary research** to go into the interview fully prepared. Most of this research should be done prior to applying for the position, but it is important now nonetheless. If you haven't taken the time to learn about the position or the department, you are going to need to learn more for the interview. This means you need to read, read, read, and ask a lot of questions. The best ways to do this are to get copies of the PD, critical elements, and KSAs, then go beyond job description. Go online and find out what you can about the agency, department, and position. Talk to people you know who can give you a better insight as to what the job is all about, and what competencies, knowledge, skills, and abilities are necessary to succeed. You are looking for ways you can sell yourself and your skills during the interview. The more you know, the better prepared you can be.

By **practicing for each interview**, you will allow yourself an opportunity to work through your weaknesses and develop ways to more successfully sell your knowledge, skills, and abilities. Through practice, you can find ways to set yourself apart from the other candidates. You can practice in front of a mirror; into a tape recorder; in front of a video camera; with a family member, co-worker, or friend; or by participating in a mock interview.

Successful panel interview strategy for a first-time Federal job applicant:

"First, before I went to the interviews, I thought about what I could offer to the prospective employer, with an emphasis on my strengths and accomplishments. I planned to use these as my themes for the interviews. I reviewed the strengths and accomplishments that were reflected in my resume. Bear in mind, my resume, which was prepared by The Resume Place, clearly set forth accomplishments in very specific terms.

Second, once I got into the interview, I tried to be sure to cover the themes when appropriate to the questions or discussion during the interviews. I planned to mention each accomplishment somehow in response to a question. Also, my referral to the themes included mentioning that I had covered them in my resume. I did this so that the interviewers could refer back to my resume."

Continued on next page

Continued from previous page

"Third, both before the interview and during it I tried to learn something about the interviewers and the work they were doing. Then I tried to show some commonality between us, either by something I had done that they had done also, or by someone I knew that they knew or an organization that we both belonged to.

Fourth, I tried to involve each of the interviewers in my response, by eye contact, body language, and asking them each at least one question when given the opportunity to do so."

Finally, you will need to **sell yourself**. An interview is a sales pitch and you are marketing a great product—you! Often people are too modest and are not used to talking about themselves in positive, not boastful, ways. But during an interview, you have to talk about what you've done well. You need to demonstrate your speaking skills as well as your listening skills, and you will need to provide accomplishment-driven examples. Your specific experiences and accomplishments will set you apart from your competition, and you will need to be able to tell stories and talk about what you have done. With examples, you can prove you have what it takes to be the best candidate for the position.

NON-VERBAL COMMUNICATION

Before we begin describing what you can anticipate in an actual interview, it is important to first emphasize the unspoken, that is, the non-verbals. A lot of time will no doubt be spent preparing for how you will answer questions and how you will sell your skills and experience. But before that even begins, first impressions have already been made based upon how you entered the room, whether or not you made eye contact, and how you presented yourself through your dress, habits, and mannerisms. Needless to say, non-verbals can significantly influence the interview. Here are some non-verbal pointers to keep in mind:

- **Entrance.** Exude confidence.

- **Handshake.** Should be firm, but not too aggressive.

- **Personal grooming.** Clean, neat, professional dress, and do not overdo make-up, cologne/perfume, or jewelry.

- **Tone of voice and volume.** You want to sound interested (with inflection), no monotone; but don't be too boisterous, overbearing, or funny.

- **Eye contact.** Maintain eye contact with the person you are speaking to. During a panel interview, look at the person who is asking the question. It is acceptable to look up while you are thinking, or to look around at each of the interviewers, but you want to avoid staring off into space, keeping someone in a deadlock stare, or constantly moving your eyes from person to person like you are at a tennis match.

- **Enthusiasm.** Act like this is the job for you. No one wants to hire someone who isn't excited about the opportunity. Just do not come across as over-zealous.

- ✪ **Posture/body language.** Do not slump back in the chair. Do not get too comfortable because this can suggest boredom or lack of interest. However, do not seem too eager, whether by sitting on the edge of your chair or invading someone's personal space.

- ✪ **Nervous habits** (fidgeting, repeating the phrases umm and ahhh while you speak, shaking your leg, playing with a pen or paper, taking your glasses on and off, etc.). We all have nervous habits. During an interview your goal should be to minimize yours. That is why practice is so important—to help you identify what your nervous habits are. Identification is the first step to eliminating the habit. For example, if you find that you play with items in front of you, do not have them there during the interview.

- ✪ **Smile.** Again, you want to be as positive as you can throughout the entire interview.

As with many things, when it comes to non-verbals during an interview, balance is the key.

PARTS OF THE INTERVIEW

During the actual interview, you can anticipate spending between 30 minutes and one hour with the interviewer or panel. Some interviews are shorter; others can be as long as several hours to a full day. Often, you will be told in advance how long the interview should be. The interview typically begins with introductions and an explanation of the position, moves into a question-and-answer session where you are asked a majority of the questions, and ends with an opportunity for you to ask some questions about the position. Let's take a closer look.

Opening

This is your opportunity to make a good first impression— first impressions do count, and the first two minutes of the interview are critical. They will make the interviewer decide if he/she wants to keep paying attention to what you have to say. A good deal of small talk typically occurs during this time as you and the interviewer(s) get to know each other. Again, you will be given some background about the position, and this is often when you will be asked the first question, something usually along the lines of "Tell me about yourself."

"Basically, I was not concerned with the questions. Rather, my focus was on trying to get across the few basic themes that I had in mind about why I should be hired and working them into as many responses as possible, with emphasis on why my qualifications met the needs of this employer."

- Panel interview participant

235

Body

As you move into the body of the interview, you will be asked a number of questions (traditional, behavior-based, situational, difficult, competency-based, etc.) that will help the interviewer(s) determine your KSAs, competencies, and experience in relation to what the agency is seeking for the position at hand. (We will take a look at sample questions later in the step.)

In general, when responding to questions, you always want to provide examples demonstrating your KSAs and competencies. Your specific experiences and examples will set you apart from the competition, and your ability to effectively articulate how you are the best candidate for the position can make all the difference in whether you receive an offer for the position. In other words, you want to be able to show them, not just tell them, why you are qualified.

Confidence in describing increasingly more responsible and complex assignments and experiences translates into good marks on the interviewer's "scorecard," used to compare the candidates. If the interviewer has to pull information from the candidate, the resulting impression is weak.

Closing

At the end of the interview, you will be given an opportunity to ask questions or bring up any selling points that were not discussed during the interview. Take advantage of this opportunity.

You should go into the interview prepared to ask questions at the end, or during the body of the interview if the opportunity presents itself. It is acceptable to have pen and paper with you to jot down questions that may come up during the interview or to have questions prepared before you come in; however, do not rely on these notes or read them verbatim—simply use them as reminders. Refer to the Sample Questions in this step for examples of questions you can ask the interviewer.

If at the end of the interview you feel you haven't had the opportunity to elaborate on a particular experience, explain a relevant skill, or demonstrate a specific expertise, now is the time to do it. If you have a portfolio with examples of work you've done, you may bring it to the interviewer's attention at this point if you haven't already. Do not take up too much time; it is, after all, the end of the interview. Nevertheless, do not miss an opportunity to sell yourself for the position.

Once you have asked your questions, and made any extra points, do not forget to thank the interviewer for his/her time and reiterate once again your qualifications for the position. This will enable you to leave on a high note—summarizing your qualifications one last time so the interviewer(s) will remember at the end of the interview why you should be the candidate hired for the position. You may also ask when you should hear back from them and let them know you will be looking forward to that.

In addition to the basic set-up of the interview, there are some interview essentials that should be mentioned:

- ✪ Concentrate on what qualifies you for the position and sell your qualifications in every response you give during the interview. Always bring the interviewer back to the competencies, KSAs, experience, and education you have that make you the best candidate for the position.

- ✪ Always sell YOURself and why YOU are qualified. Concentrate on YOU in your examples and stories, not co-workers, team members, or supervisors.

- ✪ Think first, then respond. It is okay to take a moment to pause. If you feel uncomfortable with the silence, tell the interviewer(s), "That's a good question," to buy yourself some thinking time. Only say that once.

- ✪ Keep your responses job-related. You may recall that there are illegal questions, questions the interviewer cannot ask. It is up to you whether you volunteer personal information.

- ✪ Be accomplishment-oriented. Talk about the results you have generated—qualitative or quantitative.

- ✪ Tell stories. Give examples as often as you can to demonstrate your qualifications.

- ✪ Answer the question. Be thorough, but no need to ramble— you may go off on a tangent that distracts from the interview. Let the interviewer ask you to expand if he/she wants to hear more.

- ✪ Be specific—avoid generalizations. Interviews are limited so you want to provide your best response in a clear, concise manner.

- ✪ Ask for clarification when needed. Better to have the question repeated than to give a poor response.

- ✪ Avoid criticizing others. The interview should demonstrate your strengths, not focus on others' weaknesses. In this same vein, remain as positive as you can in all of your responses.

"Today, in addition to presenting their experience and education, applicants need to be able to talk about the competencies they possess for the position. More and more vacancy announcements are written in terms of competencies. If so, the candidates should be able to describe how they have acquired and demonstrated the competencies for the field/ position. It is worth doing some research in advance for the competencies generally sought for the field/occupation generally if they are not included in the job posting. The candidate should show clearly that he/she possesses the competencies through behavioral examples. It is also important to be able to talk about where the individual sees the field/occupation going in the future and how he/she stays abreast of technical and managerial competencies for a changing and dynamic environment. This puts the candidate more in the business-oriented frame of mind rather than that of just a job-seeker."

- Former Federal personnel administrator

✪ If some volunteer work you have done (at work, in the community) demonstrates a specific skill, use that experience as an example. You are looking for the best way to show you are qualified for the position. Sometimes that means you will go beyond your professional experiences to draw on other relevant examples.

✪ Be honest. Too much embellishing of one's experience/education, or falsifying, is a serious mistake and will have negative consequences. Do you recall how the Georgia Tech football coach who recently got the job at Notre Dame lost it immediately for having falsified his college record of 20 years earlier? In the Federal sector, falsifying an application is taken very seriously and often results in dismissal.

SAMPLE QUESTIONS

As mentioned before, many interviewers use various question formats during an interview. The best preparation is to practice responding to as many questions as possible. Take a look at your package and try coming up with some questions about your own background and experience that you could practice responding to. Try to anticipate what the interviewer could ask you about the specific position and practice responding to those questions as well. It's true, you can over-prepare in the sense that you have certain responses memorized, killing any possibility of spontaneity during the interview and often sounding like you have a canned response. But you can never practice responding to too many questions. So practice, practice, practice!

Traditional

"Tell me about yourself." (An all-inclusive question. Can also take the form of "Why should I hire you?" or "What about this job interested you?" Keep this response job-related and refer to your KSAs and competencies. Use this opportunity to package your skills. Give a two-minute commercial selling yourself for the position.)

"Are you a hard worker?"

"What are your strengths?"

"Where do you see yourself in five years?"

Behavior-Based

"Describe a situation in which you demonstrated an effective customer service skill."

"Tell me about a time when you developed a training program and presented it to a group."

"Describe a time when you recognized a problem as an opportunity."

"Describe your management style when dealing with staff or coworkers."

Situational — These questions are typically designed based on the specifics of the position.

"We are always looking for new ideas to increase productivity, improve morale, reduce costs. Tell me about an idea you have that could yield positive results."

"If you were to go in and find a center not running as efficiently as you expect it could, what would you do?"

"You find you double scheduled your manager for two appointments at the same time. How do you handle the error an hour before the appointments?"

Difficult/Negative — Remember, you want to keep your responses as positive as possible and always describe how you are improving.

"Describe a time when your work performance was poor."

"What are your weaknesses?" (List only one. Let the interviewer ask for more.)

"Tell me about a time when your work was criticized."

"Describe a difficult problem you've had to deal with." (Best to keep these work-related—i.e., not personal)

Competency-Based

Problem Solving: "Give me an example of a time when you had to develop a new solution to an old problem."

Team Work: "Describe a time when you used your teambuilding skills to gain buy-in for a project or idea."

Communication: "Describe a time when you had to communicate under difficult circumstances, either verbally or in writing."

Unanswerable

If you are asked an unanswerable question, the best thing to do is to be honest. Refocus on something you can do and demonstrate how you can meet the position's specific needs, regardless.

Questions to Ask the Interviewer

The questions you want to ask the interviewer should be ones you are truly interested in getting answers to. Asking a question for the sake of asking is a waste of his/her time and yours. You will want to limit the number of questions you ask at the end of the interview to no more than four. However, that does not mean you shouldn't ask questions during the interview. If you are interested in something the interviewer talks about during the interview, ask about it. Questions encourage dialogue, and dialogue can make the interview more conversational and more comfortable. Again, don't overdo it. The questions you ask should help you determine whether or not this is the right job for you.

In order to prepare questions in advance, take a look at the PD and KSAs—is there anything you would like the interviewer to explain or elaborate upon? See if you have generated any questions from the research you have done. Be careful that you don't ask questions that you should already know the answer to (something listed in the PD, for example). Here are a few general examples:

- ✪ "What is the most important contribution you'd like to see made in this position in the next two months?"
- ✪ "Are there opportunities for creativity and problem-solving skills to be put to use?"
- ✪ "Beyond the job description, what are the expectations of this position?"

INTERVIEW AFTERMATH

Once the interview has concluded and you have reiterated your selling points and thanked them for their time, make sure you leave as confidently as you entered. The interview lasts beyond the final questions or comments because the interviewer(s) is watching you until you leave the room.

Within the following day or two after the interview, you should send a formal thank you letter or note to the interviewer(s). It is recommended that you send thank yous to all of the interviewers. This may mean that you will need to ask for business cards at the end of the interview, or call your contact at the agency who set up your interview to get names and titles of the interviewers. It is up to you whether you write or type the thank you. Typed ones are easier because you can cut and paste information, but written notes can seem more personal. The best advice we can give here is to stay away from making the thank you sound like

"I have just completed a five-year Telecom and IT build project. My thinking is that with a brand new agency and lots of telecom and information technology that the government needs to do to be able to 'connect the dots,' whether I shouldn't at least try to see if there is a fit. My greatest concern is the way it works. I fear I am too used to the quick and responsive environment that is characteristic to private sector work."

a form letter. Try your best to throw in something specific about the position, or even a conversation you had during the interview. Also, always use the thank you as an opportunity to sell yourself, one last time, for the position.

At this point, you've done all you can do and now it's time to wait. If the opportunity presents itself, keep interviewing for other positions—nothing is a done deal until you've accepted the offer and started the job. And remember, practice makes perfect; the more you interview, the better you'll do in successive interviews.

PART VI SUMMARY

The key to successful interviewing is to be prepared—know your paperwork, do your research, know what to expect, review the interview essentials in this step, and practice answering questions to assess your verbal and non-verbal responses. Practice, practice, practice.

Good luck!

" With an outstanding federal resume, electronic resume and KSAs, you can help the government 'connect the dots'. You can also contribute toward increasing the responsiveness of government through your ideas and service. Good luck with your application."

Kathryn Troutman

APPENDIX

GLOSSARY

Application express: A name given to an electronic application system.

AVUE™: This system is similar to Quickhire, except that the AVUE questionnaire includes open-ended questions. Because the AVUE system could also be used to classify jobs, the duties and the KSAs used in the announcement flow from the job description or the classification portion of the action.

Best Qualified (BQ List): Qualified applicants who scored high and were referred to the selecting official for selection. (NOTE: The "BQ list" refers to the list of applicants referred for selection as a result of an internal merit promotion action. The "List of Eligibles" refers to the list of applicants referred for selection as a result of competitive examining.)

Competitive examining: The process used to fill civil service positions with candidates applying from outside the Federal workforce. This process requires the application of veterans preference, the rule of three (which means selecting officials can only select from among the top three candidates), pass-over and objection procedures (which means if the selecting official wants to hire a non-veteran over a veteran with a higher score, the selecting official must justify passing over the veteran and be approved by OPM), and full public notice (posting the job in USAJOBS).

Delegated examining unit: It is the unit within the human resources office responsible for conducting competitive examining. OPM has the statutory authority to conduct competitive examining, but may delegate this authority to agencies. (See also competitive examining.)

Eligibles: List of applicants who met the qualification requirements for a specific vacancy announcement.

External applicant: An applicant who has not worked for the Federal Government or held a permanent appointment in the competitive service.

Internal applicant: An applicant who is a current or former Federal employee who has held a permanent appointment in the competitive service.

Inventory-building announcements: Much like the open-continuous announcement. Applicants may apply at any time during the time the announcement is open for receipt of application. Applications may have a limited shelf-life, like three or six months after receipt.

KSAs: Acronym for Knowledge, Skills, and Abilities also referred to as Quality Ranking Factors. Knowledge (K) means the facts and data a person knows gained through education or training. Knowledge is the foundation upon which abilities and skills can be built. Skills (S) means the observable demonstration of proficiency to do a task, such as typing skills or driving skills. Ability (A) means the capability to perform a job function.

Merit promotions: The process used to fill job vacancies through competition open only to current or former Federal employees with competitive status. Merit promotion generally results in movement from a lower-graded job to a higher-graded job.

Non-status candidates: Are individuals who have never worked for the Federal government or held a permanent appointment in the competitive service. In short, these are applicants outside the Federal workforce.

Open continuously announcements: Vacancy announcements with or without a closing date. If it has a closing date, it generally is for an extended period, such as one year. Applicants may submit their application at any time and will be rated, ranked, and referred to selecting officials any time there is a vacancy. Applications are held active for the life of the announcement.

Open to anyone: This is a type of "Who May Apply." Internal/status and external/non-status applicants may apply.

Optional Form OF 612: This is the optional application form for Federal employment. To obtain a copy of the form, go to http://www.usajobs.opm.gov/EI25.htm. It is available in TXT, DOC, and PDF formats.

Person with special appointment eligibility: These are people who could be appointed into a competitive position without going through the competitive examining process. Examples of special noncompetitive appointing authorities include the Veterans' Readjustment Appointment (VRA), the special authority for 30% or more disabled veterans, and the Peace Corps.

Qualifications questionnaires: This is the term used by the automated system described above for the questionnaire portion of the system.

Qualified: Applicants who meet minimum qualification requirements.

Quickhire™: This is also an automated staffing system. It is different from Resumix in that it requires applicants to respond to a series of questions to determine eligibility and qualification. Based on the answers provided, applicants are given a score, after which they are ranked in score order, from highest to lowest. Selecting officials may view the list of rated applicants on line. This system requires submission of an electronic resume and completion of the questionnaire online.

Rating and ranking: The process of identifying the best-qualified candidates from among the qualified candidates. The process generally involves the scoring of the candidates' education and experience against certain criteria listed as knowledge, skills, and abilities (KSA).

Reinstatement eligibility: The eligibility of former Federal employees to be re-employed by the Federal Government. Former employees who attained career status (had three years of Federal permanent employment in the competitive service) may be reinstated for life. Former employees who had less then three years of permanent employment may be reinstated within three years after leaving civil service.

Resume Builder: This is part of an automated staffing system where applicants may create their resume. Some systems may allow applicants to store their resume into the system for a limited period of time, but almost all systems enable applicants to submit their application directly from the builder. Depending on the system, the built-in resume builder is preferred because it formats the resume in accordance with the system's specifications.

Resumix™: An automated staffing system generally used by the Defense Department entities. It scans resumes for keywords (generally related to the job being filled), to determine whether the applicants have the necessary qualifications for the job. The system requires that the resume be submitted in a certain format and length. (A HotJobs.com company)

Self-nomination: Commonly used in Defense. Defense generally maintains inventory of resumes. When a position opens up, all applicants have to do is send a self-nomination by e-mail or FAX to be considered.

Standard Form (SF) 171: SF-171. This was the old application form for Federal employment. The SF-171 is obsolete and is generally no longer accepted by Federal agencies. The Office of Personnel Management no longer prints this form, but applicants may still use the format of the SF-171 for their application.

Status candidates: Are individuals who have held a permanent appointment in the competitive service and individuals eligible under special appointing authorities whose appointment affords them non-competitive eligibility in the competitive service. In short, these are applicants who are current or former Federal employees with permanent appointments.

Supp sheet: Same as supplemental data sheet.

Supplemental data sheet: This could mean different things. In Resumix, this is used to call the list of personal information (such as SSN, availability for travel, locations of interest, etc.) that must be attached to the resume. In others, this could mean the narrative describing related knowledge, skills, and abilities that must be attached to the application.

USAStaffing: An automated staffing system similar to Quickhire and Avue except that this system is marketed by OPM. Also, unlike Quickhire and Avue, USAStaffing offers applicants various methods of submitting resumes and answering the questionnaire. USAStaffing allows applicants to submit their application and questionnaire by mail or respond to the questionnaire by phone.

Who may apply: Listed in vacancy announcements and is the source from which the agency will consider for its vacancy. "Who May Apply" is also known as the "Area of Consideration." The sources in which an agency may consider could be as broad as "Any US Citizen," or as limited as current employees of the agency within the commuting area.

SAMPLE FEDERAL RESUMES AND KSAS

Medical Billing Associate Resume for Administrative Assistant, GS-301-09

Event Manager Trainee Resume for Administrative positions, GS-301-07/9

Sr. Information Systems Engineer Resume for Information Technology Specialist, GS-2201-13

Equipment Repair Resume for Equipment Specialist, WG-4749-10

Recent Graduate Resume for Criminal Investigator, GS-1811-07

Police Officer Resume for Civil Aviation Security Specialist, FV 1801-I

Recent MS/BS Graduate to Criminal Investigator, GS-1811-05/07

Peace Corps / Americorps Volunteer resume for Public Affairs Specialist, GS-1035-05/07

KSAs for an International Trade Specialist, GS-301-09

Samples in the book and on the CD-ROM are based on real people. They are fictionalized to ensure privacy. Information that is changed includes: name, address, phone, email, SSN, employer names, supervisor names and phones. The samples have been volunteered for this book by the Federal job applicant.

These samples and many more different resume samples are on the CD-ROM.

RAMONA ASKEW

3245 Pennsylvania Avenue, NW
Washington, DC 21228
(202) 555-0033
Ramona99@aol.com

Citizenship: United States of America
Social Security No.: 999-11-5555

Veteran's Status: N/A
Highest Civilian Grade: N/A

Objective:

Administrative Associate (GS-0301-09), Health and Human Services Administration, Health Resources and Services Administration, Rockville, MD, Announcement #WA-ID-6-0411.

Skills & Qualifications:

Administrative professional with 14 years experience managing medical office billings, client relations, records management, and office operations. Excellent people, skills, equally good at leading and serving on teams. Outstanding oral and written communication skills. Adept at identifying and solving problems. Proven track record for establishing and reaching goals. Technically proficient in Microsoft Word, Access, Excel, E-mail, and Internet. Typing speed 60 wpm.

Employment History:

MEDICAL BILLING ASSOCIATE
Maryland Family Practice
8000 Rockville Pike, Suite 900, Rockville, MD 20333
Supervisor: Ms. Sarah Pickering, you may contact at (301) 888-3333

October 2000 – Present
40 hours/week
Salary: $32,000/year

Administer step-by-step collections program for a busy cardiology practice. Track, handle, and follow up with late payments from insurers and patients. Bill secondary insurers. Identify and correct errors in billing and coding.

MEDICAL BILLING ASSOCIATE
Sports Medicine Associates
33 Broadway, Los Gatos, CA 95030
Supervisor: Ms. Connie Locke, you may contact at (408) 770-8333

April 1997 – July 2000
35 hours/week
Salary: $14/hour

Managed patient accounts for a large medical practice. Entered and tracked billing charges. Posted payments from patients and third-party sources. Followed up with problem accounts and collections. Responded to heavy volume of calls to and from patients and insurers. Generated and submitted itemized statements.

CONSULTANT
Recovery Care
4000 Connecticut Avenue, Bethesda, MD 20814

June 1994 – November 1998
8-10 hours/week
Salary: $15/hour

RAMONA ASKEW, SS# 999-11-5555

Supervisor: Ms. Anne Kelly, you may contact at (301) 953-8642

Provided support services on an as-needed basis for an organization that provides home health care, particularly for children with chronic diseases. Assisted in writing the organization's policy and procedure manual and job descriptions. Organized orientation programs and in-house training for LPNs, RNs, physical therapists, occupational therapists, speech therapists, CNAs, and home health aides.

MEDICAL RECEPTIONIST February 1993 – February 1997
Roger Williams, M.D. (Dermatology) 40 hours/week
50 Drake Street, Menlo Park, CA 90227 Salary: $12/hour
Supervisor: Dr. Roger Williams, you may contact at (650) 222-8844

Served as front desk receptionist for busy dermatology practice. Scheduled and confirmed patient appointments. Called pharmacies for patient prescriptions. Ordered supplies. Authorized patient insurance and followed up on problem accounts.

MEDICAL RECEPTIONIST January 1989 – January 1993
Kate Robinson, M.D. 40 hours/week
88 University Drive, Palo Alto, CA 94304 Salary: $11/hour
Supervisor: Dr. Kate Robinson, you may contact at (650) 555-8200

Performed front desk receptionist functions for busy obstetrics and gynecology practice. Handled heavy volume of incoming telephone calls. Scheduled and confirmed patient appointments. Called pharmacies for patient prescriptions. Authorized patient insurance.

INTERN, UNIVERSITY OF CALIFORNIA BERKELEY January 1988 – September 1988
Adult Day Care Centers (ADCC) 30 hours/week
Community Services, Inc., San Francisco, CA Salary: None

Served as an intern to Adult Day Care Centers. Reviewed delivery of quality health care services focusing studies on legislation, regulations, and policies affecting Adult Day Care Centers.

- **Studied trends.** Identified patterns in service delivery, quality management, and financial resource management.

- **Wrote portions of documents that supported funding.** Assisted in the writing and implementation of multiple grant proposals.

Education:

Bachelor of Arts, Psychology. University of Michigan, Ann Arbor, MI, 1990.

Diploma. Great Lakes High School, Highland, MI, 1985.

Event Manager Trainee transitioning to Staff Assistant-Officer
GG-0301-07/09, Defense Intelligence Agency, DoD

SAMANTHA GOLDMAN

111 South Caton Avenue
Baltimore, MD 21200
(410) 765-4321
SamanthaGoldman@hotmail.com

Social Security No.: 111-22-3333
Citizenship: United States of America

Veteran's Preference: N/A
Highest Federal Civilian Grade: N/A

OBJECTIVE:

Staff Assistant-Officer, Department of Defense, Defense Intelligence Agency, GG-0301-07/09.

PROFESSIONAL SUMMARY:

More than ten years experience in a variety of management, supervisory, sales, and customer service positions. Excellent skills in project management, research, organization, and communication. Demonstrated ability to solve problems and achieve results in high-stakes, high-pressure situations. Work extremely well with others and maintain a can-do attitude.

EDUCATION:

Bachelor of Arts, Political Science. Millersville University, Millersville, PA, 1995
Diploma. Lancaster Catholic High School, Lancaster, PA, 1991

EMPLOYMENT HISTORY:

EVENT MANAGER TRAINEE
Jackson Catering
60 Light Street, Baltimore, MD 21200
Supervisor: Susan Arnold, may contact at (410) 881-2468

March 2001 – Present
40 hours/week
Salary: $11/hour

Assist in managing all aspects of logistics, planning, and staffing for catering events.
- Act as primary customer contact for event design and preparation, ensuring company maintains professional image and excellent reputation.
- Create catering menus to meet customers' specific needs.
- Handle event logistics and event details.
- Accomplishment: implemented more effective method of documenting party information, resulting in increased operational efficiency.

CENTER MANAGER
Weight Busters
3000 New York Drive, Centreville, MD 21000
Supervisor: Melissa Stone, may contact at (410) 444-0090

August 2000 – November 2000
50+ hours/week
Salary: $350/week + bonus

Managed all aspects of creating and maintaining a successful weight loss center. Generated revenue, handled client issues, managed staff of four or more employees.
- Increased weekly sales by 41% in two months through focused efforts in marketing, employee development, and customer appreciation and recognition.
- Performed weekly audits to ensure center was meeting or exceeding corporate guidelines. Consistently exceeded guidelines.
- Motivated and rewarded staff for sales efforts and performance that contributed to staff being recognized as top in region.

EXPEDITED PACKAGES SERVICE CONSULTANT
March 2000 – August 2000
Express Services
40 + hours/week
65 Mellon Drive, Peachtree, GA 30006
Salary: $2,000/month + commission
(Worked from home-based office)
Supervisor: Vernon Walker, you may contact at (888) 421-7777

Sold domestic and international mail products to generate revenue in a pilot program for the United States Postal Service (USPS).
- Managed downtown accounts for small and medium businesses, considered to be one of the most difficult advertising markets, and significantly increased overall sales.
- Identified and researched a situation in which a local hospital was not receiving the full value of USPS services. Product usage and revenues increased as a result.

ACCOUNT EXECUTIVE
February 1999 – November 1999
Future Concepts Media
40+ hours/week
700 East Pratt Street, Baltimore, MD 21000
Salary: $38,000/year
Supervisor: David Thompson, you may contact at (410) 632-9550

Handled sales and marketing for billboard advertising in six states and the District of Columbia.
- Developed successful customer relationships and landed new customers by staying abreast of current market trends, targeting specific markets, and aggressively following leads. As a result, increased sales by 35%.
- Recognized sales potential of dot.com clients and brought a number of new dot.com accounts to the company.

CUSTOMER CONSULTANT
February 1996 – July 1998
East Coast Energy
40+ hours/week
700 Market Street, Philadelphia, PA 19106
Salary: $17.18/hour (hired at $14.28/hour)
Supervisor: Paula Johnson, you may contact at (215) 444-8123

Maintained excellent customer relations. Managed customer efforts concerning regulatory requirements, billing, electric and gas usage, and technical details of accounts.
- Researched customer complaints and inquiries to determine if errors had occurred in the billing process, and rendered significant savings for several customers by identifying problems or inconsistencies.
- Only five months after completion of training, selected to work in the "High Bill Queue" to investigate commercial customer complaints, a position generally reserved for department veterans.
- Conducted "teambuilders" training sessions to encourage staff to work more collaboratively.

ASSISTANT TO SITE COORDINATOR
July 1994 – September 1995
ABC – East Coast Energy
35 hours/week
East Coast Atomic Power Station, East Coast, PA 17098
Salary: $10/hour
Supervisor: Larry Pine, you may contact at (717) 765-1234

Performed various site Human Resources functions. Processed payroll, conducted background and security checks, handled fingerprinting, and completed numerous administrative projects. Part-time position during college.

COMPUTER SKILLS:

Microsoft Word, Access, Excel, E-mail, Internet

Senior Information Systems Engineer transitioning to Information Technology Specialist GS-2210-14/15 (Security)

FRED SMITHFIELD

1000 Apple Tree Ct, Oxnard, CA 93030 • Home: 805.567.4455 • Cell: 805.765.0330 FSmithfield@msn.com

Social Security Number: xxx-xx-xxxx
Citizenship: United States of America
Federal Civilian Status: N/A
Veterans Preference: N/A

OBJECTIVE:

Information Technology Specialist (Security) GS-2210-14/15
Announcement Number: OXN-0987-Q

SUMMARY OF QUALIFICATIONS:

√ **Certified Information Systems Security Professional (CISSP)**

√ **Cisco Certified Network Associate (CCNA)**

Experienced Systems and Network Administrator. Eight and nine years experience, respectively, performing Windows NT and UNIX systems and network administration. Extensive experience administering NT4.0/3.51, WIN98, WIN95, WFW, WIN3.1, and DOS. Substantial expertise supporting Silicon Graphics IRIX, including operating system upgrades and security patch installations. Actively learning Sun Solaris 8, Linux (Mandrake 8.1), WINXP, and WIN2K on home network, including researching and implementing recommended security practices, and evaluating newly released security applications.

Skilled Leader and Manager. Unsurpassed creativity, resourcefulness, and leadership in three high-tech startup companies. Excellent communications skills, including proficiency preparing written reports and spreadsheets, and superior ability to communicate with individuals at all levels of technical expertise. Adept at promoting teamwork among employees. Outstanding rapport with subordinates and all levels of management. Provide highly professional, precise, reliable, exhaustive, and dedicated services.

Professional with cutting-edge skills. Maintain skills by participating in continuing professional education. Active member of Computer Security Institute, and Information Systems Security Association. Subscribe to various Information Security (INFOSEC) advisory groups. Monitor federal government security web sites for latest advisories and new developments. Attend pertinent security conferences to stay abreast of the rapid evolution of INFOSEC.

PROFESSIONAL HISTORY:

Senior Information Systems Engineer   12/2000 – 3/2001
EAGLE TECHNOLOGIES, INC., 75 Dell Place, Suite 100, San Jose, CA 95000
Supervisor: Peter Sullivan   Telephone: 408.444.3992
Salary: $92,500 per year   Hours: 40+ per week

- Assessed computer, network, and physical security vulnerabilities, and reported findings to senior management with recommended corrective action.
- Collaborated on security issues with systems and network administrators at Ireland headquarters.
- Supported and managed Virtual Private Network (VPN) accessibility to company intranet for traveling sales force and telecommuters.
- Configured and managed user access, passwords, permissions, and restrictions on Sun Solaris and Windows NT local and wide area network.
- Configured tape autoloaders, verified backed up data integrity, and initiated offsite data storage and tape rotation service with special vendor.

FRED SMITHFIELD, SS# xxx-xx-xxxx   **2**

Network & Security Administrator *(defunct Internet startup)*   4/2000 – 12/2000
E*SOLUTIONS, INC., 50 N. Salem Boulevard, San Jose, CA 95000
Supervisor: Randy Windsor   Telephone: 650.78.0440 (cell)
Salary: $70,000 per year   Hours: 40+ per week

- Installed and configured Cisco 3640 router, including configuration and deployment of standard and extended access control lists to protect LAN from hacking.
- Configured packet filters for Netopia Synchronous Digital Subscriber Line (SDSL) router to restrict external access into network, and installed router as T1 line outage backup.
- Researched, installed, configured, and assessed evaluation copies of WebTrends Security Analyzer, Sniffer Pro LAN, VisualRoute Traceroute Utility, HP TopTools, and SolarWinds Network Management Tools for overall applicability and security utility.
- Installed, configured, and maintained secure heterogeneous network, involving direct, hands-on work with servers, hubs, routers, switches, and all communications resources.

NT Network Systems Administrator *(at now defunct Internet startup)*   11/1999 – 3/2000
FUTURE DIRECTIONS, INC., 85 Oak Bucket Lane, San Francisco, CA 94100
Supervisor: Paul Ciccone   Telephone: 415.881.1990
Salary: $70,000 per year   Hours: 40+ per week

- Installed and configured Watchguard Firebox II firewall to create "demilitarized zone" for company web server, and to restrict and log external access, and attempted access, into company LAN.
- Configured VPN using Point-to-Point Tunneling Protocol (PPTP), lmhosts files, and PC Anywhere to provide secure transmissions for traveling employees and local employee telecommuting.
- Reconfigured existing NT Workstation LAN with NT Server to create NT domain for robust, centralized security features.
- Transitioned company LAN from one Internet Service Provider to another for increased reliability and performance, requiring all-new Class C network, and reassignment of Internet Protocol addresses on all network nodes.

NT/UNIX Network Systems Administrator   7/1993 – 11/1999
SUMMIT, INC., 60 Jefferson Avenue, Glendale, CA 91244
Supervisor: Steven A. Martin   Telephone: 818.345.9922
Salary: $56,000 per year   Hours: 40+ per week

- Created, cultivated, and managed Information Technology Department for start-up company, including researching, selecting, purchasing, installing, configuring, maintaining, troubleshooting, repairing, and upgrading all hardware and software.
- Wrote security policy governing access rights to computers and network; configured and managed security levels, passwords, permissions, and restrictions.
- Configured network address translation on Covad SDSL router to protect LAN.
- Installed anti-virus protection, automated routine nightly scanning, proactively monitored virus bulletins and alerts, and regularly downloaded and installed latest virus signatures.
- Sourced, installed, and configured Redundant Array of Independent Disks (RAID) Level 5 server for failover protection, and to facilitate LAN backups.
- Utilized various third party tools for checking, optimizing, monitoring, securing, and troubleshooting Windows NT.

Senior Material Planner   3/1987 – 7/1993
PACIFIC AIRWAYS, INC., 5500 World Wide Way, Los Angeles, CA 90000
Supervisor: Bruce Light   Telephone: 213.446.4750
Salary: $36,000 per year   Hours: 40+ per week

- Conceived, created, and maintained electronic spreadsheet for mathematical analysis of detail parts requirements for high profile, cost-saving, provisioning project to move overhaul of aircraft components in-house.

- Presented weekly, summarized report to senior management showing cumulative progress of, and total expenditures for, this $6 M piece parts provisioning project.
- Supervised three junior planners performing parts data entry, issuing Requests for Quotes, and placing on-line purchase orders.
- Exclusively developed and maintained electronic database for procurement planning of B-777 buyer furnished equipment.

EDUCATION:

B.S. Aeronautical Operations, San Jose State University, School of Engineering
    Business minor, 1976
H.S. Degree, Glendale High School, Glendale, CA 91205, 1970

Information Technology Certificates, University of California, Santa Cruz (UCSC)
    Network Engineering Certificate (6 courses), 7/01
    Internet Security Certificate (5 courses), 6/01
    Network Management and Administration Certificate (7 courses), 5/01

Additional Security Training
    Intrusion Detection, Attacks, and Countermeasures - CSI / NSA 2-day seminar, 3/02
    Advanced UNIX Utilities and Shell Programming - UCSC - 28 hours, 5/01
    UNIX Security for System Administrators - UCSC - 21 hours, 3/01
    Solaris 8 System Administration I - Sun Microsystems 5-day class, 2/01

PROFESSIONAL CERTIFICATIONS and AFFILIATIONS:

CISSP - Certified Information Systems Security Professional #26900
CCNA - Cisco Certified Network Associate - #CSCO18451410
Member - Computer Security Institute (CSI) - I.D. 749033
Member - Information Systems Security Association (ISSA) - I.D. 83956

Equipment Specialist transitioning to Equipment Repair and Maintenance Worker
WG-04749-10, Office of Emergency Preparedness, U.S. Public Health Service

HAROLD SPRINGFIELD
22 Canterbury Road, Hagerstown, MD 21700
Home Phone: (410) 342-7005
Cell Phone: (410) 740-0668
hspringfield@hotmail.com

Social Security Number: 734-02-9966	Citizenship: United States
Highest Federal Civilian Position:	Veteranís Preference: N/A
Emergency Response Coordinator, NDMS/USPHS, GS-13	

OBJECTIVE: Equipment Repair and Maintenance Worker, WG-04749-10, USPHS
Announcement Number: OS-11-436

EMPLOYMENT HISTORY:

NATIONAL DISASTER MEDICAL SYSTEM
Office of Emergency Preparedness, U.S. Public Health Service
700 Overbrook Parkway, Rockville, MD 20500
May 1999 to June 2001

EQUIPMENT SPECIALIST, full-time, 50+ hours/week
Supervisor: Arthur Houston, (301) 444-5100; contact may be made

EQUIPMENT MAINTENANCE AND REPAIR:
- Test performance of engines. Diagnose, determine and perform needed repairs. Test small gasoline and diesel engines auxiliary generators, compressors, etc. Repair and carry out preventive maintenance on automotive and mobile equipment such as trucks, all-terrain vehicles, trailers and forklifts.
- Repair diesel or gasoline powered forklift trucks to move, stack, load and unload materials in warehouses, storage areas, and loading docks.
- Inspect, repair, and maintain shipments of equipment to emergency response teams.
- Complete troubleshooting, installation, repair and maintenance work on medical and other emergency response equipment, including x-ray machines, mobile equipment, portable laboratories, power generators, portable morgues, etc.

EQUIPMENT PLANNING AND MANAGEMENT:
- Receive, inspect, maintain, store, tools, equipment, vehicles, and parts.
- Review, coordinate and oversee the inventory process for emergency response and medical equipment and supplies.
- Proficient in using the automated data processing tracking system.
- Evaluate and research new equipment including four new vehicles.
- Relocate equipment using an accountability system.
- Maintain inventory and Management Support Team (MST) equipment data records in accordance with the appropriate federal regulations.
- Supervised the replenishing of OEP equipment necessary for future disasters, including the replenishing and preparing of five trailers with logistical, administrative, medical, and personal supplies.
- Assisted with the re-supply of the Disaster Medical Assistance Teams (DMAT) basic load.

WAREHOUSE IMPROVEMENTS:
- Designed the new warehouse layout to increase storage area from 5,000 to 20,000 square feet. Improved organization, efficiency, and customer response time.
- Trained a new OEP warehouse supervisor in operations, policies and procedures.
- Created and monitored a key control log Data Base to ensure that access to warehouse property is limited to authorized personnel.
- Monitored the use and proper return of Federal Property in accordance with the appropriate federal regulations following the deployments in Colorado, New Hampshire, Georgia, Pennsylvania, and New Mexico, all of which occurred simultaneously.
- Initiated the use of three part-time Emergency Response Coordinators to be deployed to the Warehouse to meet property needs of the National Disaster Medical System (NDMS) missions.

SHIPPING AND RECEIVING:
- Created and implemented a shipping and receiving data base to assist in tracking of new and deployed equipment including medical supplies for DMAT, administrative supplies for the MST, and the Disaster Portable Morgue Unit for the Disaster Mortuary Operational Response Teams (DMORT).
- Prepared and adapted inventory templates to meet the tracking needs of OEP.
- Experienced with purchase order procedures.
- Replenished inventory supply request using the Federal database.

EMERGENCY RESPONSE SUPPORT:
- Supervised three part-time Emergency Response Coordinators following activations of the NDMS.
- Arranged for Clean Harbors to complete decontamination process on refrigerated trailers following deployments.
- Coordinated with Perry Point to ensure that purchase order numbers be placed on the outside of requested supplies and equipment to assist in their proper tracking and logging thus improving the distribution to numerous NDMS teams.
- Participated in conference calls with OEP staff and NDMS team members in order to be briefed on the status of ongoing missions.
- Comprehend and adhere to the Federal Property Management Rules and Regulations including HHS, GSA, and GAO.

EQUIPMENT DISPOSAL AND INVENTORY CONTROL:
- Disposed of federal property in accordance with appropriate federal regulations.
- Audited equipment and supplies following the completion of an NDMS mission.

DEPLOYMENT EXPERIENCE

EMERGENCY RESPONSE COODINATOR, up to 84 hours/week
Supervisor: Donald Frazer, (800) 784-9778; contact may be made.

- Logistics Chief, Egypt Air, Flight 990, Providence, RI;
  November 1, 1999 to November 18, 1999; December 17, 1999 to January 15, 2000
- Transportation Officer, World Trade Organization, Seattle, WA; Hurricane Floyd, Tarboro, NC;
  November 27, 1999 to December 4, 1999; September 24, 1999 to October 9, 1999
- Liaison, Hurricane Floyd, Fort Jackson, SC; September 13, 1999 to September 18, 1999
- Liaison, Hurricane Brett, San Antonio, TX; August 21, 1999 to August 24, 1999
- Logistics, Property Management Officer, Operation Provide Refuge, Fort Dix, NJ;
  May 15, 1999 to June 10, 1999
- Facilities Officer, Operation Provide Refuge, Fort Dix, NJ; May 15, 1999 to June 10, 1999

SPRINGFIELD CONSTRUCTION
22 Canterbury Road, Hagerstown, MD 21700; (410) 342-7005   1996 to 1999

OWNER/OPERATOR
- Supervised preventative maintenance on all vehicles and equipment such as generators, air compressors, and electrical tools.
- Maintained all tools and equipment.
- Inventoried tools, equipment, and supplies.
- Insured preparedness for the next working day.
- Negotiated contracts.
- Ensured that projects were completed on time and within budget.
- Scheduled sub-contractors to perform services and deliver supplies.
- Supervised up to 30 people for larger projects.

EDUCATION:
Francis Scott Key High School, Union Bridge, Maryland, High School Diploma, 1986
Carroll County Vo-Tech, Machine Shop, Westminster, Maryland, Graduated 1986

TRAINING AND DEVELOPMENT:
Emergency Program Manager ñ NFA
Firefighter 1 ñ University of Maryland
Hazmat Awareness ñ University of Maryland
Hazmat Operations ñ University of Maryland
Basic Farm Equipment Rescue ñ University of Maryland
Basic Rough Water Rescue ñ NASAR
Incident Command System ñ National Fire Academy
Terrorism ñ National Fire Academy
FIT Test for Self Contained Breathing Apparatus ñ State of Maryland
Emergency Program Manager ñ National Fire Academy
Emergency Preparedness-USA ñ National Fire Academy
Radiological Emergency Management ñ National Fire Academy
The Professional in Emergency Management ñ National Fire Academy

COMPUTER SKILLS:
Windows 95 and Windows 98
Inventory Data Base for OEP Warehouse
Designed Shipping/Receiving Data Base for OEP Warehouse
Designed Key Control Data Base for OEP Warehouse and Equipment
Proficiency in Word, Excel, Access, PowerPoint
Data communicator and E-mail systems

AVAILABILITY:
Flexible to work weekends, holidays, or after hours, when necessary.
Available for on-call emergency duty outside normal duty hours.
Possess and maintain a valid, state-issued motor vehicle operator's permit.
Willing to travel on an extended or frequent basis to perform tasks related to emergency preparedness responsibilities.

Recent Graduate transitioning to Criminal Investigator
GS-1811-07, Drug Enforcement Administration

SYLVIA NELSON

3 Cherry Blossom Avenue • Baltimore, MD 21228 • (410) 545-3942
SylviaNelson@aol.com

SSN: 411-78-9844
Citizenship: United States
Veteranís Preference and Federal Civilian Status: N/A

OBJECTIVE: Criminal Investigator, GS-1811-07, Drug Enforcement Administration, Ann. #GA-2002

EDUCATION:

UNIVERSITY OF DELAWARE, Newark, DE 19711
B.A. Degree, May 2001
Dual Major: Criminal Justice and Psychology
Cumulative GPA: 3.12   Criminal Justice: 3.53   Psychology: 3.63

UNIVERSITY OF SCHOLCHERE, Fort De France, Martinique
French Studies, Winter Session 2000

Catonsville High School, Baltimore, MD, 1997

ACADEMIC HONORS:

Deanís List for Academic Excellence, University of Delaware, 1999
Golden Key National Honor Society, University of Delaware Chapter, Nov.1999
National Psychology Honor Society, Psi Chi, May 1998

PAPERS and PRESENTATIONS:

ADHD: The Current Epidemic. Research paper on the application of the biomedical model to the construction of Attention Deficit Hyperactivity Disorder and its treatment, March 2001.

The Myth of Emotional Venting. Discussion paper summarizing Moore and Watsonís research on the ill effects of uncontrolled anger expression and possible coping strategies to combat emotional flooding. Presented to a select inmate population at Baylor Womenís Correctional Institution in Delaware on April 11, 2001.

Differences in Heart Rate Variability and Facial Expressions Across Cultures and Conditions. Pseudo study designed to measure physiological arousal and emotional expression across Japanese and American cultures, May 2001.

COMPUTER SKILLS:

Microsoft Excel, Microsoft Word, WordPerfect for Windows, various specialized databases (for research, and data entry and retrieval). Typing speed: 60 wpm.

LEADERSHIP and ATHLETIC ACTIVITIES:

Avid Sports Participant, Adult Field Hockey League	Current
Field Hockey Coach, Girl Scouts Association	Fall 2000
Club Field Hockey, Secretary and Player	Fall 1998
Varsity Field Hockey Team, Player	Fall 1997-Spring 1998

WORK HISTORY:

REHABILITATION SPECIALIST   October 2001 - Present
Community Health Systems, Savage, MD 20789 $23,000/year
Supervisor: Amanda Doe (410) 722-7333, contact may be made   40 hours/week
Provide quality rehabilitation training and support services to mentally ill adults. Develop and facilitate individual rehabilitation plans, and provide ongoing support counseling and crisis intervention to Associates when needed.

ASSISTANT TO THE CORRECTIONAL PSYCHOLOGIST   February - May 2001
Baylor Correctional Institution, New Castle, DE 19721   Salary: N/A
Supervisor: Florence Smith (302) 444-8911   2 hours/week
Worked with the womenís institutional mental health therapist in group therapy activities. Organized and implemented exercise programs in order to combat the stress and depression of inmates.

TUTOR   February - May 2001
University of Delaware, Newark, DE 19722   Salary: N/A
Supervisor: Jason Waters (302) 222-9667, contact may be made   2 hrs/week
Implemented an emotion-centered program facilitating the development of childrenís understanding, regulation, and appropriate use of emotions to an eight-year old child in a classroom setting.

PRIVATE NANNY   December - May 2001
Robert and Sarah Newman, Newark, DE 19672   Salary: $8/hr
Supervisor: Sarah Newman (302) 993-3287   20 hours/week
Provided personal care to two young children and facilitated daily activities to occupy afternoons.

RELEVANT SKILLS:

Research ñ Conduct extensive research across multiple media to support team-oriented projects. Apply analyzed data to current research.

Written Language ñ Organizational skills utilized to develop adhesive thought patterns. Construct clear, precise, audience specific reports and summaries.

Leadership ñ Interpersonal skills used to relate to and motivate professionals toward desired goal. Design and present informative and demonstrative speeches.

PROFESSIONAL TRAINING: Functional Assessment; Programming Skill Use

Police Officer transitioning to Civil Aviation Security Specialist (Investigations)
FV-1801-I, Federal Aviation Administration
(Electronic Resume)

Norman Cain, SSN: 570-99-8231
7 Lucky Lane
Las Vegas, NV 77711
Office: 702-222-9999
Home: 702-433-3887
Email: NormanCain@aol.com

Work Experience

01-1999 to Present, 40 hours per week, POLICE OFFICER II, Salary: $55,000.
Las Vegas Metropolitan Police Department, 800 Cactus Avenue, Las Vegas, NV 89100. Supervisor: Sergeant Ron Kim, 702-222-9999, May be contacted.

Serve as Patrol Officer for LVMPD. Respond to Calls for Service, conduct preliminary investigations, enforce Las Vegas city and Clark County ordinances. Identify potential problems in assigned area of responsibility -AAOR- and develop solutions based on Problem Oriented Policing -POP- and Community Oriented Policing -COP- concepts and guidelines.

ACCOMPLISHMENTS: Received nine Letters and Citations of Commendation for superior service to date including: Arresting two armed suspects of kidnapping and car jacking two women. Suspects were booked on eight felony counts including Kidnapping and Robbery.
Officer of the Month for June, 2000: located three Methamphetamine labs, made six felony arrests and recovered $2000 in AAOR during May, 2000. Commendation for defusing a potentially serious community disturbance when showing great restraint and compassion toward a hostile crowd and family members of the victim when responding to a situation where shots had been fired and a male subject was suffering from a gunshot wound to the chest.

07-1994 to 01-1999, 40 hours per week, POLICE OFFICER, Salary: $64,000.
San Jose Police Department, 470 Market Street, San Jose, CA 95000. Supervisor: Sergeant Alan Kent, 408-202-8888.

Maintained law and order, cited and arrested violators; executed search and arrest warrants; testified in court proceedings; participated in initial investigations; maintained proficiency in law enforcement procedures, techniques, methods and equipment; dictated and wrote reports, letters, memos, observations, affidavits and legal paperwork. Received 14 Letters and Commendations for superior service.

03-1992 to 07-1994, 40 hours per week, POLICE OFFICER, Salary: $36,000.
Watsonville Police Department, 19 Washington Street, Watsonville, CA 95700.
Supervisor: Captain E. Gonzalez, 831-581-4433

Performed same duties as above for the San Jose Police Department. Received seven Letters and Commendations for superior service.

08-1990 to 03-1992, 20 hours per week, COMMUNITY SERVICE OFFICER—COLLEGE INTERN PROGRAM, Salary: $11.00 per hour. Gatos Police Department, 2 Summer Street, Los Gatos, CA 97890. Supervisor: Captain D. Brooke, 408-312-4144

Performed a variety of law enforcement duties including: taking police reports, impounding vehicles, issuing parking citations, directing traffic, participating in high-level visible patrols, and responding to non-dangerous calls. This was a uniform, tested position worked on a part-time basis. Monthly reviews and review of college grades were required to be maintained at a high level to continue the employment.

06-1990 to 03-1992, 40 hours per week, SECURITY OFFICER, Salary: $10.00 per hour. Macy's, Washington Avenue, San Francisco, CA 90076. Supervisor: Susan Todd, 408-414-0987.

Worked undercover to reduce company loss through external and internal theft and conduct fraud, forgery, vandalism and embezzlement investigations. The embezzlement cases were complex, involving hundreds of hours of surveillance, plotting of accounting media, and detailed interviews and interrogations. Exercised sole responsibility to conduct audits and determine the probabilities of expected losses in Women's Clothing Department. Dramatically reduced losses in Department during tenure

10-1989 to 06-1990, 40 hours per week, SECURITY OFFICER, Salary: $8.00 per hour. JC Penney, 4000 Valley Road, Pleasanton, CA 98711. Supervisor: Eleanor Bickel, 408-654-6789.

Undercover security position to act as a shopper to arrest or prevent shoplifting.

EDUCATION

AA, Liberal Arts, West Valley College, Saratoga, CA, 1993
Diploma, Los Gatos High School, Los Gatos, California, 1989

PROFESSIONAL TRAINING AND CERTIFICATIONS

Certificate: Basic Category I, State of Nevada, 711 hours, 1999
Certificate: Field Training Evaluation, Las Vegas Police Department, 760 hours, 1999
Intermediate Certificate: Law Enforcement, State of California, 1996
Certificate: Basic Law Enforcement, State of California, 728 hours, 1992
Various Courses: 539 hours, 1992 to date -Detailed list available-
Firearms, Field Techniques, Investigation, Interviewing, Criminal Law, Equipment, Law Enforcement Techniques, Informant Management, etc.

AWARDS AND RECOGNITION

30 Letters and Certificates of Commendation for superior service, 1990 - 2001

OTHER INFORMATION

United States Citizen: Yes
Federal Status: N-A
Veterans Status: N-A

Carlos Mercado

8766 Royal Street
Arlington, TX 76000
Home: (817) 788-5933   E-mail: CMercado@yahoo.com

Social Security Number: 743-55-2994
Citizenship: United States
Clearance: TOP SECRET

Federal Civilian Status: N/A
Veteran's Preference: 5 Points

Objective

Criminal Investigator, GS-1811-5/7, Immigration and Naturalization Service
Vacancy Announcement PJN-03-PPP-739

Profile

Currently a full-time graduate student in Criminology/Criminal Justice, degree expected May 2000. Previous experience includes 2-1/2 years active-duty military (enlisted) service followed by ROTC training while an undergraduate, and 3 years US Army National Guard service. Commissioned Combat Engineer Platoon Leader (2LT) December 1998. Bilingual. Strong computer skills.

Recent Accomplishments

Designed and implemented a burglary survey to analyze and predict criminal activity trends that was adopted for use by the Arlington Police Department. Examined all cleared burglary offenses to determine activity patterns; looked for areas of heightened criminal activity utilizing SPSS software for City of Arlington, TX.

Commissioned Second Lieutenant, US Army, December 1998.

Education

MS, Criminology/Criminal Justice, University of Texas, Arlington, TX, expected Dec. 2000
BA, Criminal Justice & Spanish, University of Texas, Arlington, TX, May 1999
Academic Honors: Spring 1997, Fall 1997, Summer 1998
Diploma, Chaffey High School, Ontario, CA, 1992

Employment History

Combat Engineer Platoon Leader, 2LT   7/96-Present
Texas National Guard Corps of Engineers, Plant City, TX   60 hours per month
Supervisor: Mark Hamill, (972) 772-8585   Salary: $275 monthly
Commissioned Dec. 1998 – ROTC Cadet prior. Supervise combat readiness, yearly training, MOS certifications, field training exercises (6 per year) of 28-man platoon. Serve as Company physical fitness training (APFT) coordinator.

Warehouseman – labor, forklift driver   4/97-Present
Air Freight Express, Irving, TX   36-40 hours per week
Supervisor: Keith Cox, (972) 673-0011, may be contacted.   Salary: $15.00/hour

Carlos Mercado, SS# 743-55-2994 2

Crime Analyst (Summer Intern) 5/99-9/99
Arlington Police Department 16 hours per week
Beacon Street, Arlington, TX Salary: $6.00 per hour
Supervisor: Rodney Downs, (817) 312-5865
Received, analyzed, and assessed information of a criminal nature, and disseminated information in the form of operational output.

- Collated information pertaining to criminal activity and prepared assessments of police data, and detecting patterns, structures, trends and movements of the criminal.
- Designed and implemented a burglary survey that was adopted for use by the Arlington Police Department.
- Examined all cleared burglary offenses to determine activity patterns – looked for areas of heightened criminal activity utilizing SPSS software.

Combat Engineer Team Leader, Sp/4 10/92-2/95
United States Army Corps of Engineers 40 hours per week
Supervisor: Maj. O'Brien Salary: $1200/monthly

- Responsible for the accountability, maintenance and repair of all small arms (worth over $800,000) as battalion armorer.
- Planned and coordinated for monthly, quarterly and yearly inspections of company's weapons.
- Top Secret Clearance. Honorable Discharge, 1995.

Professional Development

ROTC, University of Texas, Arlington TX, 1996-1999
Controlled Dangerous Substances, University of Texas, Arlington TX, Winter 1999
Hazardous Materials Training, Roadway Express, Irving, TX, Fall 1998

Computer Skills

Microsoft Windows, Microsoft Office, SPSS, scanning technology, Internet searches

Languages

Fluent Spanish – Bicultural

Peace Corps / Americorps Volunteer transitioning to Public Affairs Specialist
GS-1035-05/07, U.S. Department of Commerce
(Electronic Resume)

LISA PINKERTON

SSN: 322-89-0404
1010 Nevada Avenue
Washington, DC 20006
Home Phone: 202-744-4368
E-mail: LisaPink@earthlink.net

WORK EXPERIENCE

01/1999-05/2001; 40 hours per week; **Peace Corps Volunteer; TRAINER, SMALL BUSINESS COUNSELOR**; $2700 per year. The Peace Corps, Guatemala, Guatemala City, 01009, Guatemala, Central America. Supervisor: Gary Day, 502/909-8638.

TRAINING COUNSELOR, SEMINAR COORDINATOR: Provided business and life skills training to small business owners in Micro-Credit Banking Program. This included customer service, cost analysis, sales process, product presentation, and marketing, Counseled and trained small business owners on ways to improve their businesses. Planned, organized, developed, and coordinated cross-cultural exchange seminar for Micro-Credit Banks representatives and host organization co-workers.

Wrote technical topic material for technical business training manual. Facilitated local small business project experiment for 20 people. Assisted training staff in selecting current Peace Corps Volunteers for diversity panel discussions. Designed clear and concise informational materials to support these training efforts. Position required extensive knowledge of small business development and the ability to identify and analyze problem areas and communicated solutions to business owners in the local community. Taught English to local residents and business professionals.

8/1997-12/1998; 40 hours per week; **AmeriCorps Leader; MEETING PLANNER, RECRUITER, WRITER, EDITOR and PRODUCER**; $250 per week; AmeriCorps Leaders Program, Corporation for National Service, 867 New Jersey Ave., NW, Washington, DC 20500. Supervisor: Ann Marie Davenport, 202/744-4324.

Planned, facilitated and coordinated meetings and service activities for AmeriCorps Members. Served as liaison between Local Initiatives Support Corporation AmeriCorps Members, staff, and the Corporation for National Service. Assisted in volunteer recruitment for service projects. Communicated with members on a bi-monthly basis to give advice and support. Assisted the national Local Initiatives Support Corporation AmeriCorps Staff with the planning and coordination of national and regional training sessions. Developed and presented training programs for Local Initiatives Support Corporation AmeriCorps and other National AmeriCorps programs on the following topics: Journal Writing and Reflection, Public Speaking, and National Service History, etc.

WRITER and EDITOR of Local Initiatives Support Corporation AmeriCorps quarterly newsletter designed to keep workers informed of activities of the organization and matters affecting them. Edited and proofread documents.

PRODUCED and CO-DIRECTED the first Local Initiatives Support Corporation AmeriCorps video used for the support of the organizations recruitment and fundraising activities. Collected, prepared, and disseminated information to internal and external audiences both orally and in writing. Utilized interpersonal skills to maintain internal and external contacts. Team player with other New York AmeriCorps Leaders in starting the New York InterCorps Council for AmeriCorps programs throughout the state and City of New York. Skilled in audiovisual production and editing.

09/1996-07/1997; **AmeriCorps Member**; $200 per week. Task force for the Homeless AmeriCorps; 700 Peachtree Ave., SE, Atlanta, GA 30300; Supervisor: Nancy Miller, 404/333-4444.

EMERGENCY CRISIS COUNSELOR. Provided emergency crisis counseling to families and individuals, and referred homeless families and individuals to shelters, clothing centers and employment programs. Served as the only interpreter for Spanish speaking clients. Performed renovation projects at service provider facilities throughout the State of Georgia.

WRITER, EDITOR, PHOTOGRAPHER. Wrote articles and contributed photos to quarterly AmeriCorps Newsletter. Audiovisual experienced included the video taping of special projects and events pertaining to the organization's activities. Edited the Taskforce AmeriCorps Video Yearbook. Prepared public speeches to present information on AmeriCorps and homeless issues to schools, colleges and community organizations. Edited and proofread all written documents.

05/1995-08/1995; 40 hours per week; **BUSINESS NEWS REPORTER** Intern; $365 per week; Johnson City Times Dispatch Newspaper; P.O. Box 987, Johnson City, TN 23200; Supervisor, Richard Miller, 401/333-1225.

Interviewed local contacts and wrote daily and weekly news and feature stories on many topics for the Business News Section. Assisted the Business News Editor in editing and proofreading weekly news publication.

05/1994-08/1994; 40 hours per week; **CITY NEWS REPORTER** Intern; $250 per week; The Daily-Star Newspaper; 950 Riverfront St., Roanoke, VA 22000; Supervisor: Jean Tobin, 540/555-1212.

Wrote news and special feature stories for the city news desk on a variety of topics ranging from city government to community organizations. Wrote a series of feature articles highlighting outstanding academic and community-oriented high school students.

05/1992-08/1992; 40 hours per week; **REGULATORY INFORMATION ASSISTANT INTERN, GS-03**; 40 hours per week; $6.75 per hour; Office of Hearing and Appeals, Department of Energy, 1000 Constitution Ave., NW, Washington, DC 20321. Supervisor: Avery Dick, 202/737-8637.

Researched and maintained customer applications for granting refunds and approved refunds based on submitted information. Assisted lawyers and analysts with application processing. Interfaced with customers to gather pertinent application data. Recommended refunds based on data gathered. Wrote weekly status reports related to the application process.

EDUCATION:
Davis University, Davis, GA 30314, Certificate of Completion, 1995; Host Training Program, Minor Spanish, 9 sem. hours. Virginia State University, Richmond, VA; Mass Communications; 1995; Bachelor of Science; 2.9 GPA, 131 sem. hours. National University of Pedro Enriquez Urena, Santo Domingo, Dominican Republic, Study Abroad Program, 1994; Major, Dominican Culture and Spanish; Minor, Television Production Internship, 7 sem. hours.
Gerald Ford High School, Fairfax, VA 1990; 1964; High School Diploma.

PROFESSIONAL TRAINING:
Spanish Language Training, 2000; Small Business Consulting 1999; Non-formal Education, 1999; Guatemala Culture Adaptability Training, 1999; Community Development, 1999; Dimensions of Leadership, 1998; Facilitative and Situational Leadership, 1998; Handling Transitions, 1998; Successful Business Meeting Course, 1998; Project Planning, 1997; Presentation Skills, 1997; Sharing and Inspiring Visions in Others, 1997; AmeriCorps Member/Volunteer Skill Building, 1997; American Red Cross Disaster Relief Training, 1997.

PERFORMANCE RATINGS, AWARDS, HONORS & RECOGNITIONS:
Certificate of Appreciation from State of New York Executive Chamber, 1998; Norfolk State University Certificate of Achievement, 1996; Who's Who Among Students in American Universities and Colleges, 1994; Norfolk State University School of Arts & Letters Distinguished Scholars Award, 1994; Media Awards for Student Print Investigative and Feature News Reporting, 1994; Recognition of Service Award, Spartan Echo Staff Writer, 1993.

OTHER INFORMATION:
Fluent in Spanish and English. Proficient in Excel, Word Perfect, and navigating the Internet. Willing to relocate.

U.S. DEPT. OF COMMERCE
International Trade Administration, Ft. Lauderdale, FL

Title of Position: International Trade Specialist
Announcement Number C/ITA/85673.CPK

Candidate:
LAURA L. DAVIS
SSN: 326-86-8600

KNOWLEDGE, SKILLS, AND ABILITIES

1. **Knowledge of export marketing promotion, foreign trade practices and government international trade programs and policies.**

Three experiences have provided me with a broad base of knowledge about export marketing promotion, foreign trade practices, and government international trade programs and policies. First, I studied these subjects extensively while earning my International Marketing Certificate at Miami Dade Community College. Second, I applied this knowledge in hands-on experiences in my internship at the U.S. Department of Commerce. And finally, I continue to apply, hone, and increase my skills and knowledge of these subjects in my current position as the only Trade Information Specialist for the World Trade Center Miami.

For my International Trade Certificate, I completed several semester-long courses that prepared me for my work in export marketing promotion and foreign trade, and that provided a solid foundation in government international trade programs and policies. These included courses in Import/Export Marketing, Foreign Trade, Import/Export Documentation, and Transportation Geography. I was an excellent student and earned my certificate with a 3.94 average.

In my U.S. Department of Commerce internship, I counseled local firms about their export potential by providing them with information on foreign markets, including economics and political factors. I served as an expert knowledge source to identify federal programs that help U.S. companies export their goods and services around the world. I also provided instruction to businesses on how to access reports and statistical information from the computerized National Trade Data Bank. I answered questions regarding local and foreign trade practices as well as government international trade programs and policies.

My role as a Trade Information Specialist for World Trade Center Miami has further increased my knowledge of export marketing programs, foreign trade practices and government international trade programs and policies. I advise our members about where to get information they need about regulations and how to comply with U.S. laws and policies. I work directly with individual members to identify overseas trade opportunities and I steer them through the proper channels. I also help our members understand how they must modify their products and shipping practices to conform to foreign government regulations, geographic and climatic conditions, buyer preferences, and standards of living. I help our members learn about appropriate trade regulations, customs and standards, and how to gather useful economic and trade statistics.

Others regard me as an expert source of reliable and accurate information. As the Center's Point of Contact, I collect daily e-mails and answer questions about foreign trade practices and government international trade programs and policies. I also field telephone questions from members and others about international trading practices. In addition, I convey a great deal of information on these topics in our weekly electronic newsletter, which I edit.

Finally, I have increased my knowledge of government international trade programs and policies through extensive work on the Internet. I am knowledgeable about all of the relevant websites that provide needed information to our members, and frequently help them navigate through the appropriate sites and links. I have also done extensive work to promote export marketing by organizing numerous buying missions, trade missions, and matchmaking programs.

U.S. DEPT. OF COMMERCE
International Trade Administration, Ft. Lauderdale, FL

Title of Position: International Trade Specialist
Announcement Number C/ITA/85673.CPK

Candidate:
LAURA L. DAVIS
SSN: 326-86-8600

KNOWLEDGE, SKILLS, AND ABILITIES

6. Ability to effectively utilize information technology (IT) resources and tools in support of client exporters.

I am knowledgeable of the vast array of information technology (IT) resources and tools available to support client exporters. As an International Trade Specialist with World Trade Center Miami, I work with IT resources every day. Frequently, I bring useful IT resources and tools to the attention of our members, and as needed, walk them through the process of using them.

For example, the World Trade Center Association headquarters in New York has an excellent website (WTCA.org). Using it, members of any World Trade Center can post their companies online without charge. However, many members find it difficult to navigate through this website. I have therefore personally walked more than 50 World Trade Center Miami members through the website and steered them through the process of putting their products online.

I am also very well versed in the use of USATRADE.gov, BUYUSA.com and Export.gov. I have used these resources many, many times to access global listings of trade events, market research, and other tools that help with virtually every aspect of the export process. Whenever I identify an online matchmaking opportunity, I inform members of the date, time, and industry, both through the weekly electronic newsletter I edit and through personal phone calls. I am very experienced at using these websites to identify on-line buying missions, trade events, international partners, exporters, and tool kits.

I use many other IT resources to help World Trade Center Miami members as well. For example, I use the National Trade Data Bank (www.stat-usa.gov) quite often to provide members with Best Market Reports. As well, I regularly access the Foreign Trade Division's website (www.census.gov/foreign-trade) to gather information on the U.S. trade balance, import and export totals, and general commodity groupings and country totals.

The Department Office of Trade and Economic Analysis website (www.ita.doc.gov) provides useful information on aggregate foreign trade data. These include historical data on U.S. trade in goods and services and a breakdown of the United States' top 50 trade partners. It also offers a great deal of information about export documentation, regulations, information on SEDs, invoices, licenses and the Harmonized Tariff Schedule. I frequently gather information for members about export licensing requirements and regulations from the Bureau of Export Administration (BXA) website (www.bxa.doc.gov).

Finally, I frequently advise World Trade Center Miami members where to advertise using technology. For example, I often suggest that members become familiar with Commercial News USA (CNUSA), an official publication of the U.S. Department of Commerce's U.S. Foreign and Commercial Service, which is now available online. Commercial News USA Online offers excellent overseas exposure for U.S. companies, and is a website designed to assist importers around the world in their efforts to find American products or services they would like to buy.

ABOUT THE AUTHOR

Kathryn is shown here with Donald Colada, Dennis Chiu, Nadine Bayne, and Jeff Wataoka at the Pearl Harbor Naval Shipyard, Honolulu, Hawaii, following a Resumix training workshop for Navy civilians in 2001.

Kathryn Troutman is credited with being the pioneering designer of the Federal resume for the Federal government in 1995 with the publication of her book, *The Federal Resume Guidebook*. Her Federal resume style is used on the OPM Web site, www.usajobs.opm.gov, and is accepted throughout government as the standard for Federal resume writing.

With this accomplishment, Ms. Troutman is recognized as the leading expert on Federal resume writing by Federal human resources directors and civil service senior executives. As the founder and director of The Resume Place, Inc. in Baltimore, Maryland, Kathryn and her team of writers have written more than 100,000 resumes since 1973. Her Federal job search expertise covers both Federal-to-Federal and private-industry-to-Federal—each being different and uniquely challenging.

Navy Civilians at Pearl Harbor listen intently to tips on How to Find Keywords and Write a Better Resumix from Ms. Troutman in 2001 and 2002.

I really like your "tough love" approach and respect your efforts to investigate the federal hiring process and to simplify and streamline a difficult and complicated process.

Career Consultant Program
Manager

As Kathy Troutman showed in her two years as GovExec.com's "Career Corner" columnist, there's no better person to lead Federal employees through the wilderness of new electronic resume requirements. She knows how to craft a Federal resume; she's mastered the new rules; and she'll help you find the job of your dreams!

Tom Shoop, Executive Editor,
Government Executive Magazine
(http://www.govexec.com)

As a career motivator, Kathryn has also trained more than 25,000 Federal employees in 33 Federal agencies in the U.S. and Europe on resume and KSA writing techniques that will result in promotions and career change in government. She is a keynote speaker and trainer for human resources professionals who want to stay on the cutting-edge of applicant challenges. She was the Career Corner columnist for www.govexec.com for two years and is quoted frequently by syndicated career columnists and career Web sites on the subject of Federal employment. She is a popular radio and TV talk show guest on the subject of Federal employment and host for human resources training videos, adding a real human element to the complex Federal job search process. She is a fast typist and a popular Federal job search advisor on the Washington Post's Federal Diary Live On-line programs with Steve Barr.

Kathryn is a passionate proponent for change in the Federal hiring process and has been quoted in numerous on-line and print publications and Web sites concerning changes needed to simplify the hiring process.

Kathryn travels extensively training throughout the U.S. and Europe, while directing the resume writing and federal job search consulting services provided by her expert team of federal resume writers out of Baltimore, MD. When she has time in airports and evenings, she writes books that help people land their first Federal job or get promoted to a new position in government.

In addition to *Ten Steps to a Federal Job,* her previous books include *Federal Resume Guidebook, Electronic Federal Resume Guidebook, Reinvention Federal Resumes, 171 Reference Book*, and *Creating your High School Resume*. She is the publisher of www.resume-place.com, the leading Federal resume-writing site on the Web since 1995. She is a member of many professional resume-writing associations. She is a founding board member of the National Association of Women Business Owners.

Kathryn lives in Baltimore and is the mother of three college-age children who are commencing careers in publishing and marketing, retail and merchandise management, and hi-tech sales.

ABOUT THE CONTRIBUTING AUTHORS

Step 2. Review the Federal Job Processes. Michael Ottensmeyer is a retired Civilian Human Resources professional with the Air Force and currently a consultant to Senior Executive Service and other Federal Job Applicants for Resume Place. His most recent position as a civilian human resources professional was as the Senior Staff Classification and Human Resources Consultant for the Air Force Materiel Command Headquarters at Wright-Patterson covering 13 separate Air Force Personnel Offices with a total of 65,000 civilian employees in Air Force Research Laboratories, Product Development Centers, Air Logistics Centers and Test Centers across the United States. Mike holds an M.A. in Public Administration and Human Resources Management.

Step 6. Write Your Electronic Resume. Mark Reichenbacher has a distinguished career of over twenty-four years of Federal service. He has acquired a well-rounded portfolio of experience, having held generalist, specialist, supervisory, and managerial positions at the field and headquarters levels in labor-management relations and program management. Currently, he serves as Special Assistant to the Deputy Administrator, and coordinates special projects dealing with workforce transition issues. Mark designed and edited the electronic resume samples in the *Electronic Federal Resume Guidebook,* CD-ROM. Mark holds a Master of Science degree in Labor Studies and a Bachelor of Arts degree, with a double major in Psychology and Economics.

Step 7. Writing your KSAs. Laura Sachs has more than 20 years experience as a journal author, newsletter editor, freelance writer, management consultant, lecturer, and trainer. She is the author of two successful management books published by Prentice-Hall and is a regular columnist for a leading bi-monthly healthcare management journal. Ms. Sachs serves on the faculty of the Northern Virginia Community College Continuing Education division where she teaches a number of one-day business and writing courses. She is well regarded for writing effective KSAs that inject a refreshing human quality into the application package. Ms. Sachs graduated cum laude and with distinction with a B.A. in English from Rutgers College. She was elected to Phi Beta Kappa and is certified to teach high school English grades 7–12. She is currently pursuing an M.A. in English at George Mason University and focusing her studies on drama. Ms. Sachs is a co-trainer with Kathryn Troutman in Federal Resume and KSA writing workshops throughout the Washington, DC area.

Step 10. Interview for a Federal Job. Jessica Coffey brings to The Resume Place over nine years of experience providing career management strategies to all levels of government and private sector employees, displaced professionals, and college students and alumni. Jessica's background includes training and development, and she is certified as a Professional in Human Resources (PHR). Jessica is an expert in interview training and recruitment consulting. Jessica is an experienced Federal resume and KSA editor with several of her resumes included in this publication. Jessica received a B.S. in Business Management and a M.Ed. in College Student Personnel Administration from Virginia Tech.

ABOUT THE RESUME DESIGNERS, PROOFREADERS & WRITERS

Bonita Kraemer, Bonny Kraemer Day and Kathryn Troutman

Bonny Kraemer Day has been the Head Resume Designer for The Resume Place, Inc. for 20 years. She has set the quality and design standards for The Resume Place, Inc. publications and client services. Bonny is an expert at crafting resume designs in Microsoft Word balancing space, type fonts, margins and readability. Sisters Bonny and Kathy have worked well together at Resume Place for 20 years. In addition to establishing Resume Place's reputation for the highest-quality designs, Bonny was the General Manager for the business for more than 10 years. Bonny has recently left The Resume Place to pursue her dream of teaching music to elementary students and professional singing.

Bonita Kraemer is the veteran proofreader and editor for this publication and all of Kathryn's books. Mrs. Kraemer is a graduate of Union College in Union, Nebraska (1941). She became a champion typist in Idaho in 1935 in order to avoid picking potatoes in the fields. She holds a B.A. in English and Journalism. She is a master at proofreading and is an "old school" grammarian expert. As Kathy and Bonny's mother, she has held a full or part-time Editor's position at the Resume Place for 29 years – all of the years in business. Mrs. Kraemer is also a Vice President at the Catonsville Senior Center and is actively taking almost every class they offer.

Alan Cross is a Senior Writer and Trainer for The Resume Place, with more than 25 years experience as a public affairs officer, journalist, free lance writer, career strategy consultant, job search consultant and resume/job application writing instructor. Alan is expert in translating private industry skills for positions in law enforcement, criminal investigations, accounting, business, contracts and finance, as well as administrative positions. Alan is a USDA Graduate School instructor and a trained and experienced Resumix trainer with Army, Marines and Navy departments. He is a Certified Resumix© Desktop Workstation Recruiter and Resumix© Desktop Workstation Operator and has received extensive training in Job Analysis and KSA Examining from the Office of Personnel Management. Alan holds a B.S. degree in Human Resources from Columbia Union College in Takoma Park, Maryland.

Evelin Letarte is an expert in translating information technology private industry language into Federal job skills for Resume Place clients as a freelance writer, editor and job search coach. Evelin began work at University of Maryland University College and joined the Career and Cooperative Education Center in 1999 to help adult students in their career searches. Evelin works with undergraduate and graduate students and alumni transitioning from one career to the next, advising them on everything from skills assessment to interviewing to resume writing. In addition, Evelin in on the faculty of University of Maryland University College as an Adjunct Assistant Professor teaching a Cooperative Education course to help students earn credit for their new learning experiences on the job. Evelin holds a Master of Education from the University of Massachusetts, Amherst.

William Partridge retired from the Senior Executive Service of the Federal Government as the Deputy Inspector General of the Federal Emergency Management Agency (FEMA). As a freelance executive writer for The Resume Place, Bill writes, edits and translates private industry skills into law enforcement, inspector general, engineering, legal, science, engineering and criminology for Federal jobs and Senior Executive Service positions. The range of his work experience covered Federal, state, and local government as well as private business, large and small. In recent years his field of concentration was governmental program evaluation and policy analysis. Prior to joining FEMA he was on the Surveys and Investigations Staff of the U. S. House Appropriations Committee. Prior to that he was Assistant Inspector General for Inspections of the U.S. Department of Energy. Bill holds an MBA in Operations Research from UCLA, as well as an MPA from Syracuse University.

Back Row: Randy Sweetman, Alan Cross, Bonny Day, Bonita Kraemer, Diane Beall, Mark Reichenbacher
Front Row: Margie Tufty, Kim Hall and Kathryn Troutman

Carla Waskiewicz, staff writer for The Resume Place, has over 24 years professional writing experience in corporate communications, employee recruitment communications, public relations, and advertising. Carla is highly skilled in translating the skills from private industry professionals to Federal jobs and occupational series. For the past 15 years she has worked as an advertising consultant providing communications and advertising services to businesses in the Baltimore area. Carla earned her Bachelor of Arts degree in Communications from Penn State University and has completed post-graduate work in business management at the University of Baltimore.

THE RESUME PLACE, INC.— HOME OF THE FEDERAL RESUME

Need help with your package?
www.resume-place.com

CHECK OUT OUR PROFESSIONAL WRITING SERVICES:

Federal Job Search Consulting and Professional Writing Services

Professional writing, design, editing, and consulting services including: electronic resumes, private industry resumes, one-page networking resume, Federal resumes, KSAs, Federal job qualification analysis, professional critiques, and senior executive service applications, interview training, and role-playing.

Full Service Writing and Editing

Need help writing an outstanding professional resume that presents the best experience and skills you have to offer? Want a free estimate for professional services? Not sure what your next step in your Federal job search should be? Send your most recent resume, past applications, position descriptions, and any vacancy announcements to us by mail or e-mail. We will contact you with a complete recommendation and estimate of services.

Federal Job Qualification Analysis

Are you a first-time Federal job applicant and unsure how your private industry experience equates to Federal positions? We will analyze your education, experience, knowledge, skills and abilities, and provide you with Federal job titles, grade levels, and ideas for the best agencies for you. We will review your qualifications against Office of Personnel Management Classification Standards and provide your Federal Job Qualifications Analysis Report.

Professional Editing and Design Services

Have you written your resume already, but would like an editor to review your content and improve your format? Our Edit-Design service to improve your draft is outstanding. Our editors will improve the format, presentation, and readability of the resume; edit and reorganize the content; check verb tenses; highlight any accomplishments that you might not feature as well as you should; and make sure your skills are clear in the content.

Professional Critique

Are you sure your resume is focused, written at the appropriate level, clear to the reader? We'll tell you if it is or isn't.

Resumix and Electronic Resume Writing Service

The Resumix resume format, used by the Department of Defense civilian military personnel agencies, can be edited or written by Resume Place writers. We are experienced in all formats: Army, Navy, Marines, Air Force and other Defense agencies. Our Resumix resumes will maximize your success. We will maximize skills and keywords so that you will be as successful as possible with both the database query and the selecting official.

SES Services:
Consulting, Critique, Interview and Full Service Writing

The Resume Place, Inc. is the leading executive Federal resume-writing firm in the world. We know what's important and how to present your package at the executive level. The SES package is a major executive writing project. We are experts in marketing executives and writing about their accomplishments, expertise, and career history in the most impressive, succinct, and persuasive way!

The SES package includes the following components: Cover Letter, Executive Federal Resume, Executive Core Qualification (ECQ) Statements: Leading Change, Leading People, Results Driven, Business Acumen, Building Coalitions, and Technical and Managerial Factors. Total package average: 18 to 25 pages.

Would you like a Senior Executive Service Federal Employment expert to review your materials to determine what it would take to write your SES package? Write to us at resumeanalysis@resume-place.com. Subjectline: SES service information

The Resume Place, 89 Mellor Ave., Baltimore, MD 21228

Email attached files to resumeanalysis@resume-place.com

Fax: 410-744-0112

Questions? Call 888-480-8265

Federal Job Search Discussion Board – Free!
Ask your Federal job search questions

www.resume-place.com

Federal Career Corner Newsletter – Free!
Sign up for a monthly email newsletter
by Kathryn Troutman

www.resume-place.com

BOOKS BY KATHRYN KRAEMER TROUTMAN

Ten Steps to a Federal Job: Navigating the Federal Job System

Federal job expert Kathryn Troutman explains how to get a well-paid, career civil service position with a mission. She clarifies the Federal job process in ten straightforward steps, making the daunting task of applying for a government job simple.

Ten Steps to a Federal Job outlines what kinds of jobs are available, what agencies are hiring, how to match your skills and resume to Federal jobs, how the hiring process works, and how to write a successful Federal application. Troutman explains the entire process, from the decision to apply for a Federal job to the final interview. The book also includes a CD-ROM with resume samples and templates.

ISBN 0-9647025-3-3 / $38.95

ELECTRONIC Federal Resume Guidebook

Learn how to write a successful electronic Federal resume, including keywords and how to find them, how and where to submit your resume online, and in-depth resume formatting instructions.

Applying for a first-time civilian job or getting promoted in a Department of Defense agency is easier than ever. Simply write your electronic resume, post it on the databases, and self-nominate for most jobs!

Includes:

- ✪ Electronic resume samples
- ✪ Private industry resume samples
- ✪ In-depth instructions for resume writing
- ✪ Keywords, KSAs, and Skills Buckets
- ✪ CD-ROM with more electronic resume samples, skills buckets, plus keywords for civilian jobs and official job kits

ISBN 0-9647025-2-5 / $44.95

The Federal Resume Guidebook & PC-Disk, 2nd edition

Think writing a Federal resume is difficult? Let Kathryn Troutman lead you through the complexities of finding job announcements, writing Federal resumes, and packaging your resume to meet both Federal and vacancy announcement criteria. This is an essential resource for anyone applying for a Federal job. Includes over 20 sample resumes, KSA and ECQ samples, Job Kits, Federal Operational Group listings, and Federal Employment forms. Over 40,000 copies sold.

ISBN 1-56370-545-1 / $36.95

Creating Your High School Resume

Originally written and published in 1997, this book is used in career centers, English classes, entrepreneurship, business, and community service classes throughout the U.S. It includes samples of all student level resumes—gifted students, hard-working average students, technical achievers, and students barely making it through school. All students need a good resume, no matter what their career objective!

ISBN 1-56370-508-7 / $12.95

BOOK ORDERS: WWW.RESUME-PLACE.COM or (888) 480 8265

INDEX

C

G

H

I

J

Q

Federal Job Search Certificate

Congratulations!

You have completed the Ten Steps to a Federal Job... the BOOK!

This certifies that you have spent approximately 40 hours researching vacancy announcements, determining job titles and series, writing your federal and electronic resume and applying for Federal jobs. Good luck with your application and Step 10 - Interviewing for a Federal job!

Kathryn K. Troutman

Kathryn Kraemer Troutman
Author, Ten Steps to a Federal Job

First Federal application was mailed: _____

The Resume Place, Inc.
www.resume-place.com